ABSOLUTES IN
MORAL THEOLOGY?

Absolutes in Moral Theology?

EDITED BY

CHARLES E. CURRAN

GREENWOOD PRESS, PUBLISHERS
WESTPORT, CONNECTICUT

Library of Congress Cataloging in Publication Data

Curran, Charles E
    Absolutes in moral theology?

    Reprint of the ed. published by Corpus Books, Washing-
ton.
    Includes bibliographical references and index.
    1. Christian ethics--Catholic authors--Addresses,
essays, lectures. I. Title.
[BX1758.2.C8 1975   241'.04'2   75-3988
ISBN 0-8371-7450-3

Originally published in 1968 by Corpus Books, Washington

Reprinted with the permission of Charles E. Curran

Reprinted in 1975 by Greenwood Press, a division of Congressional
Information Service, 88 Post Road West, Westport, Connecticut 06881

Library of Congress catalog card number 75-3988

ISBN 0-8371-7450-3

Printed in the United States of America

10 9 8 7 6 5 4 3 2

Contents

5

The Contributors

CHARLES E. CURRAN—Associate Professor of Moral Theology, School of Theology, The Catholic University of America, Washington, D.C.

DENNIS DOHERTY, O.S.B.—Assistant Professor of Moral Theology, Marquette University, Milwaukee, Wisconsin.

DANIEL C. MAGUIRE—Assistant Professor of Moral Theology, Department of Religious Education, The Catholic University of America, Washington, D.C.

JOHN G. MILHAVEN, S.J.—Professor of Pastoral Theology, Woodstock College, Woodstock, Maryland.

KIERAN NOLAN, O.S.B.—Professor of Moral Theology, St. John's University, Collegeville, Minnesota.

MARTIN NOLAN, O.S.A.—Professor of Moral Theology, St. Patrick's, Rome, Italy.

ROBERT H. SPRINGER, S.J.—Professor of Moral Theology, Woodstock College, Woodstock, Maryland.

CORNELIUS J. VAN DER POEL, C.S.SP.—Professor of Moral Theology, St. Mary's Seminary, Norwalk, Connecticut.

CHARLES E. CURRAN

Introduction

Renewal and aggiornamento characterize contemporary Roman Catholic life and theology. In the area of theology, the scientific study of the Scriptures has been most drastically affected by renewal. Biblical scholars and exegetes have employed the auxiliary sciences to come to a better understanding of the Word of God in the words of men. Form criticism, literary genre, midrash, and myth are now commonly employed tools in Roman Catholic scriptural study. In fact, it is improper even to speak of Roman Catholic scriptural study, since scriptural study is now truly ecumenical.

Dogmatic or systematic theology is also experiencing the currents of renewal. The insights of modern scientific findings together with a better understanding of the Scriptures have brought Catholic theologians to see the cultural and historical accretions which have become a part of our theological heritage. The teaching on original sin serves as an excellent example. Scripture studies confirm the non-historical character of the Genesis account of original sin; evolutionary theories cast doubt on monogenism; the influence of a classical worldview is present in the teaching on the handing down of original sin. Theologians today are struggling with the problem of original sin in terms of the sin of the world.

Less than a few decades ago, a more rationalistic approach argued that man could know and demonstrate the existence of God from reason. Now theologians realize the embarrassing inadequacies of a one-sided rationalistic apologetics. Contemporary Catholic theologians are also calling into question the real existence of angels and even devils. Theology has previously maintained that faith is a firm and certain assent, but modern theologians speak of faith existing side by side with unbelief in the same person. An older theology stressed divine providence; today theology speaks to men come of age in terms of responsibility. Contemporary theology admits the ecclesial realities of other Christian Churches. All these changes and others have brought to the forefront the important question of the development of doctrine. Advances in man's knowledge of history, culture, philosophy, anthropology, and the empirical sciences have all played a part in such change and development.

Moral theology, or Christian ethics, can be no exception to the theological renewal in the Church. The same factors that are operative in the area of Scripture and dogmatic theology are also operative in the area of moral theology. In fact, one should expect greater change and development in the area of moral theology, since moral theology deals with man and his actions. In the last two or three centuries our understanding of man and his world has dramatically changed. The industrial, scientific, democratic, and educational revolutions have all taken place. Unfortunately, all the changes in man's understanding of himself and his world have had little or no effect as yet on Catholic moral theology.

A call for change and development does not imply a disrespect of tradition and what has gone before. A proper attitude toward tradition and previous teachings avoids the opposite extremes of either canonizing the past or forgetting about the past. A non-historical approach frequently forgets that a previous teaching was deeply affected by the historical and cultural circumstances in which it arose.

The developing Catholic teaching on religious liberty and on the separation of Church and State serves as a good illustration. The union of Church and State was proposed as an ideal. However, a difficulty arose because in certain countries it was impossible to have a union of Church and State. Theologians conceived the distinction between thesis and hypothesis. The thesis or the "ideal" calls for union, but in practice the opposite may be tolerated. Bishop Dupanloup of Orleans wrote a pamphlet after Pope Pius IX's encyclical *Quanta Cura* and the *Syllabus* in which he mitigated the harshness of the papal teaching by employing a distinction between thesis and hypothesis.[1] The distinction itself finally appears in the documents of the papal. magisterium only with Leo XIII, the successor of Pius IX.[2] However, Vatican Council II accepted the fact that the distinction between thesis and hypothesis did not really do justice to the question of Church and State and religious liberty. Today no Catholic theologian would uphold the union of Church and State as an ideal toward which all Catholics must strive. History has taught us that the "ideal" was really not an abstract ideal at all, but rather the canonization of a particular historical manifestation. The "ideal" was greatly influenced by the cultural and historical conditions of the time. (In somewhat the same way the universal condemnation of usury canonized and absolutized a concept of money that was historically conditioned.)

A theologian sins against a proper understanding of history and tradition if he merely repeats formulae and conclusions from the past and completely forgets the different historical and cultural settings in which such conclusions were formed. Theology remains true to the past and to the present when it tries to interpret the present and the future in the light of the past. Good theology avoids the opposite extreme of paying no attention to the past. A proper understanding of Christian experience and teaching in the past enables the theologian to interpret the present better and to avoid the absolutizing of any moment in history—either past or present.

John Kenneth Galbraith has said that the problem with most economic theories is not original error but uncorrected obsolescence.[3] The theories no longer fit the facts and circumstances of the present. Bernard Lonergan has wryly commented upon the same phenomenon in theology. Lonergan observes that Catholic theology usually arrives on the scene a little breathlessly and a little late.[4] Catholic theology in general and moral theology in particular have not kept pace with the revolutions which have characterized man's understanding of himself and the world in which he lives. A historical overview of moral theology will help to explain the gap between moral theology and modern man's understanding of himself and his world.[5]

Since the sixteenth and seventeenth centuries moral theology has undergone very little change either in the structure or in the content of the manuals of moral theology. A cursory reading of the textbooks of the seventeenth century and those used in Catholic seminaries and colleges until the last few years shows there has been no real change and development. After the sixteenth century, moral theology became very practically oriented and lost contact with both dogmatic theology and philosophy. Speculative theology and philosophy among Catholics were themselves in a poor state because of the nominalistic and positivistic approach of the times. Moral theology became more aligned with canon law than the more speculative sciences. But practical reasons were primary in diverting the attention of moral theology to the narrow and practical scope of training confessors for the sacrament of penance.

The historical needs of the Church have often been influential in determining the shape of moral theology. The general introduction of private penance in the sixth century gave rise to the penitentials, books which indicated the precise penances to be assigned for particular sins. In the twelfth century a new genre appeared, the *Summae Confessorum*. The insistence on yearly participation in the sacrament of penance by the Fourth Lateran Council (*DS,* 812)[6] encouraged the formation of this type of penitential handbook containing the necessary moral and canonical information for the confessor. The *Summae* evolved through the fifteenth century into the alphabetical *Summae* which abandoned any attempt at a logical and speculative explanation of the material and just listed and explained the necessary items according to alphabetical order. However, the more theoretical and speculative aspects of moral theology or ethics were still retained in the universities.

One of the aims of the Council of Trent was to provide a better training for candidates for the priesthood. The minor clergy were in no way adequately prepared for their ministry. Most of the lower clergy could never attend the protracted university course of fourteen years which led to the doctorate in theology. Also a number of abuses had contributed to the inadequate training of the lower clergy. The Council of Trent again called for a renewal of the sacrament of penance and legislated the necessity of yearly confession (*DS*, 1683). The Society of Jesus was quick to carry out the reforms intended by Trent, especially in the renewal of the sacrament of penance. According to the Jesuit *ratio studiorum* of 1586, the candidates for the priesthood were to be given a two-year course which would properly prepare them for their priestly ministry in the confessional. The approach was very practical and pastoral. The first-year course contained tracts on human acts, conscience, laws, sins, and all the commandments except the seventh. The second-year curriculum included the seventh commandment (especially contracts), the sacraments, censures, the duties and obligations of the various states of life. The *Institutiones Theologiae Moralis* were textbooks based on the plan of the *ratio studiorum*.

The manuals of theology which were seminary classroom fare until just a few years ago follow the same structure and contain almost the same content as the seventeenth-century *Institutiones*. The references to anything happening in other areas of Catholic thinking or to "secular" thinking are very conspicuous by their absence. The manuals merely added the various encyclicals and directives issued by the hierarchical magisterium. The most widely used manuals of moral theology were written in "the Jesuit tradition." However, the textbooks in the Dominican school had the same practical orientation, although there was a more speculative approach on some issues. In nineteenth-century Germany, moral theologians began to widen the scope of moral theology to embrace a consideration of the whole Christian life. The newer German manuals of moral theology did not really have much effect outside Germany until the appearance of Bernard Häring's *The Law of Christ* in the 1950s and 1960s.

The very practical scope of moral theology was not the only factor that isolated such theology from other intellectual currents of thought. All Roman Catholic theology was isolated from the philosophical and empirical insights developed since the seventeenth century. The great revolutions in man's understanding of himself and his world had little or no effect upon Catholic thinking until recently. Ever since the Reformation, Roman Catholic life and theology have tended to exist in a ghetto and react defensively to any of the advances of the time. The Reformation, the Enlightenment, and scientific advances were looked upon as threats to Catholic belief and teachings. The Catholic Church in general opted for a position of intransigence and opposition to the thinking of the modern world.

The nineteenth century witnessed the confrontation between the Church and the modern world.[7] Would Catholic thought make any accommodation to the stirrings in the modern world or would it rigidly refuse any accommodation? The confrontation centered especially on the question of liberalism and the freedoms advocated by the spirit of the revolution in France. The liberal and secular thinkers advocated freedom of religion, freedom of speech, freedom of the press, and freedom of intellectual inquiry. There were definitely unacceptable aspects to the liberalism and the thinking of the nineteenth century, but the general attitude of the Church was a rigid condemnation rather than an attempt to purify and assimilate the acceptable parts of the thinking of the age. Catholics themselves were divided on the approach to the contemporary world, but the intransigent attitude finally emerged as the official policy. In France and Belgium "Catholic liberals" supported the notion of separation of Church and State and religious liberty—a free Church in a free State according to the dictum of Montalembert. In Italy the liberalism of the day assumed primarily a political stance in working for the unification of Italy and the elimination of the Papal States.

In Germany the primary area of conflict was more in the

call by some Catholic thinkers for an accommodation with the thinking of the modern world. A congress of Catholic intellectuals was convened in Munich in 1863 to bring Catholic thinking abreast of the best thinking of the day. However, the reaction of Rome was negative. The general Roman reaction was to oppose rigidly all accommodation and to call for a return and renewal of the theology and philosophy of St. Thomas. In the light of this historical background, one can better understand the meaning and importance of Leo XIII's encyclical *Aeterni Patris* (1879), in which the pope called for the revival of Thomism in Catholic schools and seminaries. The directives imposing Thomism increased with the years.[8] The Code of Canon Law which went into effect in 1918 states that philosophy and theology in Catholic schools and seminaries are to be taught *"ad Angelici Doctoris rationem, doctrinam, et principia...."* (Canon 1366, §2). In this manner Catholic philosophy and theology were supposed to be insulated from much of the dangerous thinking of the day. The twentieth-century revival of Thomism had little effect on the manuals of moral theology because of their practical scope and isolation from dogma and theology. However, the exclusive emphasis on Thomistic theology and philosophy prevented any possible dialogue of moral theology with contemporary thought.

This brief historical overview shows the need for a renewal in moral theology. Interestingly, the nineteenth-century opposition to the modern world in the form of opposition to religious liberty and unification of Italy has already ceased. However, moral theology has not undergone a renewal through contact and dialogue with modern man's understanding of himself. The renewal in moral theology in the last few years has been through the scriptural and liturgical renewals.[9] Such a renewal has been most beneficial in trying to indicate the true vocation of the Christian constantly striving for the reign of God. But the process of renewal now calls for a dialogue with modern philosophical thought, with the natural and social sciences, contemporary human experience and man's understanding of himself in the modern world. The Pastoral Constitution on the Church in the Modern World has recognized the great changes that have occurred in man's understanding of himself and the world (n. 44). The last three centuries have seen revolutionary changes in science, technology, and knowledge. The world and the Church have also recognized the dignity of man and his need for freedom and liberty to live as a responsible person in the modern world. Moral theology is just beginning such a dialogue.

The present volume will not consider the most important problems facing contemporary Catholic moral theologians and ethicians. Moral theology is a reflection on the Christian life and experience. Christian life today struggles with the acute problems facing modern man in a technical and urban society and in a world of pluralism. Theology can no longer merely consider the question of individual actions but must consider the meaning and relevancy of Christian life in a world come of age but beset with its own problems and insecurities. Peace, poverty, human dignity, and cooperation among races and countries and peoples of different ideological backgrounds are the primary issues facing the Christian and all men today.

The contributors to this volume are addressing themselves to a comparatively minor, although still important, question— the existence of negative, absolute norms of morality. The contemporary discussion about situation ethics and the new morality has given impetus to such an inquiry. There is a need to rethink the traditional teaching of moral theology in these areas. Will a dialogue with the natural and social sciences, the modern philosophies, the changed understanding of man and his place in the universe, and contemporary human experience result in a change in the older teaching on negative, absolute norms of conduct? The general thrust of the following chapters affirms the need for such a change.

As an example and illustration of the purpose, scope and methodology of this volume, consider the moral teaching on masturbation.[10] Roman Catholic theologians have taught since the seventeenth century that masturbation always involves grave matter (*materia ex toto genere suo gravis*). On the level of popular teaching, the distinction between grave matter and grave sin is often lost, so that masturbation is taught to be always a grave sin. However, the theologian today must ask if masturbation is always grave matter. The contemporary theologian knows much more about masturbation than the theologians of previous centuries. He cannot merely repeat what St. Alphonsus said in the eighteenth century. St. Alphonsus knew nothing of the findings of modern psychology. However, psychology tells us that masturbation is not always "objectively grave matter." Masturbation is generally symptomatic behavior. It could be symptomatic of a matter of great importance but often in adolescents masturbation is just not that important a matter. The experience of many confessors seems to dovetail with the findings of psychology and psychiatry. Perhaps Catholic over-emphasis on the great importance of masturbation impedes true maturity and at times leads to severe guilt feelings.

The older theologians could only consider masturbation according to their limited knowledge. St. Alphonsus and his predecessors had to consider masturbation almost exclusively from a physiological viewpoint. However, even then, their physiological information was quite inadequate. St. Alphonsus derived most of his biological information from Galen and Aristotle, who had lived about two thousand years earlier. The fault was not St. Alphonsus'. It is only in the last few centuries that science has come to a knowledge of the process of human reproduction. Van Leeuwenhoek in 1677 with his microscope discovered spermatozoa. Some of his followers even published pictures of the "homunculus" they found in the sperm. Obviously they thought that the sperm contained the man in miniature who only needed the warmth and protection of the womb. The actual ovum of the woman was not discovered until the eighteenth century, and the process of fertilization was described as the union of the nuclei of the sperm and the ovum in 1875 by Oscar Hertwig.[11] The inadequate biological knowledge which did not know the exact contribution of the woman in the reproductive process may have given too much importance to the male sperm. Obviously, if someone believes that the sperm contains the "homunculus," then he would attach an inordinate importance to the sperm. (I am not maintaining that Alphonsus held such a notion, but his inadequate understanding of the female role in reproduction could have influenced the importance he attached to human semen.) However, modern psychology and physiology, as well as contemporary experience, call for a change in the older understanding of masturbation as matter which is always grave.

The need to re-think some of the teachings of moral theology in dialogue with contemporary man and modern scientific findings is obvious. The contributors to this volume are arguing for a change in the area of some negative, absolute norms in moral theology. The difficult questions confronting contemporary theologians are faced—conscience, natural law, the magisterium of the Church, the principle of double effect, the principle of totality, abortion, divorce, and medical ethics. However, the contributors have not neglected the teachings of the past. A number of chapters specifically consider the past so that the present can be better understood. Also one chapter is devoted to St. Thomas' explanation of the exceptions to absolute moral norms in the Old Testament. All the contributors are, or have been, teaching moral theology in Catholic seminaries and universities. The essays are not intended to be definitive but only to express the theological convictions of the authors. As theologians and scholars all are engaged in the search for truth. Catholic theology needs to be in dialogue with the modern sciences and philosophies. Likewise, Roman Catholic theologians must encourage dialogue among themselves. This volume of essays is merely trying to contribute to the dialogue which is absolutely necessary for the science of moral theology and for the Church. As editor I would like to thank the contributors for their efforts. In particular the Rev. Daniel C. Maguire has been most helpful in the work of editing this volume. Finally, I want to express my appreciation to the Rev. John P. Whalen and Mr. Joseph Caulfield of Corpus Instrumentorum for their help and encouragement in this venture.

ROBERT H. SPRINGER

Conscience, Behavioral Science and Absolutes

Vatican Council II summoned the Church to the renewal of moral theology: "Let them [the faithful] blend modern science and its theories and the understanding of the most recent discoveries with Christian morality and doctrine." This text points to both the direction that renewal should take and to a deficiency in pre-conciliar moral theology. The deficiency was the failure to "harmonize culture with Christian teaching," and to "show [the gospel's] relevance to the conditions of human life." The new direction is that of "the secular sciences, especially of psychology and sociology," of "literature and the arts."[1] In a word, our moral theology had gotten out of touch with the times. In this chapter we will follow the conciliar mandate to the extent of calling upon psychology and sociology, leaving the natural sciences, literature and the arts to the more competent.

Taking a broader view of the council, theologians are commissioned to update moral also in the overall call to the reform and renewal of the Church itself. For the Church is not just the community of Christians in their spontaneous, pre-reflective living out of their divine vocation. It is also the articulation of a theory of Christian living, the result of the reflection of the community on its religious experience, called theology.

In the passage cited the council itself draws upon the sociology of religion. Indeed, the dominating viewpoint of the

19

whole of the Constitution on the Church in the Modern World may be said to be sociological. It sees "a change in attitudes and in human structures." As a result of such change, "the institutions, laws and modes of thinking as handed down from previous generations do not always seem to be well adapted to the contemporary state of affairs."[2] The constitution goes so far as to recognize the existence of superstition in religion: "a more critical ability to distinguish religion from a magical view of the world and from the superstitions which still circulate purifies religion . . ." The reference here is to religion in general, but nowhere in the text is Catholic religion exempted from the predication of this error.

What had happened to moral theology that it should be out of step with reality? The times had changed but moral had not kept pace. It had stayed too exclusively within one "traditional" framework, retaining an earlier worldview no longer adequate. A theology that does not develop has only the limited relevance of history.

Concretely, the fixation of moral was evidenced in that it had become a code morality. Instead of a flexible set of moral rules going beyond the basic principles in the area of moral, these rules were elevated to the status of universal, unexceptionable principle. In theory they remained rules and therefore had exceptions, as Aquinas had taught. But in practice, in pulpit and classroom, in the lives of the faithful, they were the predetermined and predetermining norms of behavior. They should have been guidelines for decision allowing for the particularity of each moral choice, the *contingens singulare* of St. Thomas, and the changing situation of mankind. Now conscience had only to apply the right rule and the answer was almost automatic, a kind of computerized morality. You feed the data into the machine (object, purpose and circumstances) and conscience selects the pertinent norm. Whereupon out comes the answer.

This absolutizing tendency of ready-made, unvarying norms extended in practice beyond the rules of conduct to the level of moral conclusions, to concrete decision making. The reference here is to casuistry. The fault was not with casuistry as such, for it has a valid function in moral science. Indeed it has been one of the strengths of scholastic morality through the centuries as compared with some other moral systems which limited themselves to the elaboration of basic principles. The fault was with casuistry as taught. Typical cases were studied in the various areas of moral and solutions worked out; the subject in the case should do thus and so. Unfortunately the learner did not grasp that they were only typical, pattern solutions, models of what to do in matters of justice, veracity or chastity. He set about life thinking he had only to connect a decision with the relevant case he had studied, in order to know what he should do.

Two methodological weaknesses were concealed in this approach. Model cases for the most part give generic answers, not the final decision for the unique, singular situation. Secondly, the models themselves are subject to modification, or substitution by later models, as the conditions of human existence change. Thus the absolutizing tendency extended to the establishing of, not just theoretical, but practical absolutes in the solution of cases of conscience.

To keep the record straight, the recognition of this first weakness did not have to wait upon Vatican II. Among others, in 1955 Joseph Fuchs, in his classical work, *Lex Naturae,* had clearly pointed out the distinction between cases of conscience and situation. Councils, of course, do not spring full-blown from the head of Zeus. They are in part conceived in the womb of prior theological speculation. Nevertheless, the conciliar impetus to this recognition, and the freedom the council accorded the theologian, have been necessary for the beginnings of a general acceptance in the Catholic community.

This epistemological defect of moral rules and case solutions which are totally decisive of present decision must be avoided in the future. It involved the forcing of categories of thought, elaborated from earlier historical contexts, upon a present reality which had changed; accordingly, the categories no longer adequately fitted the changed situation. The consequence was to "load men with burdens hard to bear, and you yourselves do not touch the burdens with one of your fingers" (Lk 11:46).[3] Beyond the range of basic moral principle, norms for conscience are to be guidelines. The movement characteristic of historical reality, recognized by Vatican II, precludes permanent, unchanging moral norms in this area.

By the same token the new trend in moral, by which it is more open to the demands of love and the particularity of the situation, must avoid the same pitfall. A solution, for example, allowing the fallopian tubes to be tied in a mother with a badly scarred uterus in an individual case should not be made into a general rule. To do so would be to fall into a new tryranny of absolutism in place of the old.

So much for the mandate of Vatican II for aggiornamento in moral in general. What is the council's specific teaching on conscience? It is expressed in two earlier sections of the same constitution entitled "The Dignity of the Moral Conscience" and "The Excellence of Liberty."[4] The doctrine contains both old and new. It is not a synthesis, a systematic moral theology of conscience. The elements of future synthesis, however, are there for the theologian to systematize into a coherent whole.

The teaching may be summed up under four headings: 1) conscience is subject to objective norms; 2) yet it is personal, escaping complete objective conceptualization; 3) conscience is the recipient of a unique divine word; 4) it is communal. Let us examine each of these in turn.

THE PROBLEM OF CONSCIENCE

"In the depths of his conscience, man detects a law which he does not impose upon himself, but which holds him to obedience."[5] The source of this law is in part ecclesial: "In the formation of their consciences the Christian faithful ought carefully to attend to the sacred and certain doctrine of the Church."[6] This is traditional teaching which must be retained in any theology of conscience. Otherwise we fall into the morass of subjectivism. It means that a Christian moral theology must give centrality to the Christ event, God's gracious intervention into human history, with the consequent objective response this demands of man.

Yet this objective law must be seen in conjunction with the responding subject. Man is not an automaton spontaneously reacting to objective demands, but a person responding to the objective as perceived. We do not know reality pure and simple. Reality as experienced by man is the object of our knowledge. Accordingly, when we say conscience must respond to objective demands this means that conscience is responsible for objective moral good as perceived. The objective is no longer quite as objective as we had previously conceived it. This is one conclusion from the insight into subjectivity which recent philosophy has established.

Subjectivity also means that man in part escapes conceptualization. In our deepest core we are literally unspeakable. But to conceptualize is to objectify, to find concepts with a formal object to express what man is and should do. Therefore there is a limit to our ability to conceptualize, to formulate, the objective moral demands that rest upon us. This greater awareness of the subjective in modern philosophy, counterbalancing an earlier overemphasis on the objective, is reflected in the teaching of Vatican II on conscience. Instead of a doctrine couched solely in terms of response to objective norms, it recognizes a depth to the person that defies objectification: "Conscience is the most secret core and sanctuary of a man," it says in one place; in another it speaks of "the unsearchable depths of the human soul."[7]

The bishops at the council deserve credit for speaking as they did in terms of the person. They so spoke at a time when charges of personalism and subjectivism were being raised in the Catholic community against the relatively new philosophy of the person. The danger of subjectivism is, of course, perennially present, both in pre-reflective conduct and on the level of theory. The verification of the danger in the present instance, however, can only be established by refuting a whole movement in modern philosophy.[8]

At this point the question of the supposed opposition is usually raised, the conflict between the subjective autonomy of conscience and the objective demands upon it. This is a false presentation of the question. It is analogous to the question of law versus love, a dichotomy that likewise distorted morality but now is happily resolved.[9] That genuine Christian love respects and obeys law and authority is beyond question.

One may ask whether a given moral system overemphasizes law to the detriment of love, or vice versa. The same question may be posed of morality as lived: is John a legalist disproportionately oriented to law and order to the detriment of love of his fellow man? Is Paul committed to love in a manner neglectful of justice, a prerequisite for, and a demand of, the communion of love? But there is no opposition of conscience versus objective demands. Genuine morality interiorizes, makes its own, the demands of justice. Empiric psychology postulates a role for authority in the makeup of the mature person. Current philosophy makes society constitutive of the person.

Rather than opposition, therefore, we should speak of a tension or a polarity of conscience involving both objective and subjective. The sincere conscience in matters of justice must be more objective than with regard to humility. The former imposes clear, readily conceptualized demands of how much and to whom. At the same time the subjective element must be present, for example, a change of heart accompanying the objective restitution. Humility has to do with internal self-evaluation. Thus it lies more toward the subjective pole, though it should authenticate itself in externally objectifiable comportment. It is a matter then of more-or-less objective and subjective, not of either-or. Difference is maintained, but a mutual compenetration is verified.

Our question then resolves itself to, should conscience be more objectively or subjectively oriented today? No simple answer can be given. In view of a moral theology and a formation of conscience that was too juridical in the past, the answer is, more subjective. The theme of "de-legalizing" moral has been developed elsewhere. Suffice it to say that biblical theology, the primacy of charity in moral and Vatican II call for a renewed emphasis of the subjective: greater love, sincerity, freedom, openness and sense of responsibility.

From another viewpoint, that of a lived Christianity which sees true religion consisting solely or primarily in prayer, worship and the observance of the duties of positive law, greater objectivity must be demanded. "Religion that is pure and undefiled before God and the Father is this: to visit orphans and widows, and to keep oneself unstained from the world" (Jas 1:27). The message of the Constitution on the Church and the Modern World is the objective order of justice and love. Christians are urged to turn outwards to the urgent problems of fostering universal peace such as fashioning the community of nations and promoting programs of land reform.

There can be no unilateral answer to the question of conscience today. Those who raise their voices exclusively in either objective or subjective accents do a disservice to the community.

We come now to conscience as the recipient of a unique divine word. "Conscience is the most secret core and sanctuary of a man. There he is alone with God, whose voice echoes in his depths."[10] The word "alone" suggests that the word of God is spoken not only through the community but to the individual person. This is clearer in the Decree on the Apostolate of the Laity. Here the Holy Spirit "allots to everyone according as he will (I Cor 12:11). Thus may the individual, according to the gift that each has received, administer 'it to one another. . . . In so doing, believers need to enjoy the freedom of the holy Spirit who 'breathes where he wills' (Jn 3:8)." This delicate matter of the exercise of personal charisms, consequent upon hearing the voice of the Spirit, calls for discernment. The charismatic Christian must have due regard for the mind of the community, particularly of pastors. The latter, however, are not to "extinguish the Spirit."[11]

This was one of the more deplorable omissions of moral theology in the pre-Vatican II era. The word "charism" was never heard, except in terms of the apparently extinct charisms of the pristine Church. A code morality found little room for the voice of the Spirit. Supposed universal rules of conduct left the Christian's conscience unattuned to the word of his Lord—and tending to tune it out.

Little wonder that our moral system prior to the recent Council was embarrassed by the charismatic witness of those early Christian martyrs who took their own lives, SS. Apollonia, Pelagia, Sophronia and others. In the judgment of the Church their heroic act was held in esteem. Yet it clashed with the traditional moral analysis; it was the direct taking of one's own life, suicide. Two explanations were offered in the manuals. The first held that it was material suicide, excused from formal sin by invincible ignorance. The second allowed that they may have been divinely inspired. This was a recognition of a charism, but the justification given leaves something to be desired: "It is clear that God may command someone to commit suicide, for he is the supreme Lord of life and death."[12] No attempt was made to express under what conditions God might so command or norms given for determining how one might recognize such a call. It was, then, a form of theological positivism.

Both explanations discouraged the act, the first by assigning ignorance of morality to the martyrs. The second added that one should not readily presume a special call from God. The dim view of such behavior was reinforced by the restatement of the prohibition, "Thou shalt not kill" to read: one may not directly take his own life *on his own authority*. The italicized words allowed for the possible justification of the martyrs' deed, but the reformulation of the norm implied that an absolute prohibition had been achieved, apparently closing the door to such behavior for the future.

Today we would prefer to say that they gave their lives for Christ. All reality cannot be neatly fitted into the categories of direct and indirect killing. One attempts to do so at the risk of distorting reality. Even when it does neatly fit, the epistemology of moral does not justify universal norms of conduct in this area of morality. Thus conscience is better prepared to give ear to the voice of the Spirit. The explanation of a unique call by God, recognized by the Council, is more in accord with the acclaim of the early Church accorded these heroic witnesses to Christ.

Of a piece with this closed attitude to charisms and the word of God was the slight attention given to the discernment of spirits. This was consistent with the system, but it ignored Christian tradition on this subject. To the extent it did so moral theology was not traditional in the proper sense of the word. The slighting of the discernment of spirits was part of moral's divorce from asceticism and spirituality.

In a Christian situationism discernment of spirits finds a congenial habitat. To the degree that a moral system gives less emphasis to the juridical and stresses the more perfect, the greater the importance of the situation.[13] One feels he is responding not to a generic law only but to God's concrete invitation to him personally to realize the values in the situation before him which otherwise will never come into existence. The art of discernment is vital to responsible situation response, situations being contingent and singular. Karl Rahner has developed this theme in detail.[14] The more ample freedom in situationism demands greater responsibility. The Christian can no longer be satisfied with fulfilling the law. He has also to examine all the values and disvalues in the situation and weigh them to come to an authentic decision.

The fear of one segment of the Catholic community that this new direction of moral theology is irresponsible is not justified. What can be said in favor of the fear is that it rightly questions whether a person or a community is mature enough to respond with the increased responsibility called for. This is a question of fact, however, which cannot be prejudged solely in terms of the absence of such maturity in the past. A presumption from the past, yes. But the call of the Church to aggiornamento does not permit such presumptions alone to determine the decisions of the present and future. The fearful segment, then, may have an unwarranted distrust of God's people. At any rate the answer to the question of fact can only be known by experience. Vatican II not only permits but encourages the experiment to be tried.

Proceeding now to the communal aspect of conscience in the conciliar teaching, again we find a theme that must be pieced together from various statements. A striking example of adding the new to the traditional is the proposition: "In fidelity to conscience, Christians are joined with the rest of men in the search for truth, . . ."[15] Projecting this statement against the background of the Constitution on the Church, we may thematize as follows: Christian conscience, no matter how individually inspired by the Spirit, must be responsive to the community. In them the Spirit also speaks. Herein lies a theological problem.

The community in the real order is multiple, and in each community a multiplicity of authentic voices is raised. First, in the Catholic community the voice of the magisterium occupies a preeminent place of rule, of service and of direction for the people of God. This pre-eminence must be retained and held in honor. But it is not the sole repository of truth. Because it is not sole, it is subject to modification, to the Spirit speaking through other tongues. One tongue is the voice of the laity: "Christ, the great Prophet . . . fulfills his prophetic office until his full glory is revealed. He does this not only through the hierarchy . . . but also through the laity."[16] Indeed, in matters belonging to the temporal sphere, conscience must accord a primacy to the voice of the laity, though other ranks in the Church retain a right to speak out on temporal matters.

The voice of theologians also must be heard, whether they be clerics or laymen. The development of the sacred sciences is "altogether necessary for the Church."[17] Nor should we limit the role of the theologian to that of conciliar commentator. His functions are to be understood also from the status Christian tradition has accorded him. Seen in this perspective he is to develop and transcend the teaching of the Council. As John Courtney Murray has said:

But to stop with this [writing commentaries on the conciliar texts] would be to return theology to its preconciliar state, in which the theologian had been forced to abdicate his high function and to become simply a commentator on the latest magisterial utterance.[18]

Finally, to give full scope to the communal influence on conscience, other communities than the Catholic Church should shape and modify Catholic judgments. There is the community of other Christians who also incarnate Christian truth, the communities likewise of Jew, Moslem, Buddhist—even of secularists of good will. "In fidelity to conscience, Christians are joined with the rest of men in the search for truth, . . ." And in an obvious reference to non-Western, non-Christian lands, "Many nations, poorer in economic goods, are quite rich in wisdom. . . ."[19]

To conclude this first part, we have seen that a welter of objective demands compete for the allegiance of conscience. Far from solving the problem of conscience, the demand to be objective is a source of diffusion and ambiguity, far more complex and disparate than formerly and therefore more confusing to conscience. Magisterial teaching itself is in transition, developing under the open-ended impetus of Vatican II. The very understanding of what the Church is has received tremendous development in the Council, the implications and implementation of which will require years for us to realize.

We can no longer be quite so clear as to what our bishops throughout the world teach as matters of faith and morals. This primary source of guidance for Catholics is subject to modification from the faith of the laity, the voice of theologians, the beliefs of Protestants, the truths known by Jew, Moslem and other good men. No solution to the problem of this profusion of voices, all sources of objective guidance to conscience, can be found solely in a reaffirmation of prior magisterial statements or fulfillment of canon law.[20]

The law itself is being subjected to substantial revision. As a result of the Council parts of it are obsolete. Its basic orientation has to be conformed to the new understanding of the Church from Vatican II. Not only canon law but moral theology is in transition. Previous norms for the education of conscience are being restudied, inadequacies in the older moral are being hammered out, and a development of the tradition attempted.

The polarity of conscience must be respected, if a viable moral theology of conscience is to be had. This requires not only that moral attend to objectivity but that it develop a sub-jectivity. Personal responsibility must be given room to grow. Freedom must be had to respond to one's personal call from the Spirit. The art of the discernment of spirits must be cultivated. More importance should be given to the voice of God in the situation. Less reliance on moral formulations than in the past and more freedom responsibly to experience the present will be needed.

THE SOCIAL SCIENCES

The second half of this chapter attempts a solution to the prob-lem of conscience sketched above, the welter of change, the plurality of authentic voices, which the Christian conscience faces. The direction of the solution should be that of the ob-jective-subjective polarity of conscience. Sociology and psy-chology are the main sources of evidence we will draw upon. The two are not distinct disciplines. However, in general we may say that sociology provides a development of objectivity, psychology a deeper knowledge of subjectivity.

The very suggestion may strike fear because of the absence of certitude, the relativities, that characterize the social sciences. A moral theology following a methodology of openness to em-piric science necessarily incorporates this relativity. A conclu-sion is only as strong as its weakest premise. Our older moral formulations, however, have proved to contain considerably less certitude than we had thought. A closer look at these sciences actually provides greater strength to our ethical conclusions, as we shall presently try to show.

Vatican II does not share this fear, but rather deplores it.

The Church in the Modern World says that from the progress of the sciences "the nature of man himself is more clearly revealed and new roads to truth are opened."[21] This is a radical departure from the heavy emphasis on deduction and speculative reason in the past to determine what human nature is. The following presentation tries to justify this sane optimism of the council.

First, though, the limitations of an empirical approach need to be faced. One danger is playing the dilettante. A theologian may dip into, perhaps even read widely, anthropology, sociology or psychology without ever acquiring a professional grasp of any of these disciplines. What he produces is psychologism, or its equivalent in the other disciplines, much like the popular notions, say, of psychoanalytic theory. He has not conformed to the rigorous methology of behavioral science.

A second danger threatens from the opposite extreme, reductionism. Here a real professional in behavioral science, for example, psychology, goes beyond his data and the limits of his field of expertise. He reduces everything to psychology. Human behavior is adequately explained by the models and theories of his discipline. Though he may pay lip service to human freedom and God's grace if he is a Christian, there is really no room for these variables in his explanations. This is scientism, not science. A moral theology which adopts this approach is neither moral nor theology. The gospel becomes mental health, the Christian apostolate social progress.

A third difficulty is the complexity and the diffusiveness of the social sciences. There are mountains of data to be digested, a methodology peculiar to these sciences, a bewildering variety of partly conflicting conclusions. The psychoanalyst disagrees in part with the clinical psychologist, and analysts and psychologists disagree among themselves.[22]

This very disparity is at once a sign of weakness and of strength. It is a weakness in that the social sciences have not been in existence as long as the natural sciences. Hence they have not amassed a body of commonly accepted data comparable to the latter. The strength is that disparity contains a built-in corrective. Conflicting views are tested one against another. Psychoanalysis, psychiatry, experimental psychology, clinical psychology, behavioral psychology, insight and action therapy all vie for a hearing. From the confrontation comes discarding of error, modification and synthesis. Furthermore the interdisciplinary approach is operative. Increasingly sociology, anthropology and psychology are synthesized. What finally emerges is not the conclusions of one of these disciplines, but from all three a behavioral phenomenology of man and the human condition not far removed from a philosophical phenomenology.

At this point an epistemological note is in order.[23] Moral, as does any science, begins with the data, the given, which it wishes to explain. For moral science the given is human experience of the good. From a theological point of view it is religious experience. In the Judaeo-Christian tradition religious experience begins with the free intervention of a loving God into human history, a covenant of God with his people, the written record of which is the Old and New Testaments. This event culminated for the Christian in the life, death and resurrection of Jesus Christ. What Jesus had begun the Spirit continues through the community Jesus had founded and also through other religious communities, as Vatican II has taught.

This speaking of the Spirit is both communal and individual. The divine word to man continues to be uttered today in the community and in the depths of the human heart. Salvation history is happening now and will continue happening until the end of time.

But the word of God is not spoken to man in a vacuum. It is directed to believers in the historical situation in which they live and work out their salvation. They respond to his word not only as found in written revelation and the reflective experience of past centuries (theology, Church teaching, the cultural handing on of the tradition) but also as spoken in the events Christians live through. "For there is a *growth* in the understanding of the realities and the words which have been handed down. This happens through the contemplation and the study made by believers, who treasure these things in their hearts (cf. Lk 2:19, 51), through the intimate understanding of *spiritual things they experience* and through the preaching of those who have received through episcopal succession the sure gift of truth."[24] In a word, present religious experience is the context of God's loving word to his people. Here is a point of entry of the social sciences into theology. They help us understand more clearly the reality we are experiencing.

Anthropology tells of the religious experience of other cultures, thus broadening the base of and enriching the western Christian experience with which we are familiar. As Erik Erikson has said, every culture "behaves as if it were the only genuine realization of man as the heavens planned and created him."[25] Empiric psychology reveals the inner dynamics of, and clarifies, the experience in a way that the naked eye of the one experiencing cannot see, and leads to its purification from religiosity and self-seeking. Sociology presents a dimension of religious group behavior of which the group is unaware.

What we perceive as reality is often what appears on the surface, a part of the total experience which moral should have as the starting point of its reflection. Two epistemological conclusions emerge from this. To the extent that moral has done without the aid of the sciences of man, it has proceeded with an inadequate, and sometimes a false, view of the nature of man and the human condition. By these sciences, "the nature of man himself is more clearly revealed."[26] The reality we thought we perceived—and this is the second conclusion—is penetrated much more deeply, or found to be quite different, as a result of scientific scrutiny. Many of the certitudes we supposedly had are discovered to be actual probabilities, but to the extent that empiric science clarifies our perception of reality our moral knowledge acquires greater validity than in the past.

This has been verified in scripture studies. In recent decades the sciences of history, archeology, of oriental languages, the anthropology of the cultures of the Near East and the like have augmented our knowledge of Sacred Scripture enormously. What the exegetes have done is twofold. First, they transcended the limits of western thought patterns which had inevitably influenced western minds interpreting the sacred texts. Necessarily this had involved interpolating meanings and nuances of thought into divine revelation which were not there. We need only recall the impact of literary *genre* on what were thought to be historical passages of Old and New Testaments. This transcultural view of Scripture involved at the same time breaking through into oriental thought patterns which had long kept secret the meanings of words and phrases.

Exegetes (Catholic, Protestant, and Jewish) made a great act of faith—in the human sciences. They said in effect, "No matter how dear the long accepted meaning of a cherished text has been, we will subject it to the rigorous scrutiny of the knowledge these sciences establish, even though a different sense emerges." This required a courage and a dedication to truth not everywhere appreciated in the Church at the time.

When the full impact of the sciences used by exegesis broke upon the American Catholic community during the 1950s (one recalls the reaction upon first hearing that the Magi may not have been historical figures), a tidal wave was felt to be engulfing the Christian faith. We weathered that storm, to the great benefit of the faith.[27] Now a new wave is forming, the impact of a Catholic moral theology deepened and purified by the human sciences it draws upon. With the courage of the exegete, the moralist must now do what the structure of the pre-Vatican II Church did not allow him the freedom to do. Moral conclusions must be opened to the total truth about man and society which behavioral science establishes.[28]

Will this new wave be tidal in its impact or will it break gently on the community? According to sociology, the impact of change on human groups is either creative or disruptive depending on how it is received. A reaction of adjustment to the new can be expected to be creative. Defense of the old to the rejection of the new will be disruptive.

Applying this sociological conclusion to the reception so far given in our culture to the new developments in Catholic moral theology, we can expect disruption and dismay—unless the forces in the community favoring accommodation gain ascendancy. Unfortunately moralists do not yet have the freedom to prepare God's people for the calm acceptance of development of doctrine, to carry out the conciliar mandate of accommodating theology to the times. The theology of marriage and family limitation is a case in point. Chanceries still threaten to impose the penalty for solicitation or other canonical punishments on priests who follow the new view in confession. Communication is lacking; many in authority are not willing even to discuss the question. Liturgists in many areas have not the freedom to implement the Constitution on the Sacred Liturgy. Authorization to do controlled experiment in the liturgy is given seldom and reluctantly, if at all.

It is an invaluable function of social science to show us how to ease the way for the acceptance of new formulations, to set up norms for determining when a previous stage of theological development no longer fits the needs of Christians in the present. Eventually we can have an ethical system and a juridical structure that incorporates sociological norms for development and change, along with holding fast to tradition—if we but accept the data of sociology.

What does social science offer us in this trying period of transition? What must we hold on to, what adapt? It insists absolutely on the need of structure, of institutions. No person can stand apart from the community and social norms. In childhood isolation from the group certainly means that conscience cannot take shape. Moreover, socialization occurs in the early years of life; the child learns to get along with others and interiorizes the values and norms of the group. It is undisputed in behavioral science that the role of every society is to hand on its traditions.

This support for the Church is reassuring to Christians in this unsettling period of change. Social science lends no aid to throwing out baby with the bath water. The questioning of existing structure, it insists, need not imply the rejection of structure, an essential of human living.

In adolescence the person normally seeks and finds his socio-psychological identity. This is not solely the product of social influences. It contains his own ideal of what he wants to be and do. But to achieve identity requires a reasonable harmony between the ego-ideal and the expectations others have of him— family, friends, Church, the political society of which he is a member. One's identity must, of course, perdure through the adult years.

This social factor in identity does not mean absolute conformity to cultural norms. Nor does it imply that the values these norms ensure are unchallengeable and unchangeable. On the contrary, the mark of the mature adult is his ability to test values and freely to accept or reject them. Nevertheless, no human lifetime suffices for an individual methodically to question all the values of his culture, with a view to their acceptance, rejection or modification as they affect his life pattern. To do so would jeopardize his security and emotional balance. Much of his value system he must accept without testing from the community. Behavioral science, then, warns us of precipitous or total questioning of value systems.

Among these values are, of course, biological, economic, esthetic, moral and religious values. The culture, along with the sub-culture to which man belongs, transmits the moral values that guide his choices and constitute the kind of person he becomes. Organized religion, as an organ of cultural transmission, insures vital values to his existence. Religious tradition sets forth a blueprint for and gives meaning to his life. As an instance of this, Erikson points out (in his *Identity and the Life Cycle*) the value of religion for providing adults with the social source and support of the necessary qualities of faith and conviction. And without this strength in himself, Erikson maintains, the adult cannot communicate to the child that basic trust in others which is crucial to development in the early years of life.

Religious institutions give legitimation to man's activity by approving of it when it is in accord with the norms of the religious group; when it is not, sanctions exert pressure for compliance. Religion, along with law and ethics, is an integrative system, according to social science. This means that it is a strong force for unity and continuity; it promotes love and respect for others and counteracts disruptive forces, whether disease, hatreds, war or crime. But like the mature adult, religion must transcend the culture and challenge its values and norms, says the social scientist. Failure to do so leads to weak conformism and a watering down of the goals of religion to the detriment of society.[29]

Such tribute as the above to the role of religion assures us that our faith has not been in vain. Our turning to behavioral science for an evaluation of the Church as guide and shaper of conscience is greeted with the response: be your authentic self. We have more reason to hope in and less to fear from social science than we have thought in the past. On the contrary, from the respect of sociologists for the functions religion performs, we ought to welcome them as valuable allies and supporters of religion.

Particularly at this moment of the Vatican II era of the Church, social science has an important contribution to make. It can assist immeasurably in understanding change in the Church, matrix of consciences, when there is stress and strain in external structure and in the minds of Christians. Understanding can lead to peaceful transition and to control of the pace and direction of change. Here is one such sociological contribution.

What we are undergoing is a "pluralization of social worlds."[30] This can best be understood in terms of past experiences of the Catholic Church with the Copernican and Darwinian views of the universe. Christians had been living in another "world," with an image of man and his environment based on an earlier and less perfect knowledge. Within this relatively enclosed system they had an explanation of human existence which made sense and gave meaning to reality as men then experienced it—until these great scientific breakthroughs arose to challenge the existing popular, scientific, philosophical and theological explanations of reality. A universe of bodies in motion around the sun, the earth only one planet within the system in Copernicus' discovery; in Darwin's, man himself in his elemental constitution the product of evolutionary forces; these were earth-shaking revolutions. They threatened to dethrone sacred Scripture, God's own word to man, to undermine the Christian faith. Actually, as we know now, they did nothing of the sort. Rather they purified Christian faith of ignorance of man, God and the universe. They were midwife to the birth of new truth.

The consternation Copernicus and Darwin caused the Church is an example of what sociology calls a crisis of credibility. The Church's worldview no longer was adequate. Moreover, had it held on to a posture of defense instead of accommodation to the new, it would have become, humanly speaking, an archaic relic of the past and lost the following of educated men.

In our own day, multiply the sciences, add thousands of centers of scientific research, consider the expenditure of billions of dollars on scientific discovery of reality, throw in the computer which produces in days the knowledge which formerly required years of man-hours in the laboratory—in comparison with the times of Darwin and Copernicus. The result is not only radically accelerated changes in man's worldview from a continous explosion of knowledge but also a "pluralization of social worlds," the biological view of man and the world, the space age concept of the universe, the sociological explanation of man, and the like. Is there any wonder that we feel uprooted by the invasion of our previous worldview by these new systems of knowledge with their apparent challenge to cherished moral and religious values? The lessons of history and the sociology of change, however, give us pause and some degree of poise. The pains we are experiencing can be the birth pangs of new life.

If the Christian community is to be a viable institution it must accommodate its teaching to these new images of man and the world, and work out a new correspondence of revealed and acquired knowledge. The posture of defense of prior philosophical and theological explanations, which too many Catholics still maintain, creates that much more confusion for consciences, as Christians absorb the new scientific revolutions, yet find their implications for theology opposed by their religion.

Never again can we have the relatively closed and stable cultural systems that explained reality so well for Christians in the past. Feudal man, for example, knew well God's will for him. The simple catechetic: love God and serve your liege lord, was valid for his whole lifetime. God's will for the Christian today is to learn to live with, and to adapt to, multiple and rapidly developing worldviews. "In our day . . . the ways of thinking are exceedingly various," says Vatican II. "It is the task of the entire people of God, especially pastors and theologians, to hear, distinguish and interpret the many voices of our age, and to judge them in the light of the divine Word."[31] The experience we are undergoing is part of the trial of this life, of the wayfarer. We have no choice but to be a pilgrim Church, constantly on the move.

The first imperative for Christian conscience, then, is accommodation. Holding exclusively to the explanations of the past—says sociology from the study of change in all social groups—will only aggravate the confusion of conscience. The gap between those who defend the *status quo* and those who neglect the tradition will grow wider, the voices to left and right more clamorous, basic unity in the Christian community more tenuous.

The defenders of the *status quo* are not to be confused with conservatives. The true conservative, while holding to the past, remains open to aggiornamento. Yet he must be on his guard lest he fall into the posture of pure defense, the reaffirmations of old legitimations, the clinging to the absolutizing tendency of the past. This way leads to ghetto formation and loss of credibility in the many, except for the "faithful" few.

Similarly those who are emphasizing the need to change are not to be confused with the reckless innovator. Yet the genuine progressive needs in turn to be on his guard. From the sociological data, accommodation contains an escalation factor. The movement for change can go too far, to the collapse of the credibility of the tradition.[32]

The danger of credibility loss, inherent in both extremes, defense and reckless innovation, brings into play the sociological rule: when plausibility structures (for example, theological explanation, the legal system of an institution, liturgy) begin to disintegrate, then objective reality begins to lose its hold. Let us first illustrate this from the Death of God phenomenon, then apply it to our subject of change in the Church. The religious tradition of God has suffered a reality loss. This is due to a loss of credibility in such factors as theological explanations of reality, the institutionalized forms of established religion, the concerns and activities of the Churches which are felt to be out of touch with the real needs of mankind. As a result God is dead for many, only half alive for others. The only recourse is to make God real again by other plausibility structures—renewal in theology, catechetics and liturgical rites, for example.

Most Catholics, it seems, are willing to heed the call of the Church that we marshal all our forces to devise new ways of confronting the atheism of our times, that religion be made vital and God become real to men. Yet many of them resist the strengthening of our plausibility structures in other areas than belief in God, for example, the effort to develop moral theology. Accordingly, we read statements by prominent Catholics that the whole trouble with the Church today is the loss of faith. They thus commit the basic error of confusing loss of credibility in structures with a loss of belief in the essential truths of Christianity. They fail to see that the very sense of credibility loss is evidence of adherence to Christian faith which one feels to be poorly structured in existing formulations, laws and ritual.

Vatican II was very careful to make the distinction between faith and formulation, which is one form of the distinction between plausibility structures and reality, and to put its weight behind the restoration of credibility. Indeed the council takes a sanguine view of the effects of change on Christian faith, while recognizing the dangers involved. The questioning of values effects a purification of religion, it says, and "exacts day by day a more personal and explicit adherence to faith; as a result many persons are achieving a more vivid sense of God."[33]

Thus far in this second part we have turned to sociology for light on the question of objectivity and conscience. The sociology of religion says clearly that organized religion does valuable service to society; in guiding the consciences of its adherents according to its tradition, it ensures vital values to society. In this tradition, however, religious faith must be carefully distinguished from its theological, legal and ritual structures. The sociology of change provides most important norms that we ignore at our peril in this period of transition.

Next we look to empiric psychology, seeking to find what knowledge it imparts relative to subjectivity and conscience. First we shall try to discover what conscience is, according to psychology. Then we ask, what are the moral implications of the psychology of the super-ego, particularly with regard to the development of mature Christian conscience.

To find out what conscience is we turn first to that part of psychology which treats of the acquisition of moral values. From the conclusions reached there we obtain, for one thing, support for the tradition which sees conscience as a function of intellect or reason. Empiric studies reveal a definite cognitive dimension. The acquiring of morality by the person involves learning a system of rules for determining right and wrong. This is but one dimension, however. There is also the element of feeling, the experiencing of anxiety, guilt or satisfaction. Feelings—which were neglected in our recent moral tradition—are a basic determinant of morality. Scripture had always given them due recognition. Freud rediscovered them.

A further empiric finding is the low correlation between moral knowledge and feeling. The two are not connatural. One can be intellectually convinced of the rightness of his action yet feel guilty for having done it. Conversely we are capable of feeling innocent of evil in an act intellectually perceived as wrong.

A third dimension of morality is conduct. Psychology sees conduct as the field of action on which moral knowledge and feelings meet. Here psychological data corroborate what experience and philosophy establish, that doing moral good is not the necessary result of knowledge of the good. There are variables that intervene, the attraction of other values, one's physiological state of, say, energy or fatigue. Psychologically, the ideal is a harmony or integration of knowledge, feeling and conduct. The acquisition of this ideal is, however, the work of a lifetime, the creation of the moral self.

Such evidence as the above contains implications for moral theology. One of these is a more holistic concept of conscience. The definition of conscience as a function of reason in the tradition broadens to include the whole person. Thus Bernard Haering conceives conscience as "the person in his essential dynamism toward wholeness." For E. Clinton Gardiner it is "the self, the willing, acting and knowing subject who is aware that he is answerable for his action."[34] In greater detail, conscience may be described in its several dimensions as the person acquiring a set of norms for determining good and evil, developing the ability to evaluate, experiencing feelings of satisfaction or guilt and moving toward an integration of his conduct with his sense of right and wrong and with his feelings.

Proceeding now to the empiric data on the genesis of conscience, new light is shed on its nature. As elaborated by psychoanalysis the super-ego, that primitive, childhood precursor of conscience in the moral sense, is the agency of the person which interiorizes the values of authority figures, originally of parents, then of other adult influences such as teachers and religious instructors. Though it does not weigh moral values, the super-ego is important as the beginning of a development that takes place with greater or less success. The *terminus a quo* is significant as a basis of comparison with true conscience, a point of reference of the mature person with the infantile.

The super-ego and its functions, as elaborated in psychoanalytic theory, are confirmed by psychology. Dealing not with the mentally ill in the therapeutic situation but with the normal, the remarkable studies of Jean Piaget on the learning process in children are revealing. In earlier childhood, from the fourth to about the eighth year, Piaget found the norms are judged as absolute. Whether they be the rules for playing marbles or the prohibition of stealing and lying, they are changeless. Norms are given ontological status like things that exist. This attitude he terms "moral realism."[35]

Violations of rules are judged with equal absoluteness. Intention of evil or the lack thereof makes no difference. Nor are the effects on others of one's action relevant. Furthermore, the child at this age is unable to evaluate good and bad.

> Moral wrongness is defined in terms of adult sanctions; acts that are wrong are acts that adults punish. Duty is understood as obedience to authority. . . . The young child's intellectual limitations in conjunction with his respect for authority cause him . . . to believe that moral values are absolute and universal. . . .[36]

In a word, early childhood "morality" is extrinsic, simplistic and totally authority-oriented. There is as yet no awareness that obedience to authority is justifiable as promoting unity of action in the community and continuity for communal values, that commands which do not realize goals are questionable.

One legitimate function of absolutes is their value of support for the younger child. But they are supports for the immature. As such they are crutches to be supplanted by the growing ego, the maturing of conscience. The conclusion is not that all absolutes are to be outgrown to reach adulthood. Rather, one matures to the degree he outgrows the primitive morality which says: an act is good if commanded, bad if prohibited.

Children beyond eight years perceive rules as subject to change. The intention of the doer assumes its rightful place in contrast to the prior objectivistic moralizing. The consequences for others of one's action looms significant. Piaget terms this stage of moral development "moral relativism." It represents, of course, a growth in psychological maturity.

White synthesizes the original data of psychoanalysis with Piaget's findings and subsequent research as follows:

> We shall regard the super-ego as a childhood conscience, built upon moral realism, irrational in character, borrowed straight from parental sanctions *without reflection or the use of his own experience on the part of the child.* Mature conscience begins when the child's sympathy and insight get to work so that he sees a purpose—other than pleasing his parents— behind restraints and ideals. It continues when he discriminates the effects of his actions on everyone who is affected by them, judging his acts accordingly and freeing himself from blind literal obedience to a code. Murray describes this process as the integration of the super-ego into the ego, the integration being accomplished by cognitive activity and independent judgment. To the extent that this integration is accomplished, the super-ego ceases to function as an ego-alien force in the personality.[37]

What happens when this integration is not accomplished? Fixation of the super-ego, says White. The characteristics of moralizing in the fourth-to-eighth-year stage perdure as a disruptive and retarding force. Moral judgment continues to be overly objective, downplaying intention, discounting consequences, continuing to absolutize. "When the super-ego is not outgrown in the manner just described—and we must admit that much of our moral training seems designed to prevent it from being outgrown—it remains an autonomous and often rather disturbing force in personality."[38]

This immaturity can continue on into the adult years. Studies of adult morality, comparable to those of Piaget on children, have not been made. Yet White does not hesitate to identify as super-ego fixation the experientially verified moralizing of the old lady who makes clothes on the sabbath for soldiers in wartime and feels guilty about it. Or the self-accusation of sin by the young man of strict upbringing who smokes and tastes alcohol, yielding to pressure from his college peers.

From our Catholic sub-culture instances of childhood super-ego in adults come all too readily to mind. The young woman who confesses she ate meat on Friday "because I forgot," has the conscience of a child. The man who is told not to confess missing Mass when he was sick, but insists, "I feel better when I confess it," also confesses super-ego fixation. Examples could be multiplied. How pervasive of American Catholicism this primitive moralizing is, empiric studies have not shown. Experience indicates that it is all too widespread.

What are the social factors that contribute to such stunting of moral growth? Doubtless they are plural. White singles out the fear of moral chaos:

> Fixation of the super-ego is encouraged by society's timidity in allowing the individual to think for himself, especially on moral matters. The image of moral chaos, doubtless greatly exaggerated, makes men hesitate to encourage individual moral maturity. It is easier and safer to keep people in line.[39]

The freedom to develop responsibility, proportionate to the maturity of the person, has not been given.

The awful implications of this evidence for parents, teachers, clergy and hierarchy are clear. Since conscience is the person in his highest strivings, the perpetuation of this repression of growth and freedom is a sin against the person. And since grace presupposes nature upon which it builds, this sub-cultural trait holds back Christians from attaining the mature freedom of the sons of God. It sins against the coming of the kingdom.

To take one instance of this, the current handling by the official Church of the question of family limitation raises a fearful question that must be faced. The blanket of silence imposed from above on the new moral opinion and the waiting for a papal decision tend to reinforce super-ego fixation in many Catholics. The danger is that of morality-by-fiat: whether certain forms of family limitation are good or bad depends on authoritative decision, is the impression created in many minds. This is bad psychology, bad morality, and deplorable formation of consciences. Given such treatment of the question, if and when a development of doctrine is forthcoming from the Holy See, the likelihood is a conscience that judges conduct which it believed was intrinsically evil to be now permissible—by decision of authority. This would be a force for super-ego fixation, a factor retarding Christian growth.

This is not to say that the teachers of God's people are not concerned about the formation of conscience. They are aware also of the danger of loss of credibility in the tradition. This latter is a factor they have reckoned with. But insufficient attention has been accorded to a morality-by-fiat reaction by many Catholics. The crisis of credibility on the one hand and perpetuation of immaturity of conscience on the other poses a terrible dilemma for the pastors of the faithful. They need our understanding and our help. But one wonders if silence is the solution.

In another context our bishops responded with genuine leadership in an analogous crisis. Their action suggests a solution to the present question. At the annual meeting of the hierarchy in 1960 they issued a remarkable statement entitled "Need for Personal Responsibility." The background of the statement was the recognition of socialization and its effects, namely, the forces of the collectivity depersonalizing the individual. The end results of this were seen to be the shrugging off of personal responsibility in political matters, overdependence on the organization in the business world and an increase of divorce in family life. The bishops appositely cited Pope John: "Modern man sees that the sphere in which he can think for himself, act on his own initiative, exercise his responsibilities and affirm and enrich his personality is in many cases restricted to an excessive degree."

Eloquent appeal was made to the personal initiative and responsibility which have been our national characteristics. To achieve this personal responsibility the bishops called for greater scope to be given to individual freedom: "We must seek to enlarge the area of personal autonomy to protect the human personality from a greater encroachment on its freedom and responsibility."

There is a remarkable convergence of judgment between the bishops' statement and the view of scientists such as Professor White, the one from experiential observation, the other from empiric science. Lack of moral responsibility and initiative requiring that we "enlarge the area of personal autonomy" is the diagnosis and prescription of the bishops. "Individual moral maturity" is lacking, in White's analysis. He recommends relaxation of pressure from above which seeks to "keep people in line," and "allowing the individual to think for himself."

This convergence and mutual reinforcement of two independent sources indicate the direction in which the solution to the contraceptive problem should move. More than that, it is the direction to be taken across the board in matters moral, which is what the bishops and Professor White are speaking of.

By way of concluding this chapter, an epistemological analysis of the respective roles of the social sciences and of moral theology in their mutual interaction is here attempted. An earlier and familiar formulation of their relationship assigned facts as the province of the former, values of the latter. Sociology, economics and kindred disciplines tell us what man is, while moral science speaks of what man ought to do. The two fields are autonomous and their autonomy should be respected. Yet there is a simplistic ring to this division of labor, which calls for re-examination. We divide our study into what the social sciences *de facto* do in relation to moral science and what they validly and rightly do (the *de jure* question). Their *de facto* contribution is beyond dispute: they share the same field of study, complement moral, and in some areas substitute for it. The *de jure* question holds that the social sciences are in some ways normative, in themselves and in relation to moral.

De facto, social scientists study the same field as moralists: human behavior and attitudes, both in their personal and social dimensions. The aspect under which they examine human reality, the formal object of inquiry, however, differs from that of the moral theologian. So the traditional assessment reads. The least that can be said, then, is that the two disciplines should be complementary.

As complementary, social science offers valuable extrinsic helps to moral. For example, it tells the strength and weakness of moral norms to do what they are supposed to effect, the uplift of moral conduct. As Kenneth Boulding, Professor of Economics at the University of Michigan, points out, the force of a norm, sociologically measured, depends upon three factors: a) the extent to which it is consistent with the value system of society, b) its grounding in moral truth, and c) the degree of actual compliance of people with the norm.[40] Furthermore, knowledge of widespread non-acceptance may lead to a re-valuation of norms and result in a more adequate expression of moral truth. As an example of the compliance factor, knowledge of the extent of contraceptive practice no doubt has been a significant element in the non-acceptance by many Catholics of the official norms. Such sociological norms are no guarantee of the moral validity of ethical beliefs and practices in a culture. But they can be the source of valuable clues to the moralist, for example, the need of a reformulation of conjugal morality.

A second point of complementarity, now accepted by experts in moral: some ethical problems are more susceptible of a behavioral science solution than a moral one. Alcoholism and compulsive masturbation are two examples. Both yield more readily to therapy, group and individual respectively, than to solutions moralists have tried. Moreover, behavioral data enter into the moral judgment in such matters and modify it. Thus the fact of alcoholism as a sickness modifies the moral judgment of sin. Instead of a non-aggression pact between behavioral and moral scientists, agreeing that each stay within traditional fact-and-value confines, a mutul assistance pact ought to be signed.

Boulding sums up:

> I suspect that the sciences in general and the social sciences in particular are both substitutes and complements to the sacred aspects of life (law, ethics and religion), and whereas at some points they compete, at others they reinforce . . .[41]

To come to the *de jure* question, are the social sciences in some sense normative for moral science and for organized religion? The answer to this question appears to be that the conclusions of social science provide sociological norms which moral may not ignore. Secondly, sociologists and psychologists, in the areas of their competence bearing on moral, make good ethicists and sometimes theologians. Let us look at the evidence for our proposition. First, there is the literature on the sociology of religion, which has raised clerical hackles in the past. Second, there are writings by behavioral scientists which are specifically ethical or theological in character. The work of Peter Berger is representative of this category.[42] Lastly we have epistemological studies of behavioral science as it relates to moral.

From the sociology of religion we get data that are not only factual and descriptive but also prescriptive. From the study of activity in human groups in general, sociologists distill those imperatives which must be observed for any community to survive, grow and achieve its self-appointed goals. Moreover, these imperatives are not just sociological, but moral and religious. The Church, for example, is not free to officiate at her own burial, to refuse to spread the kingdom or carry out its divine mission. The assurance of divine protection unto the end of time does not exempt it from following the wisdom of experience and the science of society.

The classic example of religion running counter to sociological norms is Prohibition. It ignored the knowledge of behavioral science, a mistake that Alcoholics Anonymous, for example, has not reduplicated. The movement was too exclusively dictated by religious belief. There was too little recognition of the clash with other values in the cultural system.

The sociological norm violated is far from being for religion an ultimate, since religion must sometimes inevitably clash with values in the culture. Yet the norm can mean that in a given conflict the Churches would do better to choose other means than they have in mind, or to be silent. The latter alternative has long been acknowledged in the moral teaching of following the good element in the lesser of two evils, and allowing people to remain in good faith.

The social sciences are also normative as tracing the direction of moral reflection and of social action by the Churches. Sociological analysis discovers the needs of man in a given cultural context. It is precisely the complexity of life today, the interaction of social forces called socialization which makes aggiornamento so difficult, and requires the indispensable help of scientific behavioral analysis. Where does one begin, for example, the renewal of religious life in a particular congregation, assessing all of its ministries? Their corporate experience from the past is no substitute for an empiric study of the present.

Third, social science diagnoses and prescribes what is the common good, whether social, economic or political, and this not only concretely but theoretically. This means theoretical on the level of abstraction of behavioral phenomenology. For many imperatives of the common good are pre-metaphysically evident. With respect to the common good, then, ethics and social science are working common ground. They often reach the identical conclusions. Moral theology, it is true, brings to the confrontation with a culture a deeper vision of man and his destiny. And the social programs of the Churches make room for variables which sociology knows not of: God's grace, divine providence and a Spirit inspired charismatic role. The two disciplines, then, should collaborate more than they have in the past.

In fact, this sharing of labor has come a long way already. A glance at the social encyclicals of the Church since John XXIII's *Mater et Magistra* reveals a heavy indebtedness to social science. No doubt the movement of the Church toward secularity, discernible in the Constitution on the Church in the Modern World and culminating in *Populorum Progressio,* will provide further impetus in this direction. At any rate we have moved so far already that moral theology and the social sciences have achieved a viable rapprochement. Let us turn to the latest social encyclical of the Church to see that this is so.

In *Populorum Progressio* one can detect the hand of a group of Catholic social scientists. The Church has made its own the evidence, the idiom and the conclusions of current economic and sociological analysis as to the needs of the developing nations. Indeed the document represents a decided progression over its predecessors precisely because of the social scientists who worked on it. Socialism is no longer singled out as enemy to a Christian social program, because economists no longer see red, whether Moscow or Peking shade, in the socialisms of African and Asian nations. These peoples are seen as struggling for viable economies and national identities rather than following Russian or Chinese tutelage.

A second achievement of the encyclical is the absence for the first time of insistence on private ownership in the form of small business enterprises, homes or land. This represents a recognition of the ability of mass economic society to provide for human needs. Thereby we have a progression in the world-view of the Church from peasant-town to mass-industrial. Neither of these two major developments could have taken place without the aid of social scientists.[13]

A fourth way in which behavioral and moral science come together is verified when the social scientist speaks as a Christian. Here is a sample of this category of writing by Peter Berger:

> Just as the Christian faith cannot be identified with a particular political creed, it cannot be identified with a particular culture's value system. As soon as this happens the prophetic mission of the Church is paralyzed from the start. We suspect that any situation in which the Church exists in a culture without any noteworthy tension provides a danger signal that something seems to be radically wrong. That is, we suspect that the very nature of the Christian faith precludes the complete absence of tension within a culture. This, of course, does not mean that Christians will always be persecuted in a

violent way. There are many ways of being eaten by lions. But a situation in which the Christians are indistinguishable from all the other spectators in the cultural coliseum is hardly one in which we would find much faithfulness to the example of the crucified savior.[14]

In this literary genre of the social scientist turned theologian we have additional evidence of collaboration, this time on the specifically theological level. This kind of writing may not be theology or sociology in the ordinary sense of the terms. Call it interdisciplinary writing, if you will. But here sociological and moral-theological come together in the same person. The result is a synthesis of the two fields, the like of which we should wish to see much more.

At any rate it is more accurate to speak in terms of the relation between the roles of moral theologian and social scientist than in terms of the relation between moral theology and social science. This more subjective wording of the perennial question is preferable to the objective one.[45] The question was posed too exclusively in objective terms in the past. The two disciplines are autonomous, each with its own method and object. The aim to maintain autonomy in the past has been a legitimate one, but it has been overemphasized. Autonomy need not mean separation.

A further reason for retaining the older pattern of relationship between scientist and moralist has been the fear of the former that in bringing the subjective into social science in the form of moral and religious value judgments there is the risk of losing scientific objectivity. This has been the controlling norm in the epistemology of behavioral science until recently. But the time has come to raise the question: have not these sciences been on the scene long enough for their scientific status, and therefore their objectivity, to be firmly established and accepted? The social scientist need not feel apologetic for making moral evaluations. Not that his contribution to morality is the last or only word. The moralist for his part should welcome the collaboration of his behavioral counterpart.

The social scientist is a person, endowed therefore with reason, capable of value judgments, influenced by the religious dimension of his culture. He possesses a personal value system from which he cannot always disassociate himself in his professional capacity. Furthermore, and increasingly, behavioral scientists do not wish to abstain from religious and moral evaluation. So complicated has reality become (socialization, to take the horizontal axis; multi-determination of behavior, to take the vertical), that they ought to turn ethicists and moral theologians. They have a deeper perception of human reality in its diversity and diffuseness, a more profound command of the situation in its wider dimensions than the moral expert as such possesses.

This need not deprive the theologian of his job. By reason of their specialization social scientists, even speaking as Christians, usually do not have the command of moral theory extrapolated from the past experience of mankind by various ethical and moral systems. Even when the behavioral scientist is a believer, he is not thereby a professional theologian conversant with the scientific knowledge of Scripture and the method of theological science. The moralist need not join the ranks of the unemployed.

The conclusion reached thus far is that social scientists sometimes deliberately choose to be ethicists or theologians, and that by reason of their competence they ought to do so in those areas of their science which coincide with ethics and theology. We now examine the case for the claim: he is incapable of not moralizing, even though he may think he is sticking to his last. Take for example the neat distinction we used to make between psychoanalysis as a philosophy and as a therapeutic technique. The anti-religious, mechanistic, theoretical roots of Freudianism, we said, can be totally prescinded from. The therapy, like any technique, can be accepted or rejected on its own merits. The therapist need not impose Freud's values on the patient.

The distinction served the purpose of achieving an armed truce at a time when psychoanalysis and religion were at war.

But is it any longer tenable? More accurately, it should be said that the therapeutic technique can be grafted upon *another* theoretical base, rather than imply that it need not have any. For no therapist can prescind from a theory of personality. This means not only an empirical psychological theory but a philosophy of person. This may not be philosophy in any profound or metaphysical sense. But as a thinking human being, he has and operates from a theory of human nature. For the nature of man is a question of fact, the answer to the question, what *is* man? By elaborating their discipline, behavioral scientists are actually contributing to the definition of human nature.

Perry London, psychologist at the University of Southern California, expresses the subject as follows:

> Cannot the psychotherapist use the kinds of certainty that science can afford to induce some hints or clues to plausible morality? Can he not start off by addressing himself to the nature of man and use the information he can get about it as a means of calculating how he ought to live? He could not do so very comprehensively, but he does not need to be comprehensive; the very extent to which he can discover some limits to man's capacity and some parameters of it itself establishes some limits of his own moral schemes, for one cannot be asked to live in ways that violate his nature.
>
> In plain language, the above argues that finding out what men are like will go a long way towards determining for us what we should try to make them be like. To that extent, the moral wisdom of the psychotherapist will depend on his willingness to accept the dictates of his science.[16]

The truth is that behavioral scientists cannot escape ethical value judgments, London holds, and there is increasing recognition among them of the relevance of moral issues to the pursuit of their discipline. For example, a claim is made of the biological inferiority of a minority race. The anthropologist who refutes the claim, willy-nilly, is exercising a moral function in society and has made a moral value judgment in choosing the subject of his research.

Or demographers, brought face to face with the imbalance between population and resources in a developing nation, cannot but think of measures for population control. At the same time they are aware of cultural resistance to limiting the size of the family. The resistance may come not only from social or economic values in the culture but from moral and religious ones. As human beings demographers feel an imperative need to help the overpopulated nation. As scientists they have a grasp of the economic plight which the developing nation itself does not have. The previous concern of social science for "objectivity," for value-less judgment, would lead to an impasse. Now the question they ask themselves is, whose value judgments are correct, the developing nation's or ours? Faced with the life and death issue of fellow human beings, they no longer hold back but enter the arena of religious and moral evaluation. Not only demographers and economists but psychologists also are becoming increasingly aware of the "relevance of moral issues to their discipline."[47]

From what man is to what he ought to be is not quite the lyric leap from one level of knowledge to another we have conceived it to be in the past. A transition, yes, but a transition that leads by a kind of inexorable *élan* from fact to infra-moral and then moral values. We ought to conceive of the hierarchy of values, from the biological and economic through to the moral and religious, as a dynamic continuum. Man's perceptive powers move naturally and logically on from fact to value. Moreover, at times the possessor of the facts, by reason of his superior command of reality, is under a moral imperative to push on to moral judgment. Such, it would appear, was the experience of the physicists who fashioned the first atom bomb. It is the contention of this chapter that the brand of absolute separation we have held in the past between is and ought, between moral and social science, is untenable. It is a form of positivism with respect to the empiric.

We have come full cycle. The opening to behavioral science as a source of ethical values was dictated by Vatican II and the epistemology of moral science. This involves us in the relativity of the empiric. Yet this source of moral data will provide us with a rich accretion to our moral knowledge, comparable to biblical theology's enrichment by human science. The accretion will make moral norms more determinate.[48] Greater relativity in the abstract will yield sounder moral conclusions in the concrete.

DANIEL C. MAGUIRE

Moral Absolutes
and the Magisterium

History does not commend a simple view of the magisterium.
The magisterium may, with some adequacy, be described as
the Church's active competence to teach and bear witness to
the nature and consequences of God's revelation in Christ. This
competence has been in the Church from the beginning. The object of this competence, however, as well as its subject and
manner of realization, show the creative and passive-reactive
shifts and changes that mark the history of man.

The magisterium appears in varied ways in history depending on the prevailing ecclesiology, the status of communications, and the cultural views of authority and truth. The
incarnate Lord did not concede to his Church a disincarnate
immunity to the exigencies of essential human historicity. This
does not say that the Church has been buffeted and shaped
helplessly by "the forces of history"; it says merely that redemption is being achieved in time.

"Teaching" is not a univocal term. History shows a variety
of teaching forms. It shows us the Sophists and Socrates and
Aristotle; it shows us Jesus and Druids and the medieval university lectures; it shows us ecumenical councils, tribal elders,
Montessori schools, and Marshall McLuhan. A teacher can be
anything from an authority figure who imposes information on
his subjects to a prodding stimulator of thought. Lessons good

and bad are taught also by our actions. Thus it must be remembered that the Church acting is also the Church teaching.

From the beginning, liturgy was a primary means of teaching the good news. Important sections of the inspired Scriptures are actually liturgical documents. It is in great part the praying Church that teaches us in the New Testament.[1] The ministry of sacraments was not without the ministry of the word. Ability to witness and to teach was the prime qualification for authority in the hierarchical community (Acts 1:21-22; 6:4.).[2] Ideally, no administrative problem, not even giving food to the hungry, could distract the officers of the Church from their full-time magisterial role. "It would not be right for us to neglect the word of God so as to give out food" (6:2). It was their part to be given over "to prayer and the service of the word" (6:4). The success of the community was expressed in terms of effective teaching (6:7).

The teaching office in the early Church was not relegated to a "department"; the community itself was magisterial. The good news was lived in a spirit of proclamation so that the life of the Christians provided an instruction on the nature of the Christian way. The community, seen as a concrete and living norm of Christian existence, came to be called "the Way" (Acts 9:2). Thus, the Way was persecuted (22:4) and evil was spoken of the Way (19:9).[3] So closely identified was the living body of Christians with the Christian message that Ignatius of Antioch could refer to the Church itself as "the agape."[4]

The early magisterium, therefore, was liturgical, ecclesial, vital. It enjoyed, initially, an admirable dynamism and simplicity. Simple credal formulae and symbols were a favored technique.[5] Simplicity, however, was short-lived. The message was poured into the ears, cultures, philosophies, and languages of Parthians, Medes, and Elamites. Divisions and factions grew up in the Way. Apostles and elders soon found it necessary to meet in council to settle questions rising not so much from the kerygma as from the clash of Jewish and Hellenic cultures (Acts 15). The credal formulae grew longer and more complex.[6] Biblical language was not found suited to meet the philosophical

critics of Christianity and men of the Church agonized in conscience at the necessity of restating Christian teaching in new
words and new symbols.[7]

Councils and synods have always been a favored technique
for tapping ecclesial wisdom and for revealing the Church's
current state of doctrinal consciousness. Particular weight was
also attached to the traditions of the communities in the great
cities which had been the starting points of Christianization.
Irenaeus, for example, stressed the sureness of the traditions
of communities which boasted a directly apostolic foundation.[8]
At times, the most important magisterial figures on the scene
were individual bishops who through their eloquence and extraordinary abilities obtained a voice and influence not suggested
by their sees.

One such was Caesarius of Arles. The pope urged Caesarius to care for "the affairs of religion, both in Gaul and in
Spain."[9] Caesarius showed something more than alacrity, dis-
patching emissaries throughout Gaul, Spain, and into Italy itself.[10] His leadership was felt in thirteen church councils held
between 506 and 541.[11] Chrysostom, Epiphanius, and most
especially Augustine had an influence on Church teaching that
was nothing less than massive.

In the period from the sixth to the eleventh centuries, the
monasteries attained magisterial prominence. The penitential
books wrought by the monks were widely used to guide confessors. They were a most important means in those centuries
for the teaching of morality in the Church. This type of magisterial operation was not highly centralized; communications
and sociological conditions did not permit it to be. Some advantage accrued to this as when, for example, the Irish,
cut off from the penitential practices of Rome and the continent, developed the more benign system of private penance
that eventually prevailed.[12] Centralization became a notable
phenomenon in the modern Church with teaching and administrative burdens shifting more to the Roman See. This situation is now being altered by an application of the principles
of collegiality and subsidiarity.

At any rate, no study of the magisterium can ignore the variety of form that has characterized the magisterium in history. It is not enough to look to conciliar or Roman decrees to know what the Church has taught.

Our specific concern here is with the Church teaching morality. The nature of morality is such as to present special problems and to justify a distinct consideration of the Church's authentic teaching competence in this area.[13] It is instructive to see how the hierarchical magisterium has functioned in special moral questions in the past, to see how the magisterium can effectively function in the modern world. After seeing the magisterium in action, in our concluding section we will explore the theological implications of the historical data.

THE CHURCH ON WAR AND PEACE

History shows no one Christian position on war and peace.[13a] On this most crucial moral issue Christians have shown neither consistency nor unity. New Testament teaching did not answer the problem of war. War was a reality from which Jesus felt free to draw parables (Lk 14:31-33). He marveled at the centurion's faith without questioning his military profession (Mt 8:10). In spite of the absence of ethical casuistry, the New Testament was not irrelevant to war. Its appreciation of the dignity of persons and the power of suffering love points to the genuine source of peace; in addressing the sinfulness of man it calls for surgery on the radical causes of war. The sermon on the mount gives the maximal goals of justice and peace, to be fully realized on "the new earth where justice dwells," but to be worked toward now in creative tension. The Christian scriptures yield a vision of harmony and love among men but do not tell us how this vision can be realized in the perplexing situations of a sinful world. This scriptural revelation asks questions of the moralist; it does not provide the answers in the "deposit of faith."

Not surprisingly, early Christian reaction to war was mixed: some would serve in the army and some would not. So many would not serve that the philosopher Celsus had the impression that all Christians were pacifists.[14] Origen, responding to Celsus, supports this impression by saying that Christians do not fight under the emperor even if he should require it.[15] There is ample evidence, however, that many Christians, especially in the frontier provinces, served in the army without scruple.[16]

Pre-Constantinian Christian literature was not so ambivalent as practice. When Irenaeus wrote that Christians do not know how to fight and when struck offer the other cheek, he was speaking the language of Justin, Athenagoras, Tertullian, Cyprian, Origen, Minucius, and Arnobius.[17] The pacifism of these men was rather untested, however, because they spoke of peace when the *Pax Romana* had banished all major wars. What is clear is that the Christians had brought from their encounter with Christ an unprecedented sensitivity to the horror of bloodshed and they enunciated its basic incompatibility with the gospel ideal. Even when they were later forced to bend their principles to the needs of new situations, they usually insisted that the ministers of the sacraments abstain from war to maintain some minimal witness to the peacefulness of Christ.

A perceptible change took place with the coming of Constantine. When Jesus was credited with the military success, Christians leapt from persecution to preferment. After this, their voices did not sound the same.[18] In East and West the new regime was hailed in eschatological terms.[19] The sword had become a friend and Christians began to glory not in infirmity but in power. The sensitivity to military service so completely disappeared that by the time of Theodosius II only Christians were permitted to serve in the army.[20] The earlier Christian tension had disappeared. A new situation had yielded a new morality.

If the Scriptures did not have an ethics of war, pagan antiquity did, and Christians did not hesitate to borrow from it. Augustine, whose magisterial contribution in this matter has been endorsed by centuries of acceptance in the Church, fashioned a theology of war. With the barbarians pressing in Europe and Africa, Augustine the moralist was perceptive enough to see that love dictates not only rules but also painful exceptions. In a world where God is not yet all in all he could see that even gospel morality is susceptible to human compromise. And so the just war theory was baptized.[21]

Saddened by the need for violence in view of the gospel ideal, Augustine, who would not allow a private citizen to kill even in self defense, tended to blend the Old Testament idea of the God-inspired war with the idea that the power of the state comes from God. Thus the soldier preserved his innocence by the right order of obedience.[22] Surrender of personal responsibility to government and the holy war are foreshadowed here. This note would have a congenial ring in subsequent centuries of Christian history.

Aside from the military threat, the barbarians were a cultural and moral threat to the civilization they began to overrun. Knit into their culture was a creed of violence that was bereft of nuance or nicety. This creed would compete with the Christian creed and show that there are competing leavens in the batch of society and that the Christian leaven does not always raise the dough.

As this cultural invasion progressed, some Church efforts were made to resist. With the frenzy of violence mounting, the penitentials continued up until the eleventh century to prescribe penance for soldiers who had killed in battle, however just the cause.[23] The participation of the clergy in war was never really sanctioned. The Truce of God was a colossal, if belated, attempt to educate men to peace. But, as Stanley Windass remarks, "The disease was too radical to respond to such first aid."[24]

In effect, the Church chose to divert the violence which it could not subdue. This was the story of the Crusades. The sword was given a prime role in establishing the kingdom of God. The Crusades aimed at reuniting Christendom and establishing Jerusalem as the center of Christian holiness. With this rationale battle against the infidel came to achieve a salvific importance. Fulfilling the expressed hopes of Pope St. Gregory VII, Blessed Urban II launched the movement at the Council of Clermont, *toto plaudente orbe catholico.*[25] A plenary indulgence graced all who died in these wars that the Church began in the name of Jesus.[26] Pope, bishops, and monks scurried around the continent preaching the crusade. A cargo of noses and thumbs sliced from the Saracens was sent back as gory witness of crusading zeal.[27] Christian warriors stalked through fallen Jerusalem with blood up to their knees and bridle reins, exulting in the slaughter as "the justification of all Christianity and the humiliation of paganism."[28]

The consecration of violence was further formalized by the founding of the Knights Templar, who vowed to fight in poverty, chastity, and obedience.[29] Swords were blessed with liturgy. And not only infidels were struck with them. Indulgenced warriors struck at the Cathari in southern France. When the papal legate was asked how to distinguish between the Cathari and the Catholics, his reply shocked no one: "Kill them all; God will know which are his."[30] The important *Decretum* of Gratian said that to die in combat against the infidel is to merit heaven.[31] In a violent age, the Church was violent in word and in deed. A new situation had yielded a new morality.

Prophetic figures and sects within and without the Church arose to reassert the claims of the gospel of peace. With their plea made plausible by the collapse of Christendom and the rise of national power, reform was slowly brought about. But the road from Clermont to Vatican II was tortuous and many feel that an insensitivity to war and a sacralization of national policy linger on in the Christian conscience, an unhappy legacy of the crusading period.

THE CHURCH AND SEXUAL ETHICS

The New Testament does not provide a full ethics of sex, although it says much that is relevant to sexual ethics. Its view of marriage as an example of the love of God for his people and its concept of agapic love challenge the insight and discernment of the ethicist.[32] The idea of personhood which emerges from its pages has endless ethical implications.[33] But the problem of applying the profound personalism of the gospels to the intricacies and subtleties of sexual questions in a complex and evolving world remains to bother the Christian conscience.

In facing this problem, Christians did not hesitate to turn to the existent and popular moral philosophy of the non-Christian world, Stoicism. The Stoics had an ethics of sex. The Stoic anthropology exalted nature, reason, and decorum. It downgraded the emotions—*perturbationes,* Cicero called them[34] —and dependence on others. The emotion-laden phenomenon of sexuality thus needed a justifying rationale. The decision of the Stoic sages was this: "The sexual organs are given man not for pleasure, but for the maintenance of the species."[35] Nothing but the decent and reasonable need to procreate could justify sex. There was no link between love and sex. (This rigorous view of sex seemed all the more agreeable to early Christians in the face of the libertine gnostic reaction within the Church.[36])

Stoic rigor was not only generally accepted in the Church but was even intensified. Chrysostom could cite the Greek ideal of continence: "to fight desire and not be subservient to it . . . but our ideal is not to experience desire at all."[37]

However grim a view of sex this was, it had the undeniable advantage of ethical simplicity. The procreation rubric made it easy to ban non-marital sex of all forms and contraceptive sex in marriage. Small wonder that by the time the mighty Augustine appeared on the scene he could accept the Stoic rule as traditional teaching.[38] The rule also provided a perfect retreat for Augustine from the morbid Manichean resistance to procreation. On matters of sex and marriage, however, Augustine the Christian was never fully freed from Mani. "In intercourse," he said, man "becomes all flesh" (*Sermons* 62.2, *PL* 38:887). This he said in commenting on the biblical notion of man and wife as "one flesh." Nothing was more devasting to the masculine mind than "female blandishments and that contact of bodies without which a wife may not be had" (*Soliloquies* 1.10, *PL* 32:878). Only procreation could justify marriage, sex, or even women.

"I do not see what other help woman would be to man if the purpose of generating was eliminated" (*On Genesis According to the Letter,* 9.7, *CSEL* 28:275).

Concupiscence and sexual pleasure are suspect in Augustine's eyes. In the unredeemed, in fact, concupiscence is equivalent to sin. After baptism, "the concupiscence of the flesh" remains, "but it is not imputed as sin" (*Marriage and Concupiscence* 1.25.28, *CSEL* 42:240). Original sin is transmitted by the exercise of concupiscence and, were it not for Adam's fall, there would be no "concupiscence of the flesh" involved in generation (*ibid.* 1.18.21, *CSEL* 42:233).[39]

This is the Augustine who wrote the influential *The Good of Marriage* (1, *CSEL* 41:187). Not surprisingly, *proles* come first in his formula for the goodness of marriage. This formula, *proles, fides, sacramentum* (*ibid.* 29.32, *CSEL* 41:227), was to echo through the centuries and would, as late as 1930, provide a structural scheme for Pius XI in his *Casti Connubii.*[40]

Caesarius of Arles did much to maintain Augustine's historical resonance in the area of sexual ethics. With him, also, only the intention to procreate could justify marital intercourse. Following the Stoic bent for agricultural analogies, he compared intercourse to the sowing of a field and added his prestigious voice to those condemning intercourse during pregnancy; he even seemed to condemn frequent intercourse as unChristian.[41]

Caesarius was no outrider on this question of intercourse during pregnancy. John T. Noonan finds no Christian theologian before the year 1500 giving complete approval to this practice. Up until that time it was an integral part of the teaching of the ordinary magisterium of the Church.[42]

Pope St. Gregory the Great brought into the Christian scene an austerity that made Augustine look benign. In his *Pastoral Rule* he admonished couples not only that pleasure is not a fit purpose for intercourse, but also that if any pleasure is "mixed" with the act of intercourse the married have "transgressed the law of marriage." They have "befouled" their intercourse by their "pleasures" (3.27, *PL* 77:102). The *Pastoral*

Rule was an important magisterial document, as was also Gregory's letter to St. Augustine, archbishop of Canterbury. Augustine wondered whether he could teach "the rude English people" that they could receive communion after marital copulation. Gregory's answer was negative. It was as impossible to have intercourse without sin as it was to fall into a fire and not burn. Only a miracle could save you in either case (*Epistles* 11.64, *PL* 77:1196-1197).

This extraordinary doctrine proved magisterially viable. In the twelfth century, Huguccio, Gratian's chief commentator, taught that coitus "can never be without sin" (*Summa* 2.32.2.1). Innocent III, an expert theologian in his own right, thought of this opinion as beyond question.[43]

The somber thoughts of Jerome, Augustine, Caesarius, and Gregory were given prominent play in the penitentials and in the instruction of the people. Preachers like Bernardine of Siena proclaimed this news with eloquence. To have intercourse "too frequently or with inordinate affection" was wrong (*Seraphic Sermons* 19:3). "Of 1000 marriages," St. Bernardine declared, "I believe 999 are the devil's."[44]

We have already mentioned the unanimous disapproval of intercourse during pregnancy.[45] Other striking opinions took root and were propagated. The Augustinian doctrine about the need for procreative purpose to free intercourse from sin grew in Christendom until we find it the established opinion with few dissents by the twelfth century. The classical canonists and theologians of the thirteenth century reaffirmed it, and it became common teaching through the fourteenth and fifteenth centuries.[46] Theologians who followed St. Thomas (*On the Sentences* 4.31, "Exposition of the text"; II^a II^{ae}, q.154, a.11) taught that intercourse that deviated from the position of woman beneath the man was a mortal sin. It was commonly taught for centuries that intercourse during the time of menstruation was sinful. Indeed, some important figures held that it was mortally sinful.[47] All these opinions have since been abandoned.

Gradually, new insights begin to appear in the Church. The Council of Trent, in 1563, was the first ecumenical council to

stress the role of love in marriage.[48] Modern popes, keeping step
with theological developments, stress this theme.[49] Vatican II
shows some of the more recent progress and reveals the depth of
change in the Church's outlook on marital sexuality. It reflected
and crowned a recent theological development by acknowledging the coital expression of conjugal love as a substantial value
independent of procreation.[50] Until Vatican II it was customary
to refer to procreation and education of children as the primary
end of marriage (cf. Code of Canon Law, c. 1013, §2 and the
encyclical *Casti Connubii*). Due to advances in the appreciation of the other "ends" of marriage, this concession of primacy
to one end was deliberately discontinued.[51] The implications
of this and other advances in the understanding of marriage and
sexuality are slowly finding clarification and expression in the
Church.

THE QUESTION OF USURY

We are indebted to John T. Noonan for his careful studies of
the Church's condemnation of usury.[52] Taking 1450 as a year
when the Church's strong stand against usury was in fullest
vigor, Noonan explains what was meant by usury.

> On a loan to a poor man, or a rich man, to help the starving
> or to finance a mercantile enterprise, nothing could be sought
> or even hoped for. The risk inherent in lending was not a
> ground for taking interest; . . . Interest could never be law-
> fully sought as profit. To hope for interest, to seek profit, was
> to commit the sin of mental usury. Usury, mental or actual,
> was a mortal sin against justice.[53]

The unanimous stand against usury was grounded in the
unanimous interpretation of five scripture texts (Ex 22:25; Lev
25:35-37; Ps 15:5; Ez 18:5-9; Lk 6:33-35). The three men
who were most influential in shaping morality in the western
Church—Ambrose, Jerome, and Augustine—gave strong witness against usury. In the East, Clement of Alexandria, Basil,
and Gregory of Nyssa could find no room for interest-taking. Increase on a loan, as Gregory saw it, was a "wicked union, which

nature does not know"; such fertility is proper only to sexually differentiated animals (*Homily 2 on Ecclesiastes, PG* 44: 674). Three ecumenical councils lent their authority to this teaching, Lateran II, Lateran III, and Vienne.[54] Four popes had especially clear statements to make on the subject: Alexander III, Urban III, Eugene III, and Gregory IX.[55]

As far as can be determined, theologians and teachers all concurred in this teaching. Discontent arose, finally, from those who had experience in finance, the bankers of Siena and Florence. The first theologian to challenge the long accepted interpretation of Luke 6:35 was Dominic Soto in the sixteenth century.[56] In the same century John Medina defended risk as a ground for charging interest. One hundred years later a Roman congregation accepted this position; and, of course, by the time of the great modern social encyclicals all scruple about taking legitimate interest had disappeared from the teaching of the magisterium.[57]

THE MORAL QUESTION OF SELF-INCRIMINATION

Since the early 1700s English law has guarded the accused from compulsory self-incrimination. The notion was incorporated into the United States' Federal Constitution by the Fifth Amendment in 1791. Moralists unanimously hold today that this right to silence flows from the fundamental dignity of the human person.[58] Yet it was not until 1917 with the promulgation of the Code of Canon Law that the Church guaranteed this right to the accused in ecclesiastical trials.

Going back into Church history we see not only that the accused was denied the right to silence but also that even torture was used to induce his self-incrimination. Pope Nicholas I in 866 had condemned legal torture as immoral.[59] His intervention, breaking free as it did from the contemporary outlook, had a prophetic quality, but it did not take root in the magisterium of the Church. Patrick Granfield notes that medieval justice, "both civil and ecclesiastical," considered torture an indispensable part of court procedure:

The ordeal, with its hot iron, molten lead, and boiling water, became commonplace. From the eighth to the thirteenth century it was accepted by many local ecclesiastical courts with the approval of their bishops, who felt that it was a reliable way to discover the judicium Dei.[60]

Pope Innocent IV contradicts the opinion of Nicholas I, teaching in his *Ad extirpanda* that heretics should be forced "without loss of limb or danger of death" to admit their errors and denounce their accomplices. The pope imposed the same obligation on thieves and robbers.[61] The Catechism of the Council of Trent (Catechism of Pius V) denies the accused the right of silence. The Jubilee Decrees of 1749, 1775, and 1824 reaffirm this teaching.[62] As late as 1910 the Roman Rota issued norms which again did not exempt the accused in criminal trials from confessing his own guilt.[63] Canon 1743, §1 changed this teaching. The change, Father Granfield notes, was "abrupt." "In all the pre-Code documents there is either an explicitly or implicitly presumed affirmation of the necessity of self-incrimination."[64]

RELIGIOUS LIBERTY AND THE RIGHTS OF CONSCIENCE

Progress in the moral teaching of the Church concerning religious freedom is easily illustrated. Pius IX in his *Quanta Cura* condemns:

> that erroneous opinion which is especially injurious to the Catholic Church and the salvation of souls, called by our predecessor Gregory XVI *deliramentum* [insane raving], namely that freedom of conscience and of worship is the proper right of each man, and that this should be proclaimed and asserted in every rightly constituted society (Denz. 1690; cf. 1613).

The striking change is seen in the words of Vatican II:

> The Synod further declares that the right to religious freedom has its foundation in the very dignity of the human person. . . . This right of the human person to religious freedom is

to be recognized in the constitutional law whereby society
is governed. Thus it is to become a civil right.[65]

The Syllabus of Pius IX provides many opportunites to
study the change in moral judgment that has marked the teaching of the pilgrim Church (Denz. 1700-1780).[66]

THE THEOLOGY OF THE MAGISTERIUM

The theology of the magisterium has been until recently one of
the most important and most neglected areas of our theology.
Customarily the magisterium is spoken of as either *ordinary* or
extraordinary. The extraordinary magisterium comprises the
ex cathedra statements of the pope and the solemn statements of
bishops convoked in council in union with the pope to define
the faith. The ordinary magisterium refers to the normal daily
teaching of the bishops throughout the world.

As regards infallibility, the ordinary magisterium is considered infallible when there is "unanimity of the episcopal magisterium."[67] The concept of an infallible ordinary magisterium
presents some special problems. First of all, the determination of
what constitutes unanimity is not always an obvious matter,
especially in specific questions of morality. Secondly, unanimity
or consensus can be of various kinds. There can be reflective
or non-reflective consensus. Unanimity on some moral matters
might represent a legacy received uncritically from another age.
This is a non-reflective consensus, and it represents not an ac-
cumulation of serious human acts of moral evaluation but rather
the absence of such. Such a consensus has serious limitations.

At any rate the discussion of infallibility comes to center
more on the extraordinary magisterium. This is the case, for
example, in the *Pastor Aeternus* of Vatican I, which undoubtedly
provides the most solemn expression of the consciousness of the
Church concerning its magisterial role. This constitution centered, with unfortunate exclusiveness, on the infallibility of the

pope. Since, however, the council emphasized that the pope had the same infallibility that Christ willed his Church to have, its statement does afford us much insight into the understanding of infallibility in general that existed in the Church of Vatican I.

The Council declared it a divinely revealed dogma:

> that the Roman Pontiff, when he speaks ex cathedra, that is, when in discharge of the office of pastor and doctor of all Christians, by virtue of his supreme apostolic authority, he defines a doctrine regarding faith or morals to be held by the universal Church, by the divine assistance promised to him in blessed Peter, is possessed of that infallibility with which the divine Redeemer willed that his Church should be endowed for defining doctrine regarding faith or morals: and that therefore such definitions of the Roman pontiff are irreformable of themselves, and not from the consent of the Church:
>
> But if any one—which may God avert—presume to contradict this our definition; let him be anathema.[68]

This definition was the result of prolonged and intense conciliar discussion and debate. Its meaning is precise and finely nuanced, but a study of the text alone would not reveal that. The context must be carefully considered if we are to capture the meaning of this important definition. This is needed all the more today inasmuch as the Constitution on the Church in Vatican II repeats the words of Vatican I, without, of course, assuming the theologian's task of analysing their original import (chapter three).

Competent theological inquiry has never neglected the task of research into the *acta* of Church councils in order to discover the true significance of conciliar texts. Thanks to new understanding of the evolution of doctrine and of the historical and cultural conditioning of human thought and language, modern theologians are becoming more aware of the need for contextual analysis of past magisterial pronouncements. Recent advances in the interpretation of Scripture have also been instructive in this regard. Vatican II gives this advice to the biblical exegete:

> The interpreter must investigate what meaning the sacred writer intended to express and actually expressed in particular circumstances as he used contemporary literary forms in accordance with the situation of his own time and culture. For the correct understanding of what the sacred author wanted to assert, due attention must be paid to the customary and characteristic styles of perceiving, speaking, and narrating which prevailed at the time of the sacred writer. . . .[69]

Since magisterial Church pronouncements are no more immune to the influence of context and culture than are the Scriptures, the task of the theologian is obvious. He must face the problems of language, the influence of epistemological and theological presuppositions, the presence of limiting polemical perspectives, and the reality of dogmatic development. And when past magisterial pronouncements on morality are involved, the theologian must consider the statements in the light of the development of moral insight and the circumstances and conditions that affected the statements. To do anything less is to strip the original statement of its reality.

Debate at Vatican I was acrimonious. One bishop found the lament of Isaiah applicable: *"Videntes clamabunt foris, et angeli pacis amare flebunt."*[70] Relative peace might have obtained if the original plan of the council had been followed. It had been proposed to develop a vast schema on the Church of Christ. Chapters one to ten would treat of the Church in general; eleven and twelve would treat of the primacy of the pope. Through internal and external pressures, the decision was made to drop all the chapters except those on the pope.[71]

Many of the bishops felt that a separate discussion of the infallibility of the pope without treatment of the role of the bishops was ill considered. Bishop Moriarity of Kerry, for example, testified that in the Irish Church neither the ordinary preaching nor the catechisms stressed the infallibility of the pope, but that the subject of infallibility was always said to be the Church. In practice this meant the bishops in agreement with the pope.[72] The proposed definition seemed to be giving a power to the pope which was too "personal, separate, and absolute." These words were spoken in concern by so many that Bishop d'Avanzo remarked that the council could become known in history as "the council of three words."[73] To quell these anxieties, the Deputation of the Faith, the committee which had drafted the document, gave close attention to the clarification of these terms as well as to the notion and object of infallibility in the Church.

Speaking for the Deputation, d'Avanzo stressed that the anti-Gallican expression of the definition *ex sese non autem ex consensu ecclesiae* did not purport to separate the pope from the Church. He pointed out first that it was the same holy Spirit who was operative in pope, bishops, and faithful.[74] Secondly, the pope teaching infallibly did not do so in virtue of a new revelation but rather, with the help of the Holy Spirit; his role was to discover the truth already contained in the fonts of revelation.[75] Thirdly, it was obvious that the pope did not work privately with the holy Spirit, but rather that he must seek out the truth in the living witness of the Church.[76]

A more complete elucidation is found in the monumental speech of Bishop Gasser, the outstanding theologian and spokesman of the Deputation. He centered his discourse on the "three words." The infallibility of the pope was "personal" only in the sense that the pope was a public person and head of the Church.[77] This is better explained when he discusses the second word, "separate." He begins by saying that the word "distinct" would be more precise. The pope is part of the Church, and indeed when he speaks infallibly he speaks as one who represents the universal Church. The essential concurrence and cooperation of the Church is not excluded by the definition.[78] Since the pope has no new revelation on which to base his statement, he is bound to sek out the truth in the Church by various means. This is an obvious duty which binds him in conscience.[79]

Is the definition, then, really maintaining a union between the pope and the consenting Church? Yes. Anything other than such a union is unthinkable.[80] What kind of consent does the definition exclude? It excludes consent of the extreme Gallican style (cf. Denz. 1322-1326). It will not make it a "de iure conditio" (Mansi 52:1208). To insist on such a thing would create insoluble problems, such as determining how many bishops had to be consulted, and so forth.[81] When the truth is obvious it would be foolish to bind the pope to an extensive investigation. It is in this limited sense that the consent of the Church is not required.[82]

Concerning the question of infallibility, Gasser said: 1) Absolute infallibility is ascribed only to God. The infallibility of the Church is limited; 2) the limited infallibility of the Church, whether exercised by the pope or in some other fashion, extends to the same ambit of truths; 3) it certainly extends to the revealed truths contained in the deposit of faith; 4) the infallibility extends to those truths which, though not revealed, are necessary for the defense and explanation of the deposit. Whether the infallibility extended to these matters in such a way as to constitute them dogmatic truths (the denial of which would be heresy) was an unsolved theological question and the Deputation decided unanimously to leave the question open.[83] Doctrines noted as theologically certain (or with lesser notes) are not within the range of *de fide* infallible statements.[84]

Thus did Vatican Council I explain itself. Its explanations merit attention from modern theologians. More space than is available here would be required to discuss the total context of Vatican I and the deficiencies under which the council labored. The Church's present understanding of the doctrines discussed at Vatican I has grown and widened. As Vatican II says, "there is a growth in the understanding of the realities and the words which have been handed down."[85] Important areas touched by Vatican I have known vast development: the interpretation of Scripture, the relationship of Scripture and tradition, the concept of "Church" including the acknowledgment of genuine ecclesial reality in the Protestant Churches, the increased respect for the *sensus fidelium* and the magisterial role of the laity.[86] We cannot concede the genuine ecclesiality of the Protestant Christian Churches and then deny them magisterial significance. The doctrinal positions of all Christian bodies must now be viewed with a new seriousness. This appreciation does not simplify the theology of the magisterium, but it is a reality from which we may not flee.

Let us, however, at this point focus on certain elements of the teaching of Vatican I that are vital to our understanding of the moral magisterium. It is an important fact that Vatican I did not give special attention to the distinct problems involved in teaching morality. This was to be expected. The nineteenth century might indeed represent the nadir of Catholic moral theology. As Noonan remarks: "In the entire nineteenth century it is difficult to name a single person who displayed genius in its study and exposition."[87] Repetitious manuals that taught morality like a code had trained the council bishops and theologians. The in-depth expositions of Aquinas or Liguori were not seminary fare.[88] Until the *Aeterni Patris* of Leo XIII in 1879, a heavily Cartesian spirit pervaded Catholic thought. The Cartesian stress on clarity as the mark of truth did not dispose its students to grasp the ambiguities and complexities that are met in applying moral principles to the infinitely diverse circumstances of life.

Given the inevitable dependence of a council on the philosophical tools and principles available to it, it is perhaps not useless to speculate momentarily on how a strong Thomistic revival before Vatican I would have influenced the outcome of that council. The council bishops would have been well served by St. Thomas' reminder of the *quasi infinitae diversitates* that characterize the material of ethics (S. Th. II^a II^{ae}, q. 49, a. 3). Thomas' realism about the nature of ethics is an extraordinary insight which has never had sufficient impact on Catholic moral theology.

Following Aristotle, Thomas saw that moral principles were not the principles of speculative reason, which admit of universal application. The principle of non-contradiction, for example, properly understood, will admit of no exception. Moral principles, on the contrary, proceed from practical reason. They are indeed valid principles embodying eternal values, but, since they are concerned with the contingencies of human behavior, the more one descends into the particularities of life the more one is likely to find exceptions. Pressing the point, Thomas explains that the most general moral principles (do good; avoid evil; love God and neighbor) admit of no exception.

However, when one must decide by what he calls "secondary principles" how, in the concrete, one does good and loves effectively—and this is the heart of ethics—it is discovered that these principles are applicable most of the time (*in pluribus*); in particular cases (*in aliquo particulari et in paucioribus*) they may not apply (I^a II^{ae}, q. 94, a. 4, a. 5). Thus, he says what it is a good principle to return things to their owner; but, enter the ethically significant circumstance of the owner's manifest intention to do serious harm with the object held, and the principle can be seen as nonapplicable. A more important value takes precedence (cf. *ibid.*, a. 5). This is true for all of ethics. Monogamy is clearly a value which may be expressed as a moral principle; yet St. Thomas notes that particular circumstances may in fact permit a plurality of wives (*Supp.*, 65, 2).

Clearly Thomas does not support the attempt to do ethics by the deductive use of principles conceived as static derivatives of an immutable nature. "The nature of man is mutable" (II^a II^{ae}, q. 57, a. 2, ad 1). Unlike the divine nature, our nature is variable (*Supp.*, 41, 1, ad 3, 65, 2, ad 1; *De Malo*, 2, 4, ad 13). Almost anticipating the modern realization of the difficulty of teaching morality transculturally, Thomas wrote that law is not everywhere the same "because of the mutability of the nature of man and the diverse conditions of men and of things, according to the diversity of places and of times" (*De Malo*, 2, 4, ad 13. (For more detail, read Milhaven's chapter on St. Thomas in this volume.)

This Thomistic view obviously does not lead one to expect pronouncements on morality that would be infallibly true

for every time and place without exception. Neither do recent
biblical studies encourage such expectations. The Bible itself
attempts no such thing. We no longer look to the "deposit of
faith" for specific answers to modern ethical questions. The
temptation to feel that a system of ethics relevant to all times
is contained in revelation, to feel that the answers are there to
be wrenched out by exegetical wizardry—such a temptation
has happily been conquered. For example, no longer does anyone look in Scripture for explicit answers to questions of interest-taking. Also, however much the ingredients of peace were
in the doctrine of Jesus, he never took a position on the question of war.

Jesus neither affirmed nor denied the right to private
property, slavery, or the redistribution of wealth. As Rudolf
Schnackenburg observes: "Jesus no more intended to change the
social system than he did the political order. He never assumed
a definite attitude on economic and social problems."[89] We have
seen that revelation did not answer the multiple questions of
sexual ethics, the moral right to silence, or religious liberty. We
need hardly mention business ethics and international law. Even
when Jesus was apparently quite specific on the divorce issue,
he did not close the case.

Father Schillebeeckx writes:

> It is important to bear in mind that, although Christ declared
> that marriage was indissoluble, he did not tell us where the
> element that constituted marriage was situated—what in fact
> made a marriage a marriage, what made it the reality which
> he called absolutely indissoluble. This is a problem of anthro-
> pology. . . .[90]

The so-called "Pauline Privilege" (canons 1120-1124,
1126) which permits a person to contract a second valid marriage for reasons of faith while the first partner still lives, is
not found in St. Paul. Schnackenburg points out that the permission is based on 1 Corinthians 7:15 ff. However, "Paul is
dealing with the question whether separation is permissible in
such a case; he does not speak of remarriage."[91] In other words,

the Church went beyond Scripture here and decided that the ideal of indissolubility did not apply in this case. In this instance divorce and remarriage was seen as a value even though without scriptural warranty.

Clearly then, the "deposit of faith," whatever riches it contains for morality, does not do the moralists' work. Yet Vatican I defined that infallibility in faith and morals extends to guarding and exposing the deposit of faith (Denz. 1836). Obviously the infallibility does not extend to answers that are not there. Gasser, however, explained that it extends in some theologically undetermined fashion to those matters that, though not revealed, are necessary to guard, explain, and define the deposit of faith (Mansi 52:1226).

It would be no simple matter to show that the various moral questions we have mentioned above are necessary for guarding, explaining, and defining the deposit of the faith. Indeed Cardinal Berardi, immediately after the distribution of the final schema for the infallibility definition, pointed out the vagueness of the definition with regard to practical moral matters. He said that the wording even implied that the infallibility did not extend to decisions about the morality of actions *in concreto spectatae*.[92] His difficulty was not relieved the next day by the final exposition of Gasser.

Whatever problems the definition presents in this regard, one thing is clear: the council intended to say that in some way the teaching authority of the Church does extend to the area of morals. The practice of the hierarchical magisterium at the time and the general tone of the council leave no doubt that this was being taught. What the council did not do was explain how this teaching competence is best realized and best explained. This problem still remains and now commands our attention.

Traditionally the Church has claimed authority to teach "faith and morals." What is meant by "morals" in this expression is not clear, but the dominant opinion of late has been that it refers to the general and specific questions of natural moral law. Recent papal teaching has asserted this unambiguously.

Pius XII said:

> The power of the Church is not bound by the limits of "matters strictly religious," as they say, but the whole matter of the natural law, its foundation, its interpretation, its application, so far as their moral aspect extends, are within the Church's power.[93]

Pope John, speaking of the moral principles of the social order, said:

> For it must not be forgotten that the Church has the right and the duty to intervene authoritatively with her children in the temporal sphere when there is a question of judging the application of those principles to concrete cases.[94]

Recent discussion, however, comes to center more and more upon whether to term this competency "infallible." Gregory Baum writes:

> I realize that not a few authors in recent years have claimed that the Church, in interpreting the natural law, is indeed infallible. This is wrong. . . . The Church speaks with great authority in the area of human values but when she is not dealing with the ethics revealed in the Gospel, she is not exercising an infallible teaching office.[95]

John J. Reed, S.J., quite as apodictically, asserts the infallible competence of the Church in this area. Since the Church is entrusted with the whole of revelation, it seems obvious to Father Reed that it may teach the natural law infallibly. In some way the natural law is contained in revelation. Since this allegation is bristling with difficulties, Father Reed explains: "Evidently, as with matters of dogmatic truth, a particular demand of natural law may be contained only obscurely, implicitly, or virtually in the deposit of revelation."[96] Richard A. McCormick, S.J., applauds the position of Father Reed and notes that the disagreement between Baum and Reed "is representative of a growing body of opinion on both sides of the question."[97]

    I think that the term "infallible" does not in fact aptly describe the nature or function of the moral magisterium, and that we should discontinue using that term in describing the moral magisterium. My reasons are the following:

1. It is commonplace in discussions of infallibly defined doctrine to refer to the norm of canon 1323, §3, which says that nothing is to be taken as a definition unless it is seen to be such beyond all reasonable doubt: *nisi id manifeste constiterit*. Certainly since Vatican I, and even before that council, it is difficult to find an example of a pronouncement in the area of natural moral law that meets this requirement. The lack of examples in the writings of the defenders of the infallible moral magisterium is thus not surprising.[98]

    The Church's non-use of the prerogative of infallibility is theologically instructive. This seems to mean that in practice the Church has recognized that it has a firm grasp of the moral vision of the Gospel and that it can and should make rich and meaningful judgments on specific modern problems: but the Church seems to realize further, though the theologians have been slow to acknowledge it, that it does not enjoy an infallibly guaranteed competence to apply the moral vision of the Gospel to complex natural law questions such as are presented by medical ethics, genetics, business ethics, international law, social reconstruction, and war and peace. To allege that the Church can teach the natural law infallibly suggests the weird spectacle of a Church that has the power to settle these questions in a definitive fashion and does not do so. It is also a position that must suffer considerable embarrassment from the data of history.

    The infallibilist position has other problems. It claims that the natural law is contained implicitly or virtually in the deposit of revelation. This is not a little baffling. All ethical theory grants that concrete and changing circumstances enter essentially into the constitution of the "moral object." Hence there is an essential presentiality (*parcas*) in the natural law which precludes its being pre-given, even in an implicit and virtual way, in any "deposit."[99] Knowledge of the empirical data is essential to moral judgment; no moral judgment may be made without such knowledge.

Moral principles and examples may be pre-given; they may have been acquired from past experience or revelation. They enter into moral judgment but they are not the only requisite for moral science, which is not simply a deductive science. For particular demands of the natural law to be contained in revelation it would be necessary to say that a foreknowledge of the ethical implications of the particularities and circumstances of subsequent centuries is somehow contained in that revelation. I do not know how such a contention could be supported. It is certainly not supported or established by an uncritical repetition of past magisterial formulations. It is furthermore not at all supported by the Church's abstinence in the use of this infallibility. (We will consider below Father Baum's suggestion that the Church is infallible in teaching the ethics of the Gospel.)

2. As noted above with regard to the Thomistic notion of ethics, moral principles are, by reason of the ethical implications of circumstances, not universally applicable. The completely general principles such as "Do good and avoid evil" can be called absolute and universal precisely because of their lack of circumstantial content. When, however, you begin to apply specific principles to particular contexts, they admit of exceptions. They evince a certain essential plasticity.

This does not mean that there are no stable values in the moral realm. The sacredness of human life must always be respected, for example. However, in certain cases a man may kill. The ethical task is to determine what instances of killing are, because of special circumstances, compatible with a respect for life. A knowledge of the circumstances and the ethical implications thereof is essential to this ethical task. To say in advance that no circumstance whatever could ever justify a particular action implies a foreknowledge of the ethical import of all possible circumstances. The epistemological problem here should be obvious. In actions involving other human beings history should have taught us that the unpredictables and imponderables should not be adjudicated in advance.

Indeed, it can be stated that as the complexity of life increases, "exceptional" cases become more frequent. As Karl Rahner says: "What used to be an extreme borderline case in a moral situation which hardly ever occurred, has now become almost the 'normal' case."[100] Compare the ethical problems of a general store in the country a century ago with the ethical problems of a corporation like General Motors today to see what complexification does to ethics. Infallible guidance is not anticipated in such a situation. What is needed and to be anticipated in this situation is a meaningful and effective dialogue of experts in particular fields with moralists and other representatives of the moral magisterium of the Church. We shall return to this.

3. The very nature of truth should make us cautious in speaking of infallibility. Reality always exceeds our conceptualizations and knowledge of it. As Piet Fransen writes, the magisterial ministry "is a diaconia of the Holy Spirit and also of divine truth. This truth possesses the Church but we do not possess it."[101] Morality involves the mysterious truth of personal contact and relationship of God and man. The mystery of morality is radically ineffable. No matter how wise we become in explaining this mystery, we remain unprofitable servants and we still know, in Paul's words, only "in part." "The truth lives in us as something open, a disposition for more truth, for correction and completion."[102] In a sense, human knowledge is never free of error inasmuch as it is never complete. This is not to say that it is invalid; it embodies the real, but for *homo viator* it is never complete or entirely error-free.

This notion was quite alien to the men of Vatican I, who sought to grasp truth *nullo admixto errore* (Denz. 1786). The term "infallibility" seems to imply a completion that our groping knowledge of reality does not allow. It conforms better to Cartesian assumptions than to modern views of truth.

4. There is a conflict in the concept of an infallible statement made through the medium of fallible language. A form of words can symbolize "an indefinite number of diverse propositions."[103] The intrinsic ambiguity of language is such that many propositions can "fit the same verbal phraseology."[104] Communication, which is the goal of language, can be blocked by "a lack of shared presuppositions or shared universe of discourse."[105] Meaning has a tendency to slip out from under verbal formulae; through usage, new meanings succeed in attaching themselves to old expressions. It can happen that a verbal change is essential to recapture and conserve the original meaning. Change, in this case, is conservative.

This appreciation of the character of language is not entirely new. St. Thomas, for example, taught that the act of the believer did not terminate at the proposition but at the reality (II^a II^{ae}, q. 1, a. 2, ad 2). But it is modern linguistic analysis that has presented this insight with force.

5. Even the brief look at the history of our moral teaching with which we began this chapter should prompt us to describe our teaching competence in more modest terms. Either we must admit a drastic relativism which would allege that all of that teaching was right in its day or we must admit the presence of error in the history of the pilgrim Church. To stress this point: The *Decretum* of Gratian which taught that it was "meritorious" to kill the infidel, the teaching of Gregory XVI and Pius IX that it was "madness" to allege religious freedom as a right of man and a necessity in society, and the proclamation of Vatican II that such freedom is a right and necessity in society—such teachings are not consistent or mutually reconcilable.

Even full recognition of the historical context that spawned these statements does not establish doctrinal continuity. The change on interest-taking cannot honestly be explained by alleging simply that the nature of money has changed. Interest-taking could have served some economic purposes in the fif-teenth century at the height of the Church's condemnation. Certainly the nature of sexuality has not changed so much as to permit our justification of the opinions once taught by the universal ordinary magisterium. Similarly for the right to silence, and the others.

This, of course, is not to deny that notable good often re-sulted from positions taken. So, for example, the ravages of a usurious economy that have wracked other civilizations were largely averted. The attitude toward contraception did much to underline the sacredness of life and the life-giving processes. Analysis of the historical context often makes it quite under-standable why a particular position was taken.

Still, to assert that in all of this there is not change but simply development is to play semantic games. There has been development from blindness to sight, from incompleteness and error to fuller perception of the truth. Our reaction should be not to cover over the change, but to thank God with humility that we have alowed him to lead us into the light. Man can resist God. That is the tragic mystery of sin. Our history proclaims our resistance. Let us react with penance, not rationalization.

Some react to the discovery of past error by insisting that the doctrine in question was not infallibly taught. When the doctrine has come to be seen as largely wrong, its non-infalli-bility is hardly debatable. Behind this protest, however, there seems to be a docetist tendency to deny the incarnationalism of the Christian experience. It seems to deny the essential charac-teristics of human thought and language. Implicit in it is the failure to see us as we are, a pilgrim people who move slowly and not always directly toward the beckoning God of truth.

6. The *acta* of Vatican I show that some of the bishops were not at all happy with the word "infallible."[106] Furthermore, the use of the word "infallible" in conciliar discussion shows marked ambiguity. Gasser explained that infallibility—which had become by this point synonymous with the teaching author-

ity of the Church—extended also, in some way, to positions noted as rash, scandalous, or dangerous.[107] Such plasticity is not suggested by the word "infallible." It is difficult to describe a doctrine as infallibly rash or infallibly dangerous and scandalous. Clearly Gasser intended to assert teaching competence concerning matters related to the data of revelation. Describing this as yet theologically unrefined competence as "infallibility" was not felicitous. We are not, of course, bound to this expression.

7. We have already noted some of the difficulties encountered by the defenders of the infallible moral magisterium. We touched upon the position of Father Reed, who maintains that the natural law is contained implicitly and obscurely in the "deposit." Of interest here are the remarks of Richard A. McCormick as he comments with regrettable brevity on the position of Father Baum. He says: "The Church's prerogative to propose infallibly the gospel morality would be no more than nugatory without the power to teach the natural law infallibly."[108] This statement cannot be swallowed whole. (Indeed, as we shall suggest, the infallibility proposed by Baum is "nugatory.") But to proceed from that indictment to "the power to teach the natural law infallibly" is a huge and unwarranted step. McCormick argues from the ambiguous position that the natural law is integral to the Gospel. Hence the Church can teach it infallibly. (McCormick is close to Reed here, whose article he finds "thoroughly competent and well-documented" and a "very helpful essay."[109])

Saying that the natural law is integral to the Gospel could mean that principles concerning human dignity, the sacredness of life, the idea of morality as an operation of love, and the like, are integral to both natural law and the Gospel. From this it does not at all follow that the Church has the power to proceed infallibly through the multiple judgments and informational processes required to apply these natural and gospel values to special natural law problems. The Christian experience is certainly an enrichment of the natural law. The magisterium, if it is faithful to this experience, has much to offer those who struggle for the realization of human values. Its contribution, however, need not be infallible to be of value.

McCormick further elaborates his argument by saying that natural law is essential to the protection and proposal of Christian morality. He concludes again that particular demands of the natural law are capable of definition. Given the many meaningful and important ways that the Church can treat natural law questions, and given the way that it does in fact treat them, this seems to be a case of *qui nimis probat nihil probat*.

McCormick's concluding statement is more helpful.

> Would not, therefore, the ability to teach infallibly the dignity of man (certainly a revealed truth) without being able to exclude infallibly forms of conduct incompatible with this dignity be the ability infallibly to propose a cliché?[110]

There seems to be a legitimate concern here to avoid an irrelevant proclamation of the gospel ethos without applying it to modern life. One can readily agree that the Church must enter into the specific questions of the day in a quite specific fashion. The Church must recognize in so doing, however, that the position it in good faith assumes may, as has happened often in the past, later have to be changed because of subsequent data and insights. Infallibility is not the only escape from platitudinous clichés.

A final word on McCormick's statement about excluding forms of conduct that are incompatible with a proposed ideal: the claim that this can be done is more modest and nuanced than "teaching the natural law infallibly." The essential problem, however, remains. The Church might declare with much certitude (infallibly, if you will) that murder (unjust killing) is incompatible with human dignity. This statement is self-evident if not tautological. It is a general statement which allows for certitude precisely because of the lack of circumstantial content. To be certain about this does not mean that you can be equally certain (or at all certain) that a particular instance of killing is murder. The certitude of the general principle does not pass over into the discussion of cases as the liceity of certain abortions or pills that prevent implantation. Here moral intuition, empirical data, philosophical probings, and various forms of expertise are relevant, and the certainty of unapplied principles does not obtain.

Gregory Baum's view of the magisterium has the merit of an historical consciousness. He observes:

> We must face the fact that the development in the understanding and presentation of the Gospel has not always been positive in the Church and may not always be positive. It would not be difficult to establish the fact that certain themes of divine revelation have not always been announced and taught by the ecclesiastical magisterium with the same clarity.[111]

He still feels bound to assert some area of infallibility, and he formulates the idea that the Church is infallible only in regard to the ethics revealed in the Gospel. Such an infallible power would be, as Richard McCormick observed, nugatory since most of the current ethical questions are not answered in the Gospel. Much of the ethics of the Gospel is applied to the situation existing at that time and must be reapplied today to be of value. If Baum meant to say that the Church can be expected to have a basic sureness about the Gospel's moral ideals he might well have stated it without resorting to infallibility, and balanced it off with his realistic perception of how the sinful Church can at times obscure the gospel light.

8. In the polemics of the past century the word "infallible" has acquired connotations that are offensive and confusing to many. "The manner and order in which Catholic belief is expressed should in no way become an obstacle to dialogue with our brethren." Catholic doctrine should be presented "in ways and in terminology which our separated brethren too can really understand."[112] Words, like persons, have a history and a set of relationships from which one may not prescind. There is probably no word which more readily suggests to non-Catholic

Christians the objectionable aspects of the Catholic pre-conciliar mind-set than this word "infallible."

THE AUTHENTIC, NON-INFALLIBLE MAGISTERIUM

Since the question of infallibility has tended to loom over Catholic moral theology, casting an inhibiting shadow, it was necessary to deal with it at some length. Of more practical importance, however, is the authentic and admittedly fallible magisterium. In the Constitution on the Church, Vatican II speaks of this magisterium and the response due it:

> In matters of faith and morals, the bishops speak in the name of Christ and the faithful are to accept their teaching and adhere to it with a religious assent [*obsequio*] of soul. This religious submission [*obsequium*] of will and mind must be shown in a special way to the authentic teaching authority of the Roman Pontiff, even when he is not speaking *ex cathedra*.[113]

Pope John XXIII wrote:

> It is clear, however, that when the hierarchy has issued a precept or decision on a point at issue, Catholics are bound to obey their directives. The reason is that the Church has the right and obligation, not merely to guard the purity of ethical and religious principles, but also to intervene authoritatively when there is question of judging the application of these principles to concrete cases.[114]

We will impose upon John Reed again for an example of the way in which many theologians explained the effect of the authentic, non-infallible magisterium. From such teaching, he says, "two consequences follow, one external and absolute, the other internal and conditional. In the external order there results the obligation not to contradict the doctrine in public speech or writing." Theologians may enter into a "speculative discussion" of the doctrine taught, "supposing a discreet selection of audience and method of discourse." Still, even in such discreet discussions the matter in question "is not to be approached as something on which either side is of equal standing or could be equally followed."

So much for the external order.

> In the internal order there results per se the obligation of intellectual assent to and acceptance of the teaching. But since, in the supposition, the teaching is not infallible and there remains the possibility of the opposite, there must remain also the absolute possibility that someone, exceptionally qualified in some aspect of the question upon which the conclusion depends, may have grave reason to think that the proposition is not certainly true. In this event the individual, while bound by the teaching in the external order, would not be obliged to yield internal assent.[115]

Before commenting on this particular approach to the papal and episcopal magisterium it seems necessary to introduce more recent philosophical and theological perspectives without which the discussion is doomed to become a narrow exercise in legalistic quibbling.

THE OFFICE OF TEACHING IN THE CHURCH

Catholics have always believed in ecclesiastical offices, and linked these offices to a teaching role. It is partially in terms of teaching that theology explains the nature of the offices of deacon, priest, bishop, and pope. Catholic theology has emphasized those scriptural texts that promised the grace and blessings of God upon the preaching and teaching officers of the Church (Mt. 16:18; 28:19; Jn 21:15 ff; 1 Tim 4:14; 5:22; Tim 1:6; 2 Pt, *passim*.). In short, there has been no lack of stress upon the powers and prerogatives of the teaching officers.

As often happens in any science, certain aspects of a truth might be overly stressed due to cultural and polemical factors, with the result that other elements are neglected and an imbalance ensues. Regarding the ecclesiastical office, theological science should be especially wary. There is a deep-rooted tendency observable in man's religious history to magnify the role of religious authority figures and to view their teachings as oracular. A rather clear example of this is found in the history of the Church. The proclamations of councils in the early Church came to be viewed as inspired by the Holy Spirit. It became a widely held view that the first four councils were inspired and on a par with the four gospels. Pope Gregory the Great was merely continuing an established tradition when he asserted: *Sicut sancti evangelii quattuor libros, sic quattuor concilia suscipere et venerari me fateor.*[115a] This tradition continued through the middle ages and was carried on by various synods and popes as well as by canonists and theologians. Only after Trent did all traces of the tradition die out in Catholic theology.

To preserve us from a false estimation of the authority of the teaching office in the Church the office must be seen not only in terms of a *gift* of the Spirit but also in terms of a *task* imposed by the Spirit. We must continue to stress the supportive presence of God in the teaching Church: "And know that I am with you always; yes, to the end of time" (Mt 28:20). At the same time, we must acknowledge that the divine assistance is not foisted upon us without our cooperation and a disposition of openness on our part. It is given, in Trent's phrasing, *secundum propriam cuiusque dispositionem et cooperationem* (Denz. 799). Neither history nor theology will permit us to say that constant fidelity to the Spirit is guaranteed by the promise of the ultimate victory of Christ. We believe that the gates of hell will not prevail against God's work and we are supported by the vision of God becoming all in all. Until this is achieved, however, we must never forget the crippling and darkening reality of sin. We must never forget that the Church which is holy by the presence of God's Spirit is sinful by the presence of man. Perhaps the early Church was more aware of its frailty. Augustine wrote:

> Wherever in my books I have described the Church as being without spot or wrinkle, it is not to be understood that she is so already, but that she is preparing herself to be so when she too will appear in glory. For in the present time, because

of much ignorance and weakness in her members, she must confess afresh each day, "Forgive us our trespasses."[116]

St. Thomas wrote in a similar vein:

That the Church may be glorious, without spot or wrinkle, is the final goal to which we are being led through the passion of Christ. It will be so only in our eternal home, not on our journey there during which, if we said we had no sin we should be deceiving ourselves, as we are told in the first Epistle of St. John.[117]

The ability of the Church to be unfaithful to its Lord and to impede his saving and teaching work is a truth that we must confess. The Spirit of the Lord is with us, ready to lead us to all truth, but we can refuse to be led. "The Church is a sinful Church: that is a truth of faith, not just a fact of her primitive experience. And it is a shattering truth."[118] If we forget this truth of faith in our discussion of the magisterium, as though the magisterium were removed from the possibility of sin, we imply that God's help is given without human cooperation. This would be magic. The teaching office is not just a gift; it is a task at which we can falter.

This consciousness of sin should not cause us to overreact and lose all love for and trust in the Church as a work of God. It should prompt us rather to a realistic sense of penance and to an examination of ourselves and of the Church and of the magisterium. We should confidently expect to find in the Church the fruits of the Spirit, but we must be ready also to find the spot and the wrinkle. To remove the spots and smoothe the wrinkles that we find in ourselves, in the Church, or in magisterial pronouncements is a service to the Lord who works with us.

THE NOTION OF TEACHER

Discussions of the Church teaching tend to ignore how equivocal, mutable, and culturally conditioned the notion of teacher is. Even theologians writing to emphasize the magisterial role of the laity, and trying to temper a purely hierarchical conception of the magisterium, seem unduly concerned with finding examples of active lay participation in doctrinal developments in Scripture and in the history of the councils. Admittedly, such testimony is useful. However, recognizing with the recent council that "the human race has passed from a rather static concept of reality to a more dynamic, evolutionary one,"[119] we should be less likely to expect that teaching should occur in the same fashion in every time and culture, that it should be achieved now as it was in New Testament times or in the middle ages.

In this respect the teaching offices in the Church must be seen in an evolutionary perspective. The way they should function in the modern world will be as different as the modern world is different from the past. "The living conditions of modern man have been so profoundly changed in their social and cultural dimensions, that we can speak of a new age in human history." Thus Vatican II.[120] A new mode of teaching in this new age should be expected. It might differ from past forms as profoundly as a forty-year-old man differs from the infant he once was—*without loss of identity.*

In a paternalistic culture where there was general illiteracy, little insight into God's presence in non-Catholic and non-Christian experiences, and a view of truth as something static and given, paternalistic magisterial figures were understandable. They could take over the task of reflection, formulation, and preservation of the faith; their teaching was truly analogous to the work of a shepherd feeding his sheep.

The laity today are not aptly compared to sheep, and the Church in dialogue does not present itself in the guise of the all-knowing schoolmaster. In moral matters in the past, Church leaders could be expected to act like a parent dealing with immature children who need extensive help in making particular decisions. Today, however, Vatican II emphasizes that not even children are to be treated the same.

This holy Synod likewise affirms that children and young people have a right to be encouraged to weigh moral values with an upright conscience, and to embrace them by personal choice, and to know and love God more adequately. Hence it earnestly entreats all who exercise government over peoples or preside over the work of education to see that youth is never deprived of this sacred right.[121]

The right to weigh values and make personal decisions in moral matters is, in the council's words, "a sacred right." Those who would deprive people of this right on grounds that they would abuse it or are too immature to exercise it responsibly certainly bear the burden of proof. What the council says of children is obviously more true of adults. We can expect the maturing hierarchical Church to give fewer detailed rules of conduct to the maturing laity and to teach rather by giving broad outlines. Growing up is a painful process and people can be expected to resist the burdens of responsible freedom and the agonies of decision-making. Bishops and popes will share the experience of good parents who hate to see the children grow up. These problems are to be expected and faced.

Vatican II's reminder is a good one here: "Let the layman not imagine that his pastors are always such experts, that to every problem which arises, however complicated, they can readily give him a concrete solution, or even that such is their mission."[122] Moreover, what their pastors on the scene cannot do should not be expected from the bishop or the pope. The nature of ethics in a world of mounting complexification makes this quite impossible.

It seems today that the notion of teacher does not imply the imposition of information and decisions on largely passive recipients. Rather, the effective teacher in this age should be a stimulator of thought. He should seek to dissipate the immature desire for unreal certitudes. He should seek always to enlarge a debate and not to close it.

Let it not be thought that we are suggesting here that the hierarchical magisterium make an instant conversion to a kind of non-directive counselling technique. Whatever the ideal and whatever the progress thus far, many people will continue to function at an immature level and will continue to need very specific directions. We have not sufficiently encouraged the laity to be mature and cannot call for immediate maturity. But as we attend to these needs which our pastoral practice has helped to create, let us see the situation for what it is.

ETHICS AND THE EXPANSION OF THE SCIENCES

Regarding the various sciences, there is an expansion not only of data and expertise but also of our appreciation of the ethical significance of the sciences. (Cf. the chapters by Robert Springer and Charles Curran in this volume.) Acknowledgement of this is frequent in the documents of Vatican II. We are directed to the many new ancillae of theology: psychology, sociology, the social sciences, the science of communications, and biology.[123]

A further quite relevant observation is the following:

> Today it is more difficult than ever for a synthesis to be formed of the various branches of knowledge and the arts. For while the mass and the diversity of cultural factors are increasing, there is a decline in the individual man's ability to grasp and unify these elements. Thus the ideal of "the universal man" is disappearing more and more.[124]

So too is the ideal of "the universal magisterium" disappearing. Magisterial pronouncements will perhaps have an even greater value in such an age, as man's social consciousness grows and his need to tap communal wisdom is more felt. The magisterium must try to provide this wisdom by being as sensitive as possible to the movements of the ubiquitous Spirit. Still, both moralist and moral magisterium will have a very new look.

In a simpler age the moralist could attempt to acquire enough technical expertise to make judgments about the moral problems of the scientist. Technological growth and "the information explosion" make this impossible. In facing the moral questions posed, for example, by the science of genetics, two possibilities are conceivable: the moralist must become a geneticist or the geneticist must be made morally alert by a continuing dialogue with the ethical experts. The second is obviously preferable. The geneticist must not prescind from the moral dimensions of his science (and indeed he does not even if he pretends to). The moral questions cannot be answered by him alone; but they cannot be answered without him.

THE ECUMENICAL APPROACH TO MORAL TRUTH

This point about ecumenism can be made briefly. The Church has entered into dialogue with other Christians, with non-Christians, and with non-believers. This means that we have something to learn from them. None of the faithful, lay or clergy, can ignore the witness of these people in the pursuit of moral truth—although emotionally, it would seem, we are more ready to say this than to do it. The hierarchy may not merely proclaim their teaching prerogatives if they are not engaged in *real* dialogue with the laity, theologians, and all others who are also annointed with the spirit of truth and prophecy.

With these considerations in mind it is hoped that we will attain to some useful refinements by turning to the statements of Reed and McCormick concerning the authentic magisterium. John Reed asserts that, given a pronouncement of the authentic magisterium, there is an "obligation not to contradict the doctrine in public speech and writing."[125] This statement, for some years, was a truism among Catholic moralists and canonists. It is hardly defensible today. Reed, we saw, says that theologians may enter into speculative discussion about magisterial statements "supposing a discreet selection of audience." Presumably, if discussion is called for, theologians around the world can hardly communicate by word of mouth. They must write, and by now it would be obvious that there is no written word on theological subjects that might not be proclaimed from the housetops. Vital theological discussions can no longer be kept "under wraps." Pastoral difficulties result from this and must be met, but this new fact of life must be accepted.

More important is the internal intellectual assent which Reed states is *per se* due magisterial statements (p. 59). Enlarging on this Reed says that "it will not easily or commonly happen that the ordinary faithful, the ordinary priest, or even the ordinary theologian will be in a position to depart from the sort of authentic teaching at issue here" (p. 60). Anyone going against a particular moral teaching would appear to be imprudently exposing himself "to the danger of violating the moral law" (p. 57). The reason: "For the assistance of the Holy Spirit is always present to the vicar of Christ and the other bishops, and in their purposeful pronouncements they will have used more than ordinary human means as well" (p. 57). (Since the Holy Spirit is also present to the laity and theologians and non-Catholics, this reason is limp. It also ignores the times when hierarchical teachings were amended at the initiative of the faithful.)

Reed does, however, make an important admission. There is an "absolute possibility" that someone "exceptionally qualified" could disagree with the teaching in question and even act according to his own opinion as long as he does not shake "the external order" (p. 59). This, of course, is "a rather extraordinary thing" (p. 60).

This admission, I repeat, is important. It is, I think, quite gratuitous to assert that it is "a rather extraordinary thing" to find persons sufficiently qualified to dissent with a particular teaching. In the present question of contraception, for example, given the wide publicity afforded important studies on the subject and the deep convictions of the persons and groups with whom we are in dialogue, it seems to me that the number of those "exceptionally qualified" to dissent could be quite large. Clearly it is a matter of judgment. Reed mentions the possibility that the Church could in a particular case wish to impose a norm of conduct by using its "jurisdictional authority." If we apply this possibility to the contraception question, then the debate is no longer about natural law but is a case of positive law;

positive law, of course, is open to the soothing influence of *epikeia.*

Several points made by Richard McCormick deserve attention. He writes: "Certain truths about man's nature penetrate his consciousness gradually by historical processes and for the same reason are maintained only with difficulty."[126] He points out that it is not always easy to demonstrate the reasonableness of certain moral evaluations. Because of this, an authoritative magisterium makes sense.

It is certainly true that it is not always easy to give a fully satisfactory explanation of certain moral convictions which emerge gradually in human consciousness. The magisterium can exercise an important preservative influence here. It can preserve these nascent appreciations from an iconoclastic rationalism. We would only add to this that the developing understanding in history of a truth can also be arrested at a particular point by an inflexible magisterium which is not open to the implications of an expanding historical consciousness. The magisterium can easily fall prey to a bad spirit of conservatism. This too should be admitted and guarded against.

McCormick continues:

> Is it not, up to a point, precisely because arguments are not clear, or at least not universally persuasive, that a magisterium makes sense in this area? At what point does our healthy impatience to understand muffle the voice most like to speed the process? (p. 613)

Three comments suggest themselves here. First, precisely because the arguments are not clear it makes sense for the magisterium to be flexible and open to the possibility that when the arguments are clarified another position may be indicated.

Secondly, precisely because the arguments are not clear, the magisterium, however forcefully it presses its position, may not impose a certain obligation that only clarity makes possible. *In dubiis libertas* contains an insight that may not be invalidated by any juridical power.

Finally, one should view history closely before saying that

the magisterium is "the voice most likely to speed the process." At times, it has been such a voice, but at other times it has failed.

To conclude this section on the authentic, non-infallible magisterium: how should we react to this kind of papal and episcopal teaching? Pius XII in *Humani generis* said that "if the supreme pontiffs in their official documents purposely pass judgment on a matter debated until then, it is obvious to all that the matter, according to the mind and will of the same pontiffs, cannot be considered any longer a question open for discussion among theologians" (*quaestionem liberae inter theologos disceptationis iam haberi non posse*).[127] Vatican II, as we have seen, said that the ordinary magisterium of popes and bishops should be met with a *religiosum obsequium* (in *Documents of Vatican II, "obsequium"* is translated "assent" and "submission," perhaps not too felicitously). To determine the authority of papal statements which are not *ex cathedra* the council offers some criteria: they are to be adhered to in accordance with the "manifest mind and will" of the pope (same paragraph). "His mind and will in the matter may be known chiefly either from the character of the documents, from his frequent repetition of the same doctrine, or from his manner of speaking" (The Constitution on the Church, #25, p. 48).

Concerning the celebrated statement of Pius XII in *Humani generis,* Ford and Kelly are ready to concede that "even a non-infallible pronouncement can close a controversy among theologians." They add something of a reservation:

> We feel sure, however, that the pope himself would agree that this decisive character of the pronouncement must be evident. That is in accord with canon 1323, §3, which states that nothing is to be understood as dogmatically declared or defined unless this is clearly manifested. The canon refers to infallible teachings; yet the same norm seems to apply with at least equal force to the binding character of non-infallible teaching, especially when there is question of pronouncements that would close a controversy.[128]

We need not belabor the problems of such a position. *An admittedly fallible statement could close off discussion of the question among theologians with the possibility of error thus going unchecked.* The reservation expressed by Ford and Kelly indicates that they were not unaware of this difficulty. They do not, however, exclude the possibility of closing a controversy with fallible teaching.

John Reed prefers to translate the final words of the statement from *Humani generis* in this way: "cannot be any longer considered a matter of open debate."[129] He feels that Pius meant that the debate could go on but that both sides of the question cannot "be held and followed with equal freedom."[130] The precise cause of this limitation of freedom is not made manifest. It seems to me that whatever the presumptive value of a particular fallible papal teaching and however respectfully one receives it and studies it, it is difficult to see why the discussion should thereby have been rendered less free. At any rate, I do not think that many theologians would deny that the theology of the magisterium has advanced considerably since *Humani generis*, and that the magisteriological controversy was obviously not closed by that encyclical.

The statement of Vatican II concerning the criteria for judging the binding power of the authentic papal magisterium is not satisfying. It seems to say that the teaching is as binding as the pope wills it to be. This would be voluntarism. It also would lead theologians into fantastic probes to discover the mind and intent of the pontiff on certain questions. Some theologians, for example, trying to discover the mind of Pius XII on psychiatry after he had warned against certain attitudes and techniques, felt the need to do more than analyse his text. They also sought out "a subsequent 'inspired' comment in the pages of *L'Osservatore Romano* [which] made it very clear that he had not intended to condemn psychiatry in general or psychoanalysis in particular."[131] They also thought it relevant to report that "his *cordial* reception of the psychiatrists and psychoanalysts and the friendly words with which he closed his address showed a spirit far removed from hostility to this modern branch of science."[132]

Let us think of the statements of Pius IX on religious freedom. His manner of speaking, his frequent repetitions, and the solemn character of the language he used indicated the utmost seriousness of intention. I would not be inclined to say that those who respectfully disagreed with Pius' stand, preferring something more akin to the subsequent teachings of Vatican II on religious liberty, would have deserved any reproach.

The language of the code of canon law on the related question of the episcopal magisterium seems better: "While the bishops, whether teaching individually or gathered in particular councils, are not endowed with infallibility, yet with regard to the faithful entrusted to their care they are truly teachers and masters (*veri doctores seu magistri*)" (canon 1326). The pope and the bishops are truly teachers. Their teachings should receive deep respect. Their statements represent serious interventions by officers of the Church. Hopefully, these teachings are representative of ecclesial wisdom and thus merit religious reverence, but it is religious also to recognize that they are not infallible; they might at times come from a period when vitally relevant data, since come to light, were lacking. These teachings, after all—and we must say this to avoid a kind of magisteriolatry—are not the word of God. Indeed they must stand under the judgment of the word of God. It is not an act of disloyalty but rather a duty of the theologian to test these statements to see if they can withstand the cutting power of the two-edged sword.

To develop a new kind of magisterial approach to a new kind of world is a massive task. A thousand questions beginning with "how" await research and reply. Here I presume only to persent certain terms which might more accurately describe the essential characteristics of the Church's moral magisterium. Two terms seem particularly apt: prophetic (closely allied to creative) and dialogical.

Prophetic: The magisterium is called to prophecy. The prophet is distinguished not so much for his insight into the future as for his insight into the present. His call is to pierce the blinding clouds which inevitably envelop human consciousness. Inherent in our history is a tendency to develop a myopic and insensitive code morality which evades the agonies of the moral call to authentic personhood. This insensitive ethos tends to grip society and defy penetration. The prophet must see and penetrate.

The Church in history has had great moments of powerful prophecy. In the early centuries it became a powerful social force, championing the dignity of persons, the rights of conscience, and the power of unselfish love. It was its religious and moral intensity that made it so important on the imperial scene that Decius himself had to admit that he was more concerned over the election of a bishop in Rome than over the revolt of a political rival.[133] It was not Constantine who gave the Church status. Historians tell us that: "Sooner or later some emperor after Constantine would have had to seek an understanding with the victorious Church."[134] The Church's work in education and the care of the sick and the poor gave many effective, prophetic lessons in compassion and love of truth to the medieval world. The social encyclicals in modern times that braved charges of left wing radicalism to call for social reconstruction were genuinely prophetic. Recent papal calls for peace merit the same encomium.

On the other hand, prophecy melted in the warmth of Constantinian favor. In the medieval age of violence the Church imbibed the barbarian spirit of violence. It did not pierce the enveloping cloud. Christian consciousness was seduced by the rigors of Roman law and Stoicism for centuries. It followed when it should have led. The treatment of "heretics" and unbelievers was harsh and often ruthless. The use of torture and the ordeal provide us no happy memories. The lessons taught by these practices were not prophetic or Christian. The evils of anti-Semitism, colonialization, slavery, right wing totalitarianism, and racism were not met with distinguished prophecy.

The bane of prophecy, often enough, is a stifling traditionalism which confuses tenure with authenticity, forgetting that error too can become traditional. Traditions must be respected; they must also be critically examined to see if they enshrine insensitivity and blindness.

The true prophet is creative. The Church teaching must not detach itself from the human scene, and act as though it were called to pronounce *licets* and *non licets* from a distance. Its role is creative more than judgmental. It must not simply worry over the dangers of progress, but participate in that progress so as to minimize the dangers. A timid and negative magisterium is the irrelevant voice of uncreative fear.

Ethics can be radically divided into an ethics of survival and an ethics of creativity. A cringing, self-centered ethics of survival can never befit the Christian. And yet the way of creativity is difficult.

Sometimes the creative word will be called utopian because its hour has not yet come. Pope John's encyclical on peace was thus described by Paul Tillich at the *Pacem in Terris* convocation at the United Nations. Yet the prophetic word must be spoken and inserted into the stream of human thought so that it might slowly achieve dynamic influence.

Creativity breaks through the status quo. An institution which has allowed itself to center on survival will thus be tempted to crush the creative spirit. The long list of creative theologians who have been condemned shows that this danger is not illusory in the Church. The harassment of theologians whose work was later to find conciliar blessing in Vatican II gives a poignant lesson in this regard.[135]

Dialogical: Truth is not reached in solitude but in the processes of communitarian existence. If the Church would bear witness on the human scene, it must recognize itself as a participant in these processes. It must not enter conversation trying to say the last word; rather it must say meaningful words drawn from its vast memory and rich Christian experience. The magisterium must be honest and not pretend to data it does not have. Obviously the moral magisterium must not feel bound, by a kind of institutional pride, to past magisterial documents that through lack of insight and information taught something that can now be seen as inaccurate and unacceptable. Respect for the wisdom of the past does not impose the perpetuation of past deficiencies.

An example of a dialogical magisterium can be found in the statement on the Vietnamese war issued by the American bishops in November, 1966. Indeed, it could serve as a classical paradigm for the Church teaching on many moral questions:

> We realize that citizens of all faiths and of differing political loyalties honestly differ among themselves over the moral issues involved in this tragic conflict. While we do not claim to be able to resolve these issues authoritatively, in the light of the facts as they are known to us, it is reasonable to argue . . .

The bishops then went on to acknowledge that Catholics were free to be conscientious objectors to the position that their bishops had presented. The bishops did not content themselves with reiterating the gospel message of love and peace. They made an effort to see how this applied to the present war situation. But they allowed that Catholics with other viewpoints and insights could responsibly reach another opinion.

There is no reason why this approach could not be taken in other areas. The doctrine of conscientious objection involves a respect for the individual conscience and for the complexity of ethical decision making. These factors obtain in questions other than war. Persons of all faiths and differing loyalties differ among themselves and with us on issues such as contraception, abortion, divorce, civil disobedience, political philosophy, business ethics, etc. With the same honesty that our bishops showed in this instance, all spokesmen for the teaching Church should admit that we do not have a comprehensive knowledge of all the factors needed for a solution to these questions.

In these matters it could be said with the bishops: "While we do not claim to be able to resolve these issues authoritatively, in the light of the facts as they are known to us, it is reasonable to argue . . ." Then, acknowledging with consistency that individual Catholics might disagree, the possibility of respectful conscientious objection to the announced position should be admitted. Any other practice pretends to an omniscience regarding all relevant essential circumstances and places an obstacle before the guidance of the Spirit whose grace is the New Law.

Furthermore, should a dialogical statment such as that of the American bishops have to be amended in the light of new information, the change would not be a clumsy retreat from a position too apodictically assumed. It would represent, rather, a new phase in the enriching dialogue. It will occasion no loss of prestige among honest men. Other Christians and non-Christians will be inspired by our openness to their views and will thus be inclined to share more deeply in our experience of truth.

We are not suggesting that the Church succumb to the weakness of consensus politics and become an insipid and bland voice. Dialogue cannot always be reserved or agreeable; neither can it be reduced to a gentle, inoffensive bleating geared to the creation of a false unanimity and fellowship. Its prophetic character would thereby be lost. However, it must acknowledge a *de facto* pluralism in many moral matters, especially those which have been profoundly affected by changing conditions and new knowledge. It is naive and self-deceiving to seek one "official" Catholic position on all questions. (It would, for example, be naive and self-deceiving to allege that Catholics are one in theory and practice on the question of contraception.) However, in such less ambiguous questions as racial integration, and even in ambiguous questions, churchmen should speak out with sufficient force and specificity to be influential in national and international discussions.

Agencies should be erected also to make it possible for strong minority opinions in the Church to enter the public forum effectively as "Catholic." (The bishops' statement on Vietnam in November, 1966, did not represent the views of large segments of the Catholic population, who are thus left to protest "unofficially" without the important sociological influence of institutional prestige.)

A dialogical magisterium does not forget the integral magisterial role of the laity. The laity, Pius XII said, "are the Church" (*AAS* 38: 141). Vatican II taught: "The body of the faithful as a whole, anointed as they are by the holy One, cannot err in matters of belief."[136] Neither the magisterium nor the Church is simply hierarchical. If the laity, therefore, feel that the Church is not being effective or true to its mission they are not free simply to criticize the hierarchy. We usually get the leadership we want and then ease our consciences by criticizing it. The laity, quite as much as the hierarchy, too often work under the illusory impression that initiative and creativity always come from "above." The impression is a kind of infantilism and has been repeatedly disproved in history.

Finally, the magisterium must be served by a vigorous theological community. Theologians, bishops, and laity must concur in the service of the word. In fact, since there are and should be various agencies of witness and influence in the Church, it would be better to speak of the *Magisteria* of the Church. We would then consider not just the papal and episcopal magisteria but the equally authentic magisterium of the laity and the magisterium of the theologians. Each of these has a role of creative service to the truth; none can be considered as having a quasi-juridical power to stifle or invalidate the other. Each magisterium must be seen as open to the corrective influence of the other magisteria. Freedom and mutual respect must characterize this service. The theologian must respect the bishops' concern for the integrity of the kerygma; bishops should presume a similar concern on the part of theologians. Episcopal consecration does not convey theological expertise.

Theologians whose teachings or prudence is questioned should have the advantage of judgment by their peers. Those not active in the theological community might easily miss the implications of current debate and judge a man unjustly. Error is inevitable in the development of any science. The only way to stop it is to stop all thought. It should be noted too that bishops who create a repressive atmosphere for theologians are thereby inviting non-experts and the popular press to address themselves to the neglected subjects. Theologians, on the other hand, must respect the pastoral needs and concerns of the bishops. Mutual respect for the distinct but complementary authorities of bishop, theologian, and layman must be the goal.

Will a moral magisterium that does not call itself infallible command respect? Yes. Will an authentic magisterium that is conscious of its limitations as well as of its strength be able to exert a positive influence? Yes. In the first place, it will spare many Catholics the anguish of unexpected change that wracks so many of our people today. Unaware that the Church can in many ways change—and has changed often in the past—many Catholics today are shaken in their faith. Future Catholics, schooled in the reality of being a pilgrim people, will greet progress with joy and not with panic. Formal magisterial pronouncements which give faithful voice to Christian consciousness will be received with respect. In matters moral, such pronouncements will be treasured as an expression of the wisdom of the Christian people. Such teaching will be seen as an invaluable aid but not as a substitute for conscience, since no agency can substitute for the unique role of conscience.

Secondly, non-Catholics will react to our honesty as they did to the honesty of Vatican II. Prophets of doom feared the self-revelation that was inevitable in the council; they have not yet changed their triumphalist stance. No man of good will will think less of us if he hears in our voices the echo of him who was meek and humble of heart. A Church that is distinguished by a fervid religious life and an unmistakable concern for the good of mankind will be a powerful force for good. Its involvement, its love, and its absence of pretense will give it superb credentials in the modern world.

Catholic moral teaching will be more realistic and pertinent. The collegial character of the magisterium will free it from the impossibilities attached to overcentralization and the attempt to impose moral absolutes universally and transculturally without sufficient regard to varying contexts. The magisterium will not be thought of as merely papal or merely episcopal. Rather, the service of the hierarchy will be to vitalize and encourage the primary witness of the Church, the liturgy and lives of the people of God. This is the magisterium, the Church that will give to the world the word that is life.

CHARLES E. CURRAN

Absolute Norms
and Medical Ethics

The natural law has recently become a very important topic of
discussion in moral theology. The ecumenical dialogue has
forced Roman Catholic theologians to re-examine this theory.
Many Protestant theologians point out that the natural law
concept constitutes a primary source of disagreement between
Protestant and Catholic ethicians.[1] The ongoing dialogue with
our world has shown Catholic theologians a world and a reality
that differs considerably from the view of the world and reality
enshrined in the traditional textbook understanding of natural
law.

The entire process of renewal within the Church demands
a critical appraisal of natural law theory. The debate over contraception, for example, has evolved into a questioning of natural law itself, as a rethinking of contraception necessarily
entailed a critique of the natural law system on which it was
based. But to make a definitive critique of the natural law here
is impossible. The aims of this chapter are more modest: it
will consider the concept of natural law which underlies Catholic moral teaching on medical morals.

Medical moral has occupied a prominent place in Catholic
moral theology in the present century. In the United States
alone, a proportionately large number of books have been
written recently in this area.[2] Furthermore, many of the utter-

ances of recent popes have been concerned with the moral problems confronting modern medicine.[3] Both the papal teaching and the textbooks base their medical morality upon natural law. Thus, medical morality serves as a good illustration of the use of natural law in Catholic moral theology. This chapter will also try to show that the area of medical morality tends to show up the shortcomings in the textbook theory of natural law. (In other areas, such as social problems, where Catholic teaching has employed the concept of natural law, it has received wide-based support from many men of good will.)

POINTS OF DISSATISFACTION

There is dissatisfaction among Catholic theologians concerning a number of questions involving medical morality. Contraception comes to mind as the most obvious example. The majority report of the papal commission which examined the problem of contraception rejected the natural law arguments against contraception.[4] Even many who have upheld the ban against contraception admit that the natural law arguments are not convincing.[5] However, there are also other applications of natural law theory in the area of medicine which do not command universal assent from contemporary Catholic theologians.

Contraception and Sterilization. Logically, the question of sterilization is closely connected with contraception. Catholic theologians have generally proposed that direct sterilization (either temporary or permanent) is immoral. Sterilization is permitted only if it is indirect; that is, "if a pathological condition of the organ renders it necessary for the preservation of the patient's life or health."[6]

Traditionally, theologians have distinguished contraception from sterilization by the fact that contraception interferes with the sexual act, whereas sterilization interferes with the sexual faculty itself.[7] (According to this theological terminology, the anovulant pills involve sterilization and not contraception.[8]) Once a theologian admits that man may interfere in the reproductive process, there is no essential difference (other than the permanency of the effect) between interfering with the act of sexual intercourse (contraception) or interfering with the reproductive faculty (anovulant pills, sterilizing operations).

Interestingly enough, at one time a few Catholic theologians were willing to admit the liceity of the anovulant pill (a sterilization) and still deny the morality of contraceptive intercourse.[9] But the significant moral difference between sterilization and contraception is the fact that sterilization, especially through surgical procedures, tends to be more permanent than contraception.

Medicine itself has always maintained the principle of economy: man should interfere only to the extent that it is necessary. For example, medicine prefers to avoid surgery if other means of treatment are sufficient. Likewise, a permanent procedure should not be employed when a temporary procedure would be sufficient. The principle of economy also has moral validity. However, there are occasions when a permanent sterilization is called for, especially in those cases in which the woman can never again bear children. Thus, a change in contraception points toward a change in the condemnation of direct sterilization.

Artificial Insemination. There are other instances of dissatisfaction with textbook solutions to moral problems in the area of medicine. "The Ethical and Religious Directives for Catholic Hospitals," sanctioned by the Catholic Hospital Association of the United States and Canada, maintains: "Sterility tests involving the procurement of the male specimen by masturbation . . . are morally objectionable" (n. 38).[10] A partial reason for the condemnation is given in an earlier directive. "The unnatural use of the sex faculty (for example, masturbation) is never permitted even for a laudable purpose" (n. 29). Pope Pius XII spoke in the same vein.[11] However, contemporary theologians have not been convinced that such an action is wrong.[12]

In the past theology has perhaps tended to look at the action only from the physical and biological viewpoint. Masturbation was totally defined by its physiological properties. However, human understanding tells us there is quite a difference between masturbation and the ejaculation of semen to obtain a specimen for sterility tests. The human act seems to be the obtaining of semen for examination and not the human act of masturbation. The whole purpose and intent of the person gives a different meaning to the action. To describe the morality of an action solely in terms of the physical nature of the faculty apart from any other existing relationships and circumstances appears to be inadequate.

The basic question remains artificial insemination when the wife is inseminated with her husband's semen. Pope Pius XII taught that such artificial insemination is wrong because the act of intercourse must always be a personal action which is expressive of love.[13] Some theologians, before the papal allocutions, thought that an absolute condemnation of artificial insemination puts too much emphasis on the individual physical action as such.[14] Ordinarily the conception process begins by the depositing of male semen in the vagina of the woman through physical intercourse. However, occasionally it may happen that such normal intercourse does not provide good conditions for conception to occur. By bypassing the normal way of insemination, science can provide a better possibility for the husband's seed to fertilize his wife's ovum. It is true that insemination must take place within the context of a relationship of marital love; but the physical act of natural intercourse does not seem to be of absolute and determining moral necessity.

A concrete case illustrates the difficulties inherent in the present ban on artificial insemination in the medical moral textbooks. John is a handicapped person suffering from a partial paralysis in the legs. John is able to have sexual intercourse with his wife, but real penetration is often not attained. Yet John and Alice desperately want a family. A sympathetic Catholic doctor tried to help. After having relations with her husband, Alice rushed to the doctor's office hoping that she still retained some of the semen. The doctor then tried to gather whatever semen was still in the vagina in a syringe, and then insert the semen into the cervix, thus avoiding the harmful acids of the vagina. Such an approach did not result in a pregnancy. Then the doctor decided that John and Alice should have sexual relations in his private office. The doctor would enter immediately after intercourse and be able to gather what little semen there might be in the vagina before the harmful vaginal fluids could affect the semen.

The natural human reaction rejects such a solution as inhuman. Even though conception would then occur after a "natural act," the entire circumstances of such marital intercourse seem unnatural. To obtain the husband's semen in such a case, by voluntary ejaculation which is then medically inserted into the cervix of the wife, does not seem to be an immoral procedure.

The Double Effect. There has also been discussion in recent years about the principle of the double effect.[15] The principle of double effect has bearing on the questions of direct killing, direct abortion, direct mutilation, and direct sterilization. The principle tries to come to grips with those complex human situations where both good and evil exist intertwined. If the evil effect is only permitted (and not directly intended), then the evil effect can be permitted for a proportionate reason. The Directives of the Catholic Hospital Association, for example, describe direct killing as a procedure "whose sole immediate effect" is the death of a human being (n. 12).

In this sense the sole immediate effect of an action is determined by the physical structure of the action itself, without any consideration of the other values present in the situation. The question of ectopic pregnancy serves as a good illustration. Within the framework of the principle of double effect, the sole immediate effect of the action cannot be thought of as the abortion itself. The immediate effect of the action has to be the curing of some pathological condition. Earlier theologians maintained that an ectopic pregnancy (generally a fetus in the tube) could not be removed unless the tube itself had ruptured.

Once the tube had ruptured, it was in a pathological condition and could be removed even though it contained a fetus.

Lately, some theologians have maintained that the doctor does not have to wait for the tube to rupture. The blood of the tube is already being infected by the fetus and is thus pathological before the rupture occurs. Thus one may remove the tube with the fetus in it even before the tube ruptures.[16]

But here a further question must also be raised. What if the doctor can interfere by removing the fetus without taking out the tube? If the doctor has to remove the tube too, then the chances of the woman's giving birth again are greatly reduced. By removing just the fetus, the doctor does not impair the child-bearing ability of the mother. The doctor knows that the fetus has no chance to live and sooner or later will have to be removed. The logical solution would be to remove the fetus and save the tube, if possible. Such a solution appears to be very moral, but the usual application of the theory of direct killing or direct abortion would not admit the liceity of such a procedure.

The identification of the direct effect by the sole immediate effect of the action has caused some Catholic theologians to question such an understanding of "direct." "An act may or may not be abortion as a human act although materially and externally it is nevertheless exactly the same act."[17] Theologians are quick to point out the problems created by the notion of direct mutilation defined in terms of the physical structure of the act itself. For this reason, many theologians originally condemned transplantation of organs as a direct mutilation. To transplant an organ from one person to another, the organ obviously must be removed from the first person. However, an act whose sole immediate effect is the removal of an eye or a kidney involves a direct mutilation. The fact that it is later to be given to a person in great need of such an organ does not change the fact that the sole immediate effect of the action is mutilation.[18]

Archbishop Denis Hurley has proposed a somewhat different principle to apply in some complex situations where both

good and evil effects exist. Hurley speaks of the principle of
the overriding right, and hesitatingly mentions the possibility
of employing such a principle in the case of abortion when the
mother's right to life is put in jeopardy by the fetus.[19] The
principle of the overriding right, if logically extended, could apply to a number of other situations, even in the area of abortion.
Hurley's principle does not rely on a moral determination based
on the sole immediate effect of the action, but rather tries to
weigh the different moral values at stake in the concrete situation.[20]

Medical Experimentation. Catholic moral teaching has not been
favorable to medical experimentation. The certitude with which
some actions were proposed as immoral (if it had not been
widely ignored) would have prevented much profitable medical
experimentation. Transplantation of organs is just one example.
Many tests on human sperm would have been condemned because the sperm was held to be obtained through immoral
means. A rigid belief in the absolute certitude of the immorality
of medical procedures makes experimentation and medical progress most difficult for Catholic scientists. In the future Catholic
theologians should be wary of insisting that some actions are
certainly and always immoral.

The dissatisfaction with a number of conclusions in recent
Catholic understanding of medical morals has been sufficiently
documented. But present tensions in medical morality are nothing compared to those that will occur in trying to solve some
of the genetic problems of the future. The individual problems,
of course, are symptomatic of the underlying difficulties with
the system, or theory, of natural law upon which such conclusions are based. (This chapter assumes that the reader is
generally familiar with the theory of natural law found in the
applications to medical problems in Catholic moral textbooks.)
A general understanding of Catholic medical moral teaching
together with the dissatisfactions mentioned point to some of the
difficulties involved in such a system.

The main problem stems from the too easy identification

of the physical action itself, or the physical structure of the effects, with the moral determination of the human action. The human action cannot be judged merely in and by itself or according to its own physical structure alone, with no consideration given to the other values present in the situation. Also, the certitude with which Catholic theologians have maintained that some actions are always wrong in the area of medical morals, and the current call for change in these areas, makes one wary of any system which continues to profess such certitude.

Historical investigation will partially explain how such questionable ways of viewing morality have entered into the system of Catholic medical morality and can suggest ways for avoiding such apparent distortions in the future. By reviewing at least some of the historical antecedents of these questionable teachings in medical morals, a way may be found to avoid such distortions in the future.

NATURAL IDENTIFIED WITH PHYSICAL: ULPIAN

The danger that arises if we identify the moral action simply with the biological and physical structure of the human act is evident in the controversy over contraception and sterilization. The notion of "direct" in the principle of double effect also seems to be too closely tied both to the physical structure of the human act and the sole immediate physical effect of that action.

Ethical theory constantly vacillates between two polarities —naturalism and idealism. Naturalism sees man in perfect continuity with the nature about him. Nature shapes and even determines man. Idealism views man completely apart from nature and sees man as completely surpassing nature. Even Thomistic philosophy, the main Catholic proponent of natural law theory, knows an ambivalence between nature and reason.

The Thomistic natural law concept vacillates at times between the order of nature and the order of reason.[21] The general Thomistic thrust is towards the predominance of reason in natural law theory. However, there is in Thomas a definite tendency to identify the demands of natural law with physical and biological processes. Thomas, too, is a historical person conditioned by the circumstances and influences of his own time. These influences help explain the tendency (but not the pre- dominant tendency) in Thomas to identify the human action with the physical and biological structure of the human act. A major one is Ulpian, a Roman lawyer who died in 228.

Ulpian and Thomas. Ulpian defined the natural law as that which nature teaches all the animals. Ulpian distinguished the natural law from the *ius gentium.* The *ius naturale* is that which is common to all animals, whereas the *ius gentium* is that which is proper to men.[22] Albert the Great rejected Ulpian's definition of the natural law, but Thomas accepted it, and even showed a preference for such a definition.[23] In the *Commentary on the Sentences,* for example, Thomas maintains that the most strict definition of natural law is the one proposed by Ulpian: *ius naturae est quod natura omnia animalia docuit.*[24]

In his *Commentary on the Nichomachean Ethics,* Thomas again shows a preference for Ulpian's definition. Aristotle had proposed a twofold division of *iustum naturale* and *iustum legale,* but Ulpian proposed the threefold distinction of *ius naturale, ius gentium* and *ius civile.* Thomas solves the ap- parent dilemma by saying that the Roman law concepts of *ius naturale* and *ius gentium* both belong under the Aristotelian category of *iustum naturale.* Man has a double nature. The *ius naturale* rules that which is proper to both man and the animals, such as the union of the sexes and the education of offspring; whereas the *ius gentium* governs the rational part of man which is proper to man alone, and embraces such things as fidelity to contracts.[25]

In the *Summa Theologiae* Thomas cites Ulpian's definition on a number of occasions.[26] In the classification of natural law again Thomas shows a preference for Ulpian's definition. Thomas accepts the division proposed by Isidore of Seville, accord- ing to which the *ius gentium* belongs to the category of human law and not to the category of divine law. Thomas uses Ulpian's definition to explain Isidore's division. The natural law pertains to the divine law because it is common to man and to all the animals.[27] In a sense, the *ius gentium* does pertain to the category of human law because man uses his reason to deduce the conclusions of the *ius gentium.*

Thomas thus employs Ulpian's definition of natural law as opposed to what reason deduces (the *ius gentium*) to defend the division of law proposed by Isidore. The same question receives somewhat the same treatment later in the *Summa.*[28] The texts definitely show that Thomas knew and even accepted the definition of natural law proposed by Ulpian.

Ulpian's Concept of Natural Law. Ulpian is important for the understanding of natural law morality. The natural law for Ulpian is defined in terms of those actions which are common to man and all the animals. There results from this the definite danger of identifying the human action with a mere animal or biological process. "Nature" and "natural" in Ulpian's meaning are distinguished from that which is specifically human and derived by reason. Traditional theology has in the past definitely employed the words "natural" and "nature" as synonymous with animal or biological processes and not as denoting human actions in accord with the rational nature of man.

Moral theology textbooks even speak of sins according to nature. The manuals generally divide the sins against the sixth commandment into two categories—the sins against nature (*peccata contra naturam*) and sins in accord with nature (*peccata secundum naturam*). "Nature" is thus used in Ulpian's sense, as that which is common to man and all the animals. In matters of sexuality (and Ulpian himself uses the example of the sexual union as an illustration of the natural law), man shares with the animal world the fact of the sexual union whereby male seed is deposited in the vas of the female. Sins against nature, therefore, are those acts in which the animal or biological process is not observed—pollution, sodomy, bestiality, and contraception. Sins according to nature are those acts in which the proper biological process is observed but something is lacking in the sphere which belongs only to rational men. These include fornication, adultery, incest, rape, and sacrilege.[29]

The classification of sins against chastity furnishes concrete proof that "nature" has been used in Catholic theology to refer to animal processes without any intervention of human reason. Many theologians have rightly criticized the approach to marriage sexuality used by Catholic natural law theoreticians because such an approach concentrated primarily on the biological components of the act of intercourse. The personal aspects of the sexual union received comparatively scant attention in many of the manuals of moral theology. Ulpian's influence has made it easier for Catholic natural law thinking to identify the human act simply with the physical structure of the act.

Ulpian's Anthropology. Ulpian's understanding of the natural law logically leads to disastrous consequences in the anthropological understanding of man. The distinction between two parts in man—that which is common to man and all the animals, and that which is proper to man—results in a two-layer version of man. A top layer of rationality is merely added to an already constituted bottom layer of animality. The union between the two layers is merely extrinsic—the one lies on top of the other. The animal layer retains its own finalities and tendencies, independent of the demands of rationality. Thus man may not interfere in the animal processes and finalities. Note that the results of such an anthropology are most evident in the area of sexuality.

A proper understanding of man should start with that which is proper to man. Rationality does not just lie on top of animality, but rationality characterizes and guides the whole person. Animal processes and finalities are not untouchable. Man's whole vocation, we have come to see, is to bring order and intelligence into the world, and to shape animal and biological finalities toward a truly human purpose. Ulpian's concept of natural law logically falsifies the understanding of man and tends to canonize the finalities and processes which man shares with the animal world.

A better anthropology would see the distinctive in man as guiding and directing the totality of his being. For Thomas rationality constituted what is distinctive and characteristic in man. Modern philosophers differ from Thomas on what is distinctively human. Phenomenologists tend to view man as a symbolic person; while personalists look upon man as an incarnate spirit, a "thou" in relation to other "you's." However, all would agree in rejecting a notion of man that sees animality existing in man and that retains animal finalities and tendencies without any intervention of the specifically human part of man.

I am not asserting that Thomas always identified human actions with animal processes or the physical structure of the act. In fact, the general outlines of the hylomorphic theory, by speaking of material and formal components of reality, try to avoid any physicism or biologism. Nevertheless, the adoption of Ulpian's understanding of "nature" and "natural" logically leads to the identification of the human act itself with animal processes and with the mere physical structure of the act. Such a distorted view of the human act becomes especially prevalent in the area of medical morals, for in medical morality one can more easily conceive a moral human action solely in terms of the physical structure of that action.

Likewise, Ulpian's notion of nature easily leads to a morality based on the finality of a faculty independently of any considerations of the total human person or the total human community. One must, of course, avoid the opposite danger of paying no attention to the physical structure of the act or to external actions in themselves. However, Catholic theology in the area of medical morality has suffered from an oversimple identification of the human action with an animal process or finality.

Marriage and Sexuality. Ulpian's understanding of natural law logically has had another deleterious effect on Catholic moral theology. Until the last decade magisterial pronouncements frequently spoke of the primary and secondary ends of marriage.[30] The latest statements of Pope Paul, and the Pastoral Constitution on the Church in the Modern World (*Gaudium et Spes*), happily avoid this terminology.[31] However, such a distinction has obviously influenced Catholic teaching on marriage and sexuality. Many people have questioned the distinction as being contradicted by the experience of married couples.

The distinction logically follows from Ulpian's concept of the natural law and man, although I do not claim that Ulpian is the source of such a distinction. "Primary" is that which is common to man and all the animals. Ulpian, and Thomas in citing Ulpian, use the union of the sexes and the procreation and education of offspring as examples of that which is common to man and all the animals. "Secondary" is that which is proper to man. Since only men and not animals have sexual intercourse as a sign and expression of love, the love union aspect of sexuality remains proper to man and therefore secondary. The former teaching on the ends of marriage is logically connected with Ulpian's understanding of man and natural law. Thus the teaching of Ulpian on natural law has a logical connection with the inadequate understanding of a human action as identified with an animal process.

A MORE PRIMITIVE ATTITUDE

A second and more general historical factor has also influenced the tendency to make the processes of nature inviolable. Stoic philosophy well illustrates a more general historical factor that tends to identify the human action with its physical or natural structure. One should avoid too many generalizations about the Stoics because Stoic philosophy included a number of different thinkers who covered a comparatively long span of years. In addition, Stoic philosophers invoked the natural law to justify practices that contemporary natural law theoreticians brand as immoral.[32] However, there is a common thrust to the ethical doctrine proposed by the Stoics.

Nature: Norm or Servant. Ethics considers man and his actions. Man wants to find happiness. What actions should man perform to find his happiness and fulfillment? A more primitive and less technical society will come to conclusions different from those reached by a more technically and scientifically developed society. Primitive man soon realizes that he finds his happiness in conforming himself to the patterns of nature.

Primitive man remains almost helpless when confronted with the forces of nature. The forces of nature are so strong that man is even tempted to bow down and adore. He realizes the futility in trying to fight them. His happiness will come only by adjusting himself.

Nature divides the day into light and dark. When darkness descends, there is little or nothing that man can do except sleep. When the hot sun is beating down near the equator, he will find happiness only by avoiding work and overexposure in the sun. In colder climates, man will be happy only when he uses clothing and shelter to protect himself from nature. If he wants to be happy, he will stay under some form of shelter and avoid the rain and snow. If there is a mountain in his path, the wise man will walk around the mountain rather than suffer the ardors of trying to scale the peak. For man living in a primitive society (in the sense of non-scientific and non-technical), happiness is found in conforming himself to nature.

Stoic philosophy built on this understanding of man living in a non-technical society. As Greeks, the Stoics believed in an intelligible world. They made the universe as a whole—the cosmos—their principle of intelligibility. Stoic philosophy held that reason governed the order of nature. Man's happiness consisted in conforming himself to reason, that is, in conforming himself to the order of nature. But nature was informed by reason or even identifiable with reason. The primary norm of morality, therefore, was conformity to nature.[33]

We who live in a scientific and technological society will have a different view of man and his happiness. Modern man does not find his happiness in conforming to nature. The whole ethos and genius of modern society is different. Contemporary man makes nature conform to him rather than vice-versa. Through electricity man can change night into day. There are very few things that modern man cannot do at night now that it is illuminated by electricity.

Contemporary man uses artificial heat in the winter and air conditioning in the summer to bring nature into conformity with his needs and desires. Nature did not provide man with wings to fly; in fact, the law of gravity seems to forbid man to fly. However, science has produced the jet plane and the rocket, which propel man at great speeds around the globe and even into the vast universe. When a mountain looms up as an obstacle, modern man either levels the mountain with bulldozers or tunnels under the terrain. Modern man could never tolerate a theory which equates human happiness with conformity to nature. Contemporary man interferes with the processes of nature to make nature conform to man.

These few paragraphs have not attempted to prove the influence of Stoic philosophy on St. Thomas. Rather, Stoic philosophy was used to illustrate how the conditions existing in a non-technological society will influence the philosophical understanding of man and ethics. Thomas too lived in an agrarian, non-scientific world. The non-technological worldview would be more prone to identify the human act with the physical process of nature itself.

Reality or Facticity. A more primitive society also tends to view reality in terms of the physical and the sensible. The child, unlike the adult, sees reality primarily in terms of externals. The tendency to identify the human action with the physical structure would definitely be greater in a more primitive society. For example, the importance that Catholic theology has attached to masturbatory activity, especially the overemphasis since the sixteenth century, seems to come from viewing it purely in terms of the physiological and biological aspects of the act. Modern psychology, however, does not place very great importance on such activity.

Theologians must incorporate the findings of modern science in trying to evaluate the human act of masturbation. To view it solely in terms of the physical structure of the act distorts the total reality of this human action. Contemporary theologians cannot merely repeat what older theologians have said. Today we know much more about the reality of the human act of masturbation than, say, St. Alphonsus or any other moral theologian living before the present century.[34]

It would be erroneous to say that Catholic theology has identified the human act with the brute facticity of natural processes or just the physical structure of the act itself. In the vast majority of cases, moral theology has always distinguished between the physical structure of the action and the morality of the action. The moral act of murder differs from the physical act of killing. The physical act of taking another's property does not always involve the moral act of stealing. However, in the area of medical morality (for example, contraception, sterilization, masturbation) the moral act has been considered the same as the physical structure of the act itself.

The Morality of Lying. Another area in which Catholic theologians are moving away from a description of the human act in purely physical or natural terms is lying. The contemporary theological understanding of lying serves as a salutary warning to the medical moralist because the morality of lying cannot be determined merely by examining the faculty of speech and its finality, apart from the totality of the human person speaking and the community in which he speaks.

The manuals of moral theology traditionally define lying as *locutio contra mentem.* The faculty of speech exists to express what is in the mind. When human speech does not reflect what is in the mind there is a perversion of the faculty. The perverted faculty argument is based on the finality of the faculty of speech looked at in itself. Accordingly, a lie exists when the verbal utterance does not correspond with what is in the mind. Theologians then had to face the problem created by the fact that at times the speaker simply could not speak the truth to his hearer or questioner (for example, in the case of a committed secret). A casuistry of mental reservations arose to deal with such situations.[35]

Today most contemporary Catholic theologians accept the distinction between a lie and a falsehood. A falsehood involves an untruth in the sense that the external word contradicts what is in the mind. However, the malice of lying does not consist in the perversion of the faculty of speech or the lack of conformity between the word spoken and what is in the mind. The malice of lying consists in the harm done to society and the human community through the breakdown of mutual trust and honesty. Thus, some theologians distinguish between a lie as the denial of truth which is due to the other and falsehood which is a spoken word not in conformity with what is in the mind.

The distinction between lying and falsehood obviates the rather contrived casuistry associated with broad and strict mental reservations.[36] But what does the more contemporary understanding of lying indicate? The new definition denies the validity of the perverted faculty argument. It is not sufficient merely to examine the faculty of speech and determine morality solely from the purpose of the faculty in itself. Likewise, the malice of lying does not reside in the lack of "physical" conformity between word and thought.

To view the faculty of speech apart from the total human situation of man in society seems to give a distorted view of lying. The faculty of speech must be seen and judged in a human context. Man can interfere with the physical purpose of the faculty for a higher human need and good. Perhaps in a similar vein, the notion of "direct" in the principle of the double effect cannot be judged merely from the sole immediate effect of the physical action itself, apart from the whole human context in which the act is placed. For example, if the fetus will have to be removed in the future when the tube becomes pathological, why not remove the fetus now and save the tube for future childbearing? The morality must be viewed in a total human context, and not merely judged according to the physical act itself and the natural effect of the act seen in itself apart from the whole context.

The influence of Ulpian and the view of primitive man tend to identify the total human action with the natural or biological process. A better understanding of such historically and culturally limited views of man should help the ethician in evaluating the theory of natural law as applied in the area of medical ethics. I do not claim that the summary historical evidence partially adduced here proves that the specific dis- satisfactions with textbook medical morality are correct. Nor have I proved that the human act never corresponds with the physical structure of the act. However, I think it is clear that an ethician must be very cautious that older and inadequate views of man and reality do not influence his contemporary moral judgments. It does seem that the definition of Ulpian and the general views of a more primitive society have a logical con- nection with what seem to be erroneous conclusions in the area of medical morality. The specific disagreements with points of textbook morality in the area of medicine point to deficiencies in that theory of natural law which is the basis of medical moral ethics.

A CHANGED WORLDVIEW

A second major deficiency with the theory of natural law as applied in the area of medical morality stems from the classical worldview which is behind such a theory of natural law. Ber- nard Lonergan maintains that the classicist worldview has been replaced by a more historically conscious worldview.[37] In the same vein, John Courtney Murray claimed that the two different theories on Church and State represent two different methodologies and worldviews.[38] And today, other more radical Catholic thinkers are calling for a change from a substantive to a process metaphysics.[39] At the least, all these indications point to an admission by respected Catholic scholars that the so-called classical worldview has ceased to exist.

The following paragraphs will briefly sketch the differ- ences in the two approaches to viewing reality. There are many dangers inherent in doing this. There is really no such thing as *the* classical worldview or *the* historically conscious worldview— there are many different types of historical mindedness. By

arguing in favor of an historically conscious worldview, I by
no means intend to endorse all the theories and opinions that
might be included under such a heading.

Since this section of the chapter will argue against a
classical worldview, a reader might conclude that I am denying
to past thinkers the possibility of any valid insights into the
meaning of man and reality. Such a conclusion is far from true.
There are even those (for example, Lonergan and Murray) who
would argue that a moderate historically conscious methodology is in continuity with the best of Thomistic thought. We
must never forget that some of the inadequacies in the classical
worldview stem from the poor interpretation of St. Thomas
by many of his so-called followers.

Two Views of Reality. The classicist worldview emphasizes the
static, the immutable, the eternal, and the unchanging. The
Greek column symbolizes this very well. There is no movement
or dynamism about a Doric or Ionic column. The simple
Greek column avoids all frills and baroque trimmings. The
stately Greek column gives the impression of solidity, eternity,
and immutability. Its majestic and sober lines emphasize an
order and harmony which appear to last forever. This classical
worldview speaks in terms of substances and essences. Time and
history are "accidents" which do not really change the constitution of reality itself. Essences remain unchangeable and can
only go through accidental changes in the course of time.
Growth, dynamism, and progress therefore receive little attention.

The Platonic world of ideas well illustrates this classical
worldview. Everything is essentially spelled out from all eternity.
The immutable essences, the universals, exist in the world of
ideas. Everything in this world of ours is a participation or an
accidental modification of the subsistent ideas. Man comes to
know truth and reality by abstracting from the accidents of time
and place, and arriving at immutable and unchangeable essences.
Such knowledge based on immutable essences is bound to attain the ultimate in certitude.

The more historically conscious worldview emphasizes the changing, developing, evolving, and historical. Time and history are more than mere accidents that do not really change essential reality. Individual and particular differences receive much more attention from a correspondingly more historically conscious methodology. The classical worldview is interested in the essence of man, which is true at all times in history and in all civilizations and circumstances. A historically minded worldview emphasizes the individual traits that characterize him. Modern man does differ quite a bit from primitive man precisely because of the historical and individual traits that he has.

In the more historical worldview the world is not static but evolving. Progress, growth, and change mark the world and all reality. Cold, chaste, objective order and harmony are not characteristic of this view. Blurring, motion, and subjective feeling are its corresponding features, as in the difference between modern art and classical art. Modern art emphasizes feeling and motion rather than harmony and balance. It is not as "objective" as classical art. The artist imposes himself and his emotions on the object.

Perhaps modern art is telling the theologian that the older distinction between the objective and the subjective is no longer completely adequate. Music also illustrates the change that has occurred in our understanding of the world and reality. Classical measure and rhythm is gone; free rhythm and feeling mean very much to the modern ear. What is meaningful music to the ear of the modern is only cacophony for the classicist. Changes in art and music illustrate the meaning of the different worldviews and also show graphically that the classical worldview is gone.

Two Methodologies. The two worldviews created two different theological methodologies. The classicist methodology tends to be abstract, *a priori,* and deductive. It wants to cut through the concrete circumstances to arrive at the abstract essence which is always true, and then works with these abstract and universal essences. In the area of moral theology, for example, the first principles of morality are established, and then other universal norms of conduct are deduced from these.

The more historical methodology tends to be concrete, *a posteriori,* and inductive. The historical approach does not brush by the accidental circumstances to arrive at the immutable essences. The concrete, the particular, and the individual are important for telling us something about reality itself. Principles are not deduced from other principles. Rather, modern man observes and experiences and then tentatively proceeds to his conclusions in a more inductive manner. Note that the historical consciousness as a methodology is an abstraction, but an abstraction or theory that tries to give more importance to particular, concrete, historical reality.

As we have noted above, John Courtney Murray claims that the different views on Church and State flow from the two different methodologies employed.[40] The older theory of the union of Church and State flows from a classicist methodology. It begins with the notion of a society. The definition of a society comes from an abstract and somewhat *a priori* notion of what such a society should be. The older theory then maintains that there are two perfect societies, and deduces their mutual duties and responsibilities, including their duties and obligations vis-à-vis one another. The theory concludes that the *cura religionis,* as it was then understood, belongs to the State. The State has the obligation of promoting the true faith.

What happens when the older theory runs headlong into a *de facto* situation in which the separation of Church and State is a historical fact? The older solution lies in a distinction between thesis and hypothesis, which roughly corresponds to the ideal order which should exist and the actual order which can be tolerated because of the presence of certain accidental historical circumstances. Notice the abstract and ahistorical characteristics of such a theory.

The newer theory of Church and State as proposed by Murray employs a more historically conscious methodology. Murray does not begin with an abstract definition of society and then deduce the obligations and rights of Church and State. Rather, Murray begins from a notion of the State derived from his observations of them in contemporary sociey. The modern State is a limited, constitutional form of government.

Its limited role contrasts with the more absolute and all-embracing role of the State in an earlier society. It does not interfere in matters that belong to the private life of individuals, such as the worship of God. Murray's theory has no need for a distinction between thesis and hypothesis, since he begins with the concrete historical reality. His conclusions then will be in harmony with the present historical situation.[41] Using a historical methodology, he can even admit that in the nineteenth century the older opinion might have been true, but in the present historical circumstances separation of Church and State is required.[42]

A classicist mentality is horrified at the thought that something could be right in one century and wrong in another. (Note, however, that the historical methodology employed by Murray and Lonergan insists on a continuity in history and rejects any atomistic existentialism which sees only the uniqueness of the present situation without any connection with what has gone before or with what will follow in history.)

A New Catholic Perspective. Theologians and philosophers are not alone in speaking of the changed perspective. In the documents of Vatican II the bishops do not officially adopt any worldview or methodology. But Vatican II definitely portrays reality in terms of a more historical worldview, and also employs a historically conscious methodology. The fact that the council has chosen to call itself a "pastoral" council is most significant; but "pastoral" must not be understood in opposition to "doctrinal." Rather, pastoral indicates a concern for the Christian faith not as truths to be learned but as a life to be lived.

The pastoral orientation of the council reflects a historical worldview. The bishops at the council also acknowledged that the Church has profited by the history and development of humanity. History reveals more about man, and opens new roads to truth. The Catholic Church must constantly engage in an exchange with the contemporary world.[43]

Gaudium et Spes frequently speaks of the need to know the signs of the times. The introductory statement of this constitution asserts the need for the Church to know them and interpret them in the light of the Gospel (n.4). The first four chapters of the first section of the constitution begin with an attempt to read the signs of the times. The attention given to what was often in the past dismissed as accidental differences of time and history shows a more historical approach to reality. The constitution does not begin with abstract and universal ideas of Church, society, state, community, and common good, but rather by scrutinizing the signs of the times. *Gaudium et Spes* thus serves as an excellent illustration of the change in emphasis in Church documents from a classicist methodology to a more historically conscious approach.

The teachings on the Church as contained in the Constitution on the Church (*Lumen Gentium*) and the other documents of Vatican II also reflect a more historical approach and understanding. Previously Catholics pictured the Church as a perfect society having all the answers, and as the one bulwark of security in a changing world. However, *Lumen Gentium* speaks often and eloquently of the pilgrim Church. The charge of triumphalism rang true in the conciliar halls of Vatican II. A pilgrim Church, however, does not pretend to have all the answers.

A pilgrim Church is ever on the march towards its goal of perfect union with Christ the spouse. A pilgrim Church is constantly striving, probing, falling, rising, and trying again. A pilgrim is one who is constantly on the road, and does not know there the security of his own home. So too the pilgrim Church is an *ecclesia semper reformanda*. Change, development, growth, struggle and tension mark the Church of Christ in this world. The notion of the pilgrim Church, even in language, differs very much from the perfect society of the theological manuals.

The conciliar documents underscore the need for the

Catholic Church to engage in dialogue—dialogue with other Christians, dialogue with Jews, dialogue with other non-Christians, dialogue with the world. Dialogue is not monologue. Dialogue presupposes that Catholics can learn from all these others. The call for dialogue supposes the historical and pilgrim nature of the Church, which does not possess all the answers but is open in the search for truth. The need for ongoing dialogue and ongoing search for truth contrast sharply with the classicist view of reality and truth.

Lumen Gentium rebuilds ecclesiology on the notion of the Church as the people of God and points out the various functions and services which exist in the Church (Chapter 2). Hierarchy is one form of service which exists in it. Another office is prohecy. The prophetic function exists independently of the hierarchy (n.12). The hierarchical Church can learn, and has learned, from the prophetic voice in the Church. History reminds us that in the Church change usually occurs from underneath. Vatican Council II brought to fruition the work of the prophets in the biblical, liturgical, catechetical, and ecumenical movements.

Thank God for Pope John and the bishops at Vatican II, we can say, but there never would have been a Vatican II if it were not for the prophets who went before. Many of them were rejected when they first proposed their teaching, but such has always been the lot of the prophet. The pilgrim Church, with the prophetic office, will always know the tension of trying to do the truth in love. The Church sorely needs to develop an older notion of the discernment of the Spirit, so that the individual himself and the total Church will be more open and ready to hear its true voice while rejecting the utterances of false prophets.[44]

The Church portrayed in Vatican II is a pilgrim Church which does not have all the answers but is constantly striving to grow in wisdom and age and grace. Thus the conciliar documents reflect a more historical view of the Church, and even employ a historically conscious methodology.

THEOLOGICAL CONSEQUENCES

A historical worldview and a more historically conscious methodology will have important consequences when applied to the
field of moral theology, for the manuals of moral theology today definitely reflect the classicist approach. In fact, there is a
crisis in moral theology today precisely because such theology
seems out of touch with modern man's understanding of reality.
Of course I do not claim that everything modern man says
about reality is correct, but then not everything in the classicist worldview was correct.

　　Sin infects the reality we know, and the Christian thinker
can never simply accept as is whatever happens to be in vogue.
However, the God of creation and redemption has called us to
carry on his mission in time and space. The Christian, that is,
is always called upon to view all things in the light of the gospel
message. Whatever insights we may gain into reality and the
world of creation can help us in our life.

Change and Development. The first important consequence of
this new worldview and methodology affects our attitude towards change and development. The classical worldview, as we
have seen, had little room for change. Only accidental changes
could occur in a reality that was already constituted and
known in its essence. Naturally such a view rejected any form
of evolutionary theory because it was most difficult to explain
evolution in such a system. On the other hand, the new worldview emphasizes the need for change. Change and growth do
not affect merely the accidental constitution and knowledge of
reality.

　　Man thirsts for truth and is constantly trying to find it.
He is never satisfied with the knowledge he has at any given
moment. Modern man realizes how incomplete this is, and he
is continually probing to find out more about reality. The growth
and progress of modern society demonstrate that development
is absolutely necessary. The classicist methodology, on the other

hand, claims a comparatively absolute and complete knowledge. Change naturally becomes a threat to the person who thinks that he already possesses truth. Of course, modern man recognizes that not all change is good and salutary. There will be mistakes on the way. However, the greatest error would be not to try at all.

Let us take as an example the dogmatic truth about the nature of Christ. The early christological councils proposed the formula of one person and two natures in Christ, a formula that is not present in the Scriptures. At the time there was an agonizing decision to go beyond the language of the Scriptures. But why does change have to stop in the fifth century? Might there not be an even better understanding of the natures and person of Christ today? Modern man might have different—and better—insights into the reality of Christ. Who can say that the fifth century was the final point in the development of our understanding?

When the classical worldview does speak of development, it places much emphasis on the fact that the truth always remains the same but it is expressed in different ways at different times. The same essential truth wears different clothing in different settings. However, does not the truth itself change and develop? There is more involved than just a different way of starting the same essential reality. Even in such sacrosanct dogmatic teachings there is room for real change and development.

The historical worldview realizes the constant need for growth and development, and also accepts the fact that mistakes and errors will always accompany such growth. But the attitude existing towards theology on the part of many priests in this country epitomizes the older worldview. (Perhaps such a mentality on the part of priests has been an obstacle in the path of Church renewal.) As seminarians, they learned all the truths of the Christian faith. There was no need, in this view, to continue study after ordination. The priest already possessed a certain knowledge of all the truths of the Christian faith.

Such an attitude also characterized the way in which theology was taught. Very little outside reading was done. The student simply memorized the notes of the professor which contained this certain knowledge. But the new methodology will bring with it a greater appreciation of the need for change and development in all aspects of the life and teaching of the Church.

Theology and Induction. Theology must adopt a more inductive methodology. Note that I am not advocating a unilaterally inductive and *a posteriori* approach for theology. However, in the past theology has attached too much importance to a deductive and somewhat *a priori* methodology. (Of course, as we shall see, with a more inductive approach moral theology can never again claim the kind of certitude it once did. At best, in some areas of conduct the ethician will be able to say that something clearly appears to be such and such at the present time.)

The classical methodology was a closed system, whereas a more historically conscious methodology proposes an open and heuristic approach. It will always remain open to new data and experience. Nothing is ever completely solved and closed, for an inductive methodology is more tentative and probing.

An inductive approach recognizes the existence of mistakes and errors, and even incorporates the necessary mechanism to overcome them. The building and manufacture of the Edsel automobile illustrates the possibility of error in a more inductive approach. Obviously, elaborate and expensive tests were run beforehand to see if there was a market for a car in the class of the projected Edsel. The decision to market the car was made on the best possible evidence. However, experience proved that the Edsel was a failure. A few years later, after similar exhaustive testing, the same company produced the Mustang, which has been a great success.

Theology, of course, is not the same as the other sciences. Progress and growth are much more evident in the area of the empirical sciences. However, the historicity of the gospel message and the historicity of man and the world demand a more historical approach in theology and the integration of a more inductive methodology. Particularly in the rather detailed minutiae of medical ethics, Catholic theology must learn to abandon the desire for the kind of absolute certitude which has characterized such moral theory in the past. Medicine, like science, is a field where man is constantly interfering with the processes of nature and the natural patterns of individual powers. But here the sole immediate effect of an action considered in itself cannot be the only determining element of morality. The action must be weighed in its total impact upon the persons involved and on the total community.

A more inductive approach in theology, especially in moral theology, will have to depend more on the experience of Christian people and all men of good will. The morality of particular actions cannot be judged apart from human experience. History seems to show that the changes which have occurred in Catholic morality have come about through the experience of all the people of the community. The fact that older norms did not come to grips with reality was first noticed in the experience of people.

Changes have occurred in the areas of usury, religious liberty, the right to silence, the role of love as a motive for marital relations, and other areas.[45] Certainly the rigorism of the earlier theologians on the place of procreation in marriage and marital intercourse has been modified by the experience of Christian people—for example, they held that marriage relations without the express purpose of procreation was at least venially sinful. And when the older theory of Church and State did not fit in with the historical circumstances of our day, John Courtney Murray showed that the living experience of people in the United States was more than just a toleration of an imperfect reality. In each case, experience showed the inadequacy of the older theory.

The older casuistry of mental reservation never set well with the experience of Christian people. The dissatisfaction with such casuistry played an important part in the understanding of lying now accepted by most contemporary theologians. Of course, just as theological methodology can never become totally inductive (the theologian always begins with the revelation of God in Christ), so too experience can never become the only factor in the formation of the Christian ethic. However, experience has a very important role to play.

Since the experience of Christian people and all men of good will is a source of moral knowledge, an ethician cannot simply spell out in advance everything that must be done by the doctor. And generally speaking, in other complicated areas of human life, the theologian cannot say that this or that action must always be performed. In many matters of medicine the ethician can merely tell the doctor to exercise his own prudent moral judgment. The patient and the doctor together must decide the feasibility of performing an operation by weighing the advantages against the risks.

Perhaps in some other matters now spelled out in the hospital code, more room should be left for conscientious decision by the doctor. The problem seems to reside in a system or theory that attaches exclusive moral importance to the physical structure of an act. At the very least, theologians must listen when doctors of good will are speaking to them. In fact, theologians must ask doctors to reveal their moral experience. The doctor must at least be listened to with respect when he honestly says that he thinks a raped 15-year-old girl who is a patient in a mental hospital should be aborted.

The Empirical Approach. Since a more historical methodology emphasizes the individual and the particular and employs a more inductive approach to knowing reality, Catholic theology will have to work much closer with the empirical and social sciences. It is these sciences that help man to pursue his goal and guide his development. A classicist approach which emphasized universals and essences was content with an almost exclusively deductive approach.

The Catholic Church in America today still reflects the fact that an older worldview did not appreciate or understand the need for the empirical and social sciences. The Catholic Church is probably the only very large corporation in America—I am here using "church" in the sense of a sociological entity and its administration—which does not have a research and development arm. How long could other corporations stay in existence without devoting huge sums to research and development? Heretofore, the Catholic Church has not realized the importance of change and growth.

Perhaps the crisis the Church faces today stems from a clinging to older forms of life when newer forms are required. However, without research and experimentation, who can decide what are the new forms which are needed? The answers are not all spelled out in the nature of things.

Certitude. As we have already seen, a changed theological methodology must necessarily result in a different attitude towards certitude. The classicist methodology aimed at absolute certitude. It was much easier come by in the classical approach, for this method cut through and disregarded individual, particular differences to arrive at immutable, abstract essences. In a deductive approach the conclusion follows by a logical connection from the premise. Provided the logic is correct, the conclusion is just as certain as the premise. Since circumstances cannot change the essences or universals, one can assert that the conclusion is now and always will be absolutely certain. There is no room for any change. A deductive methodology can be much more certain than an inductive approach.

The penchant for absolute certitude characterized the philosophical system which supports the concept of natural law as still found in medical ethics. Science, in this view, was defined as certain knowledge of the thing in its causes. Science, therefore, was opposed to opinion and theory. However, modern science does not aim at such certitude. Science today sees no opposition between science and opinion; in fact, scientific opinion and scientific theory form an essential part of the scientific vocabulary.

Absolute certitude actually would be the great enemy of the progress and growth that characterize modern life. Once absolute certitude is reached, there is no sense in continuing research except to clear up a few peripheral matters.[46] In the Thomistic framework there was really no room for progress in scientific fields. And there was little or no room for development within the sciences, so conceived, because the first principles of the science itself were already known. The revolutionary approaches within the modern sciences show the fallacy in the Thomistic understanding of science.[47]

A more historically conscious methodology does not pretend to have or even to aim at absolute certitude. Since time, history, and individual differences are important, they cannot be dismissed as mere accidents which do not affect essential truth. This approach does not emphasize abstract essences, but concrete phenomena. Conclusions are based on the observations and experience gleaned in a more inductive approach. Such an approach can never strive for absolute certitude.

Modern science views reality in this more historical manner and consequently employs this more inductive approach. The progress of scientific and technical mankind demands a continuing search for an ever better way. Even the Volkswagen is constantly being improved, and may be quite different in ten years. An inductive methodology can never cease its working. It constantly runs new experiments and observations, for modern science aims at the best for the present time, but realizes that new progress must be made for the future.

The Magisterium. A historically conscious methodology also entails important consequences for a proper understanding of the role of the hierarchical magisterium. Catholic medical moralists often speak in terms of eternal and immutable moral norms. But awareness of the historical condition of man means that older statements of the magisterium may no longer be adequate today.

Scripture scholars have freed the Church from a literal fundamentalism through a demonstration of the historical influence present in the formation of the Scriptures. Unfortunately, the statements of the magisterium are still accepted in a somewhat fundamentalist manner by many Catholics. These statements must also be seen in the light of the historical, cultural, and scientific circumstances of the times in which they were composed.

Murray's claim, for example, that the newer teaching on Church and State reflects the different historical reality of the twentieth century should serve as a salutary reminder to those who feel it is enough merely to cite magisterial documents from a former time. Obviously, the theory of Church and State proposed by Murray did not become true only at the moment when *Pacem in Terris* or the Declaration on Religious Liberty were promulgated in Rome.

Even more importantly, magisterial teaching generally reflects an older theological methodology and a one-sided hierarchical view of the Church, both of which today have changed. In the past the magisterial moral teachings were stated in the form of norms that were thought to be absolutely and immutably true. However, a more inductive approach will not always claim that type of certitude.

The emphasis on human experience and the Church as the people of God will also tend to leave matters more open ended. There are many ways in which the Church does teach, and should teach, other than by pronouncements of the hierarchical magisterium. In fact, if the magisterium is going to be relevant in the modern world, then the claim to absolute certitude becomes a hindrance. To be meaningful, the magisterium has to raise its voice or try to clarify issues long before such certitude is at all possible. If one waits for absolute certitude before speaking, one can be assured that his utterance will be either meaningless or irrelevant when the pronouncement is finally made.

The whole teaching Church must be willing to assume the risk of being wrong and making mistakes. In the modern world guidance for Christians will not be given in terms of absolute statements, but in terms of what appears to be the most Christian way of acting at a given time. A more historical understanding of reality and a more historically conscious methodology definitely alter our understanding of past statements of the magisterium (not that they are necessarily wrong today) and also significantly affect the way in which the Church must teach in the future.

Positive Law. Likewise, the modern view of positive law attributes a much changed and reduced role to it. Canon law exists primarily to preserve order and harmony in the society of the people of God, and not to serve as a guide for the life of the individual Christian.[48] Nor are civil laws primarily a guide for man's moral conduct. Civil law as such is not primarily interested in the true, the good, and the beautiful. Civil law has the very limited aim of preserving the public order.[49]

Society functions better not when law dictates to everyone what is to be done, but rather when law tries to create the climate in which individuals and smaller groups within the society can exercise their creativity and development for the good of the total community.[50] No longer is society under a master plan minutely controlled by the rules of the society. Rather, modern society's progress and growth come from the initiative of people within the society. Thus, the more historically minded worldview has a different perspective on the meaning and role of law in human life. Natural and human law are no longer seen as a detailed plan which guides and directs all human activity.

The Nature of Reality. A classicist worldview tends to see reality in terms of substances and natures which exist in themselves apart from any relations with other substances and natures. Every substance has its own nature or principle of operation. Within every acorn, for example, there is a nature which directs the acorn into becoming an oak tree. The acorn will not become a maple tree or an elm tree because it has the nature of an oak tree. The growth and "activity" of the thing is determined by the nature inscribed in it. Growth is the intrinsic unfolding of the nature within the substance.

Notice how such a view of reality affects morality. Human action depends upon the human nature. Human action is its intrinsic unfolding in man. Nature, therefore, tells what actions are to be done and what actions are to be avoided. To determine the morality of an action, one must study its nature. The above description, although a caricature of Thomas' teaching, does represent the approach to morality of the kind of unilaterally substantialist view of reality generally assumed in the manuals.

The contemporary view sees reality more in terms of relations than of substances and natures. Man is not thought of as a being totally constituted in himself, whose life is the unfolding of the nature he already possesses. There seemingly can be no real human growth and history when future development is already determined by what is present here and now. This is the point of difference between a naturalist view and a historicist view.[51]

According to the modern, more relational view, reality does not consist of separate substances existing completely independent of each other. Reality can be understood only in terms of the relations that exist among the individual beings. A particular being can never be adequately considered in itself, apart from its relations with other beings and the fullness of being. An emphasis on relations rather than substances surely cannot be foreign to Catholic thinking, since theologians have spoken of the persons of the Trinity as relations.

Human experience also reminds us of the importance of relationship even in constituting ourselves as human persons. A relational understanding of reality will never see morality solely in terms of the individual substance or nature. Morality depends primarily not on the substance viewed in itself but on the individual seen in relationship to other beings. Unfortunately, medical ethics frequently derives its conclusions from the nature of a faculty or the physical causality of an action seen only in itself and not in relationship with the total person and the entire community.

Aristotle. A brief defense of Aristotle is necessary here to avoid false impressions. Aristotle did not have a static view of reality. Nature itself was a principle of operation that tended toward a goal, but the goal was specific rather than individual. The emphasis was on the species of oak tree, that is, and not on the individual oak as such. But Aristotle did not conceive of man as he did of lesser life.

As an acute observer of the human scene, he realized that most men do not achieve their goal of happiness and self-fulfillment. Man, he thought, does not possess an intrinsic dynamism which necessarily achieves its goal. Man's happiness, consequently, depends not on an intrinsic tending to perfection according to the demands of his nature, but rather his happiness depends on extrinsic circumstances.

Man has no intrinsic orientation (a nature) necessarily bringing about his perfection; rather, according to Aristotle, he depends more on the contingent and the accidental. Man needs freedom, health, wealth, friends, and luck to find his fulfillment.[52] Notice that Aristotle himself constructed a theory of man that answers many of the strictures made against textbook natural law theories today.

But the classicist worldview of the manuals tends to see the world in a very detailed pattern. The function of man is to corespond to this structure (the "natural law") as minutely outlined. Man puts together the different pieces of human behavior much like putting together the pieces of a jigsaw puzzle. He finds the objective pieces already existing and just fits them together. The more historically minded worldview, on the other hand, sees man as creating and shaping the plan of the world. Man does not merely respect the intrinsic nature and finalities of the individual pieces of the pattern. Rather, man interferes to form new pieces and new patterns.

A Transcendental Methodology. A different worldview, as we have seen, affects our understanding of reality. The older stressed the objectivity of reality. In this view truth consists in the mind's grasp of the reality itself. A clear distinction exists between the object and the subject. Meaning exists in the objective reality, and the subject perceives the meaning already present in reality. A historically conscious methodology must avoid the pitfall of a total relativism which occasionally creeps into Christianity in various forms of cultural Christianity. Man needs to understand the ontological foundations of historical development; the Christian needs to understand all things in the light of the uniqueness of the once-for-all event of Christ Jesus. Both contemporary Protestant (for example, Macquarrie, Ogden) and Catholic (Rahner, Lonergan) scholars are addressing themselves to this problem.

Modern thought and culture stress more the creative aspects (both intellectual and affective) of the subject. Modern art reveals the feelings and emotions of the subject rather than portraying an objective picture of reality. The modern cinema confronts the viewer with a very subjective view of reality that calls for imagination and perceptivity on the part of the viewer. Catholic theologians are now speaking in somewhat similar terms of a transcendental methodology in theology.

Karl Rahner has observed that natural law should be approached in this way.[53] A transcendental methodology talks about the conditions and structure in the subject necessary for it to come to know reality, for this very structure is part of the knowing process. Bernard Lonergan speaks about meaning in much the same way.[54] Man's meaning can change such basic realities as community, family, state, etc. Meaning involves more than just the apprehension of the objective reality as something "out there."

A note of caution is necessary. Although Lonergan, for example, espouses a more historical consciousness and a transcendental method, at the same time he strongly proclaims a critical realism in epistemology. Lonergan definitely holds for propositions and objective truth, and truth as a correspondence. However, for Lonergan human knowing is a dynamic structure; intentionality and meaning pertain to that objectivity. He reacts against a "naive realism" or a "picture book" type of objectivity.

The problem in the past was that the objectivity of knowledge was identified with the analogy of the objectivity of the sense of sight. "Objective" is that which I see out there. Such a concept of objectivity is false because it identifies objectivity with just one of the properties of one of the operations involved in human knowing. Lonergan rejects both a naive realism and idealism.[55] It seems, however, that the objectivity talked about in medical moral textbooks is often a naive, picture-book objectivity.

The concept of natural law presupposed in Catholic medical ethics definitely reflects a classicist worldview, which sees a very precise and well-defined pattern existing for the world and man's moral behavior. This ordering and pattern is called the natural law. Natural law reigns in the area of the necessary.

Within the area marked out by the pattern showing the absolute and the necessary is the contingent and the changing. Just as natural law governs the life of man in the area of the principles common to all men, so positive law, both civil and ecclesiastical, governs the life of man in the contingent and the changing circumstances of life. The plan for the world is thus worked out in great detail in the mind of the creator, and man's whole purpose is to conform himself to the divine plan as made known in the natural and positive laws. (Despite the classical worldview of his day, in his system Thomas did leave room for the virtue of prudence and the creativity of the individual. However, the place later assigned to prudence in textbooks was drastically reduced, and thus Thomas' teaching was distorted.)

But a more historically minded worldview does not look upon reality as a plan whose features are sketched in quite particular detail according to an unchanging pattern. Modern man's moral existence does not primarily call for conformity to such a detailed and unchanging plan. He looks upon existence as a vocation to find the meaning of human existence creatively in his own life and experience. The meaning of human life is not already given in some pre-existing pattern or plan.

Perhaps the characterization of the two worldviews in this chapter tends to be oversimplified. For one thing, the points of difference between them have been delineated without any attempt to show the similarities. The differences in many areas of morality—for example, the understanding and living of the evangelical norm of love and forgiveness—would be minimal. The reasoning developed in this section has prescinded, as well, from the question of growth and development in human values and morals. However, in the modern world of science and technology, characterized by instant communication, rapid transportation, and changing sociological patterns, it is clear that man needs a more historical worldview and a more historically conscious methodology than the person who lived in a comparatively static and closed society.

SOME RE-EVALUATIONS

The contemporary dialogue of Catholic ethicians with other men of good will, together with the demands of renewal, have helped Catholic ethicians in trying to re-evaluate natural law and its place in Catholic theological thought. The next few paragraphs will try to summarize briefly some of the recent investigations about natural law.

Textbooks frequently leave the impression that the natural law is a very detailed plan for human existence, inscribed in man's nature. A better understanding of man's mastery over brute nature and the acceptance of a historical worldview should do much to refute the idea of a natural law as such a plan. However, the impression still remains among Catholics that the natural law is a monolithic, ethical system with an agreed upon body of moral content.

A Changing Concept. The assertion is not true. Historical investigation shows that numerous thinkers have used the term, but the term had different meanings for many of them.[56] Aristotle spoke of nature as the principle of operation in things, but man does not necessarily have a nature which brings him to his goal.[57] The Stoics used the term "nature" in reference to the whole cosmos and the intelligibility of the order enshrined in the universe. Gerard Watson has concluded that the term "natural law" for the Stoics had a meaning about as general as our term "morality."[58]

The fact that all those who employed the term "natural law" did not mean the same thing by the term is also evident from the divergency of opinions on the morality of certain human actions. A knowledge of history should destroy the myth of a monolithic, philosophical system of natural law in existence from Greek philosophy down to the present day. The Scriptures, for example, do not use the word "nature" in a technical way. In St. Paul's famous passage in Romans 2:13-15, he does not claim that man without Christ or grace can keep the works of the law.[59] The Fathers of the Church understood nature in a historical sense; thus following them, Gratian, who codified canon law, described the natural law as that which is contained in the law and the Gospels.[60] We have already looked at Ulpian's conception of it.

The nominalistic scholastics who came after Thomas did not mean by nature the same thing he did. Those who spoke of the natural rights of man in the seventeenth and eighteenth centuries did not accept Thomistic philosophy. Nature was understood in many different ways: some opposed nature to spirit; others opposed nature to the positive laws and conventions of society that were destroying the true dignity of man; economists used nature as opposed to a controlled or regulated economy. All of these people could use the term "natural law," but they all meant something different.

Natural Law and Catholicism. Since natural law is not a determined philosophical system, with an accepted code of ethical conduct in existence from the earliest times of human history, has repercussions on the place of natural law in the development of Catholic moral teaching. Catholic textbooks give the impression that the moral teaching on a particular point came into existence through the application of the system of natural law to a particular moral problem. However, if there was no coherent philosophical system of the natural law (at least before St. Thomas), then natural law cannot be the real reason explaining why the Church judged such conduct to be wrong.

Take as an example the traditional teaching on birth control. Clement of Alexandria did not solve the moral problem by calling together a study group of natural law theoreticians.[61] The teaching on birth control, like the teaching on the vast majority of other moral matters in the Church, came into existence independently of the natural law theory. Most of our moral teaching was already formed long before Thomas ever lived.

The natural law, for the most part, has been used in recent centuries as a systematic explanation of a moral teaching that already existed independently of the theory of natural law. But in the earlier Church, the experience of Christian people seems to have been a most important criterion. Reasons were then given to bolster the already existing teachings.

Theologians traditionally have taught that masturbation was wrong and even gravely so, but the theologians could not agree on the reasons for such a condemnation.[62] Even many proponents of the condemnation of artificial contraception admit that the natural law reasons adduced are not convincing. The reasons proposed by Thomas for the malice of fornication can be obviated by the use of contraceptives.[63] It is clear that the vast majority of Catholic moral teaching did not come into existence by an application of natural law theory to a particular question. In fact, the sovereign freedom of the word of God means that theology can never be tied to any one philosophical understanding of reality, although there are some philosophical theories that are incompatible with the Christian understanding of faith. Catholic theologians do not have to defend natural law apologetically, as if Catholic moral teaching totally depends on such a theory.[64]

Absolute Norms. The characteristic of natural law that has been most attacked is the tendency to establish absolute norms of moral behavior. However, scholars are realizing that Thomas himself did not maintain, at least in theory, the existence of moral norms that never admit of exceptions.[65]

Thomas admits that once reason leaves the first principles of the natural law (do good; act according to reason), there is a possibility of exceptions to the general norm. Speculative truths do not admit of exceptions when applied to particular cases. But matter itself is changeable and, as it were, matter can get in the way of the principle and block its application because of particular circumstances.[66]

Likewise, Thomas admitted the exceptions to the absolute norms mentioned in the Old Testament: Abraham's willingness to kill Isaac, the polygamy of the patriarchs, the stealing by the Israelites, the fornication of Hosea. Thomas occasionally explains these exceptions by saying that God can intervene in the moral order by a miracle just as he can intervene in the physical order by a miracle.[67] (Interestingly, one Protestant theologian recently gave a talk on situation ethics entitled, "Law and Miracle."[68])

Thomas himself, in principle, admits the possibility of exceptions to the particular norms of morality that are derived from the first principles of the moral life. In addition to a more historical consciousness and the intervention of man in the physical laws of nature, other factors such as a knowledge of cultural relativities and anthropological data have forced theologians to reconsider the absolute demands that have been made in the past in the name of natural law.[69] One Thomistic scholar concludes that the primary principles of the natural law are merely formal and tautological, while the derivative principles are disputable and not accepted by all.[70] Thus, at least in theory, Catholic scholars admit that the natural law is not as absolute as many had thought in the past.

Two Ambiguities. There appears to be an ambiguity connected with the term "natural law." Our very brief recapitulation of its historical development shows the many different senses in which the word "natural" has been used.[71] The term is ambiguous at best, and frequently leaves the impression (if not the reality itself) of being identified with the physical laws of nature.

The term "law" also seems to be ambiguous and misleading. Contemporary Catholic philosophers and theologians point out that the Thomist notion of law has been misinterpreted by those who often call themselves Thomists.[72] Nominalistic influence has altered this notion. In general, nominalistic tendencies accentuate the role of the will: something is right because it is commanded. The Thomist notion is more realistic: something is commanded because it is good.

Some have suggested apparent deficiencies in the Thomistic understanding of law because the will of the legislator is not mentioned. However, Thomas places the obliging force of law not in the will of the legislator but in the reality itself—the ordering of reason. If he is rightly understood, he cannot be accused of legalism. Law for Thomas does not have the connotations of external obligation and legal sanctions. He makes the will of the legislator conform to the reality itself.

Law for him means an ordering of reason. Natural law is the divine plan, the divine ordering, insofar as it exists in the rational creature. If the Thomistic understanding of law were accepted, some of the ambiguities connected with the term "law" would cease. But even if his concept of law were properly understood, difficulties arise from the classical worldview inherent in such an approach.

The connotations of the word "law" definitely recall absolute norms and sanctions. The Thomistic notion presupposes that man's primary function is to conform to a plan which is already existing. Also a classical worldview at least insinuates that the plan is quite detailed and exact. However, contemporary thought accentuates man's call to become creatively a more human person within the community of mankind.

The fact that theologians are today calling into question the absoluteness of the "natural law" also argues against the retention of such a term. One receives the impression that in the past Catholic thinkers have strained to call something "natural law" just so they could justify its absolute prohibition. Nature says this; therefore, man can never change it. Both in the popular mind and also in the argumentation of theologians the term "natural law" has led to an unwarranted emphasis on the absolute character of the norms sanctioned by it.[73] The very term "natural law" thus seems inaccurate and misleading.

There does, however, seem to be a real validity for theological ethics behind the traditional theory of natural law. The basic truth is that a source of ethical wisdom and knowledge apart from the explicit revelation of God in Scripture exists. A morality based on the reality of man and his history in the world definitely is a valid source of ethical knowledge. A frequent complaint against natural law theory has been the insistence on absolute norms. However, such an insistence is not necessarily of the essence of a morality based on man and human community in the world. In the area of social morality, for example, Catholic natural law theory has spoken a relevant message.[74]

A Christian Convergence. A convergence seems to be growing in Christian ethics. More and more, Catholic theologians are coming to realize the overemphasis on absolute norms in natural law theory. In addition, a more historical worldview should overcome some Protestant fears about the Catholic understanding of natural law. The contemporary understanding of nature and grace in Catholic theology should also allay some Protestant fears about the "natural" in Catholic theology. And Catholic moral theologians are more and more realizing the presence and influence of sin in the ethical problems facing the Christian. However, many Protestant ethicians see the need for a source of ethical knowledge apart from the explicit revelation of God in the Scriptures.

Protestant ethicians have used different approaches to the problem. Emil Brunner speaks of the orders of creation.[75] Bonhoeffer shows the divine mandates at work in history.[76] Reinhold Niebuhr stresses the importance of justice.[77] John C. Bennett writes about the natural law, and lately he refers to common ground morality.[78] Paul Ramsey accepts a description of his ethical theory in terms of love transforming natural justice.[79] James Gustafson has maintained that Christian social ethics must have a number of different starting points, including Christian revelation and faith, an analysis of self, and an understanding of social structures and processes.[80]

There are many reasons underlying the realization of the need for a source of ethical wisdom apart from the explicit revelation in Christ. Perhaps the most contemporary reason in Protestant thought is the emphasis on a theology of secularity and a reaction against transcendence. The meaning of history and the importance of life in this world are the main theological issues of the day. Other reasons include: the need to cooperate in social questions of poverty, race, and peace with all men of good will; the insufficiencies of the Scriptures, especially in dealing with the complex ethical problems of urban life; and the realization that two-thirds of the world does not know Christ.

I believe that in the future the ethical convergence of Protestant and Catholic thought will be even more evident. Historical differences fade away as Christians seriously examine together the problems confronting the world today. I do not say that the future will find a perfect harmony among all Christian ethicians, but the differences will not be based on something that is peculiar to Roman Catholic thinking.

Catholic ethicians themselves will probably be divided on a number of issues, even on those issues which up to the present have seemingly been accepted by Catholic moral theologians. Catholic theoreticians realize the ambiguities and problems connected with the textbook approach to natural law.[81] Newer theories are being proposed in terms of an ethic based on person or community. These newer theories obviate some of the traditional objections to natural law theory and at the same time call for a different approach to moral problems, especially in the area of medical morality.

Recent Catholic Reconstructions. Robert O. Johann, S.J. has been proposing his understanding of natural law in various publications in recent years. Johann sees his theory in continuity with traditional natural law because morality has an ontological foundation. Johann objects to the older understanding of natural law because of its absolute character, and also because of its substantive view of reality.

Things cannot be considered only in themselves, exclusively in terms of the principle of operation which is present in each thing. Rather, reality exists in relationship with other beings, and ultimately with Being itself. There is something outside the situation which prevents morality from degenerating into sentimentality. All moral requirements are grounded in Being itself, so that moral values remain objective. Everything else is relativized by its relationship to Being. The general moral norm is the promotion of Being.[82]

Note the implications of such a theory in the area of medical morals. Johann's system logically leads to many of the conclusions about particular medical moral problems which were mentioned in the beginning of this chapter. The moral understanding of the relativizing of all individual things and actions in the light of Being leads to a denial of absolute norms based on the structure of an individual act viewed in itself apart from its relations with other beings and the fullness of being.

W. van der Marck, O.P., also rejects the textbook consideration of human acts and the natural law. An act cannot be judged merely according to its physical structure. Traditional theology has neglected the intersubjectivity of human actions. For him the ultimate norm of morality is not the nature of an individual thing or man or the physical structure of an action, but rather the community-forming or community-breaking aspect of a particular action, its relationship to the community. The human act is primarily a means of communication and a way of building up the community. Only in such a light, and not by a consideration of abstract natures or physical structures, can an action be judged.[83]

Bishop Simons of India also realizes the need to abandon a moral theory based on the inner purpose or construction of a particular organ or action considered in itself. The ultimate criterion of morality, he suggests, is what the good or welfare of man—individually or socially—demands. The moral judgment depends on all mankind and springs from truly human values. Simons calls for the need to weigh the results of the actions, but the individual act and its consequences are subordinated to the consequences that would follow if the action were permitted as a general rule.[84]

John G. Milhaven, S.J., has also questioned the principle that the essential purpose of a particular action suffices to determine its morality. Milhaven wants to see things in the light of the general purpose of God and creation; consequently, more empirical evidence would be necessary to set up an absolute moral norm.[85]

In general, the newer proposals reject the idea of a morality determined by an investigation of a particular being or a particular faculty viewed in its essential nature apart from the relationship to the person and the wider relationship to the community or even Being itself. The newer approaches have a continuity with the older understanding of natural law, but they look upon reality in a different way. Basically, the newer theories are reactions to the difficulties with traditional natural law theory mentioned earlier in this chapter.

The newer theories definitely will have an effect on the textbook understanding of natural law as applied to medical morality. Such theories would not be prone to admit, for example, that direct killing, or direct abortion, or direct sterilization, based on the sole immediate effect of the action, could become an absolute prohibition. Likewise, the newer theories do not seem compatible with the absolute prohibition of the voluntary emission of male semen, or the absolute necessity of conception taking place as the result of the act of sexual intercourse.

The call for a change in the curent Catholic understanding of medical morality has already begun. This chapter has tried to show some of the individual points of dissatisfaction with the present teaching and also to put in a historical context some of the reasons underlying them. The newer approaches to natural law theory (if the name is to be continued) all logically come to the same conclusion: the need to change the theory underlying Catholic medical morality and to work out the concrete applications of that theory.

JOHN G. MILHAVEN

Moral Absolutes
and Thomas Aquinas

The discussion of Christian ethics going on these days includes, as everyone knows, some vigorous debate, not to mention some unchristian and unethical quarreling. Arguments are often heated and *ad hominem*. Those who condemn, let us say, all divorce and abortion are called inhuman and insecure legalists. Those who recommend some freedom on the two points are accused of license and murder, and their principles assessed as moral anarchy.

Feelings are strong because the difference of opinion on a particular point reflects a deeper intellectual and emotional opposition. It is a conflict between a common contemporary mentality—perhaps *the* contemporary mentality—and an older mentality which is still with us. In Roman Catholic circles this older mentality corresponds to a natural law tradition. The division not only descends deeply between the opposing mentalities, but it extends widely in practical application. A conspicuous example concerns the practical use of means.

For the natural law tradition, the end never justifies the means. The principle, ás understood by the tradition, says two things. First, a good end can never justify the use of immoral means. Second, there are certain acts (specified by their effect) which, if used as means, are always immoral.

In the second meaning of the principle, the effect itself is defined from a purely physical, that is, a non-moral point of view (for example, direct killing of an innocent person, sexual intercourse with a woman who is not your wife).[1] Certain such physical effects are seen, when submitted to moral reasoning, to be always and under all circumstances morally wrong as means to an end, and are therefore never to be used in this way.

One can exemplify the two senses of the traditional principle by its application to murder and abortion. Murder is, by definition, a moral act, that is, an unjust killing. It can, consequently, never be used as a means. Abortion, on the other hand, is defined in physical, non-moral terms: the expulsion from the mother's womb of a living fetus which is incapable of surviving outside the womb.[2] Precisely on the basis of such a non-moral definition, natural law reasoning concludes to the fact that the act, if used as a means, is always immoral and, therefore, never justified.

The contemporary opposition to the various absolutely universal prohibitions of the tradition arises from its opposition to both prongs of the general principle of the tradition concerning the use of means. In opposition to the first sense of the principle, not a few contemporary Christian ethicians, particularly those of Lutheran background, maintain that in certain situations the only moral course is to use immoral means to achieve a good end. They envisage situations in which all practical alternatives, especially that of refusal to act, have a bad side. Instead of inquiring whether any of the alternatives are absolutely unjustifiable or whether the principle of double effect could be applied, they say, "We must do what we must do—and say our prayers." We must choose. And even if it be the lesser evil and the greater good that we choose, we still must turn to God for his forgiveness.[3] On the other hand, it is not easy to say how many of the ethicians of this stamp would come out for the direct opposite of the traditional principle in its first meaning and hold that any proportionately good end can justify any means.[4] In any case, we are not going to deal here with this first sense of the natural law principle being debated.

The more widespread opposition to the traditional principle meets it on its second meaning. Whether or not they grant, as some of them do, that *immoral* means are never to be used, a large and growing number of Christians fail to see how a specific external action, defined in physical, *non-moral* terms (as abortion or adultery), can be condemned absolutely, that is, never to be used as a means no matter what the circumstances and the end in view. In other words—to use the terminology that we will employ to express precisely this type of moral principle—they fail to see how there can be any "negative moral absolutes."

They see how a specific kind of action could be condemned generally, that is, in most cases, because the action generally does serious harm and relatively little good. Joseph Fletcher grants that sex relations outside marriage can be wrong for many individuals because it hurts themselves, their partners or others. This gives them reason to abstain altogether except within the full mutual commitment of marriage.[5] But it is the possibility of an *absolute* condemnation of any physical action, a condemnation applying in advance to all possible cases without exception, that leaves many a contemporary Christian ethicist uncomprehending.

The only thing that matters to them absolutely is to respond in love to God's loving presence in the world of men. How can one tell in advance that the physical action in question, such as abortion or adultery, in some one case at least, might not be the best or only means of serving love. Among the most decisive in their rejection of negative moral absolutes (in the sense in which we are using the term) are Paul Lehmann and Joseph Fletcher.[6] But in the current debate among American Protestants, there is widespread agreement on a contextual methodology which tends to deny any negative moral absolute, that is, any absolutely universal condemnation of a given physical means.[7]

The controversy among Christians concerning negative moral absolutes has grown far out of proportion to its importance. In application to practice, the disagreement often centers about highly exceptional cases such as those of the Resistance *Untergrundmoral*. The kind of physical actions that the natural law tradition condemns absolutely are, though important, few in number. The average Christian may well be tempted at times to fornication or abortion, but how rarely it occurs in comparison with the daily and hourly temptation to irresponsibility, selfishness, lethargy, narrow-mindedness, moodiness, etc.

It has become a scandal that the controversy over negative absolutes has absorbed so much emotional energy and ethical reflection of Christians, which is badly needed elsewhere—for example, in the problems of the inner city or of mental health or of population growth. Moreover, as a result of the controversy many on one side have come to look at the thinking of the other side with such bewilderment and even bitterness that dialogue and cooperation in non-controversial areas are also hampered.

My purpose here is to reduce the dimensions of the controversy by locating more precisely the fundamental point of division and thus, hopefully, revealing a greater common ground for dialogue. It is not my intention to take sides, but to offer a brief historical study.

Most of the present-day champions of natural law are not direct descendants of Grotius or Pufendorf or Locke, but trace their origins to one man above all, Thomas Aquinas. Thomas did not merely play a major part in the development and transmission of their natural law tradition, which he had inherited from the Greeks and Romans, but his positions and arguments are frequently advanced by natural law proponents today as they stand in his text.[8]

It is a truism that one can often see more clearly and deeply into an intellectual movement at its source rather than in its tributaries—in Hegel or Augustine rather than in Hegelians and Augustinians. It might not be of merely historical interest to examine the mentality of Thomas Aquinas in the matter of negative moral absolutes. Is his mind as foreign and incomprehensible to contemporary ethicists as that of his followers today? What is the fundamental point of division? Is there any common ground on which each side could meet and learn from each other? In other words, if Thomists of today saw more clearly what was the position of Thomas, and if it was with this position that they confronted contemporary Christian ethics, could there be a more fruitful dialogue than is now going on?

Thomas does agree with present-day natural law tradition in affirming unequivocally certain negative moral absolutes: certain actions, identifiable by their physical effect, are never to be used as means.[9] Many of Thomas' examples correspond to those given today: direct killing of an innocent person, extramarital sexual relations, stealing, etc. But like twentieth-century Christian ethicians, Thomas also brings into the picture the God of Abraham, Isaac and Jacob and the fact that he could command Abraham to kill the innocent Isaac.[10] In fact, Thomas draws out the implications by recalling, too, that the God of the Old Testament ordered Hosea to have sexual intercourse with a prostitute[11] and bade the Israelites despoil the Egyptians.[12] Similarly, Thomas condemns, on the basis of natural reason, a man's taking his life and any private person's execution of criminals.[13] He maintains that both divorce and polygamy are against the natural law.[14] Yet he recalls, precisely in connection with the four negative moral absolutes, that the God of the Old Testament has on occasion commanded or permitted each of the condemned acts.

The above incidents reinforce for Thomas the same thing that, in general, Abraham's faith symbolizes for the twentieth-century theologian: God's sovereign freedom in dealing with man and things human.[15] As Thomas sees it, at least some of the negative moral absolutes do not bind God. But if this is the solution of one problem, it is the datum of another. How is it possible for God to authorize what otherwise would be absolutely wrong for a man to do? Like twentieth-century theologians, Thomas recognizes that the revelation of God's sovereign freedom must tell us something about man and the morality that binds him. That God could command Abraham to kill Isaac cannot fail to put into new perspective why Abraham could not do it on his own. That certain negative moral absolutes do not bind God should cast light on why and how they bind man. Thomas' view on this is the subject matter of the present historical study.

Thomas, like Barth, Brunner, Bultmann and Tillich, knew he stood at a historic confluence of thought, and welcomed the new and the old. In moral theology, he welcomed the newly translated ethics of Aristotle. He fitted the enclosed humanism of Aristotle's ethics into a theistic metaphysics that owed much to Stoicism and Platonism. The gradual accrual of Stoic elements in the medieval worldviews (for example, the Stoic theory of natural law) had been effected particularly by Cicero and the influence of Roman law and lawyers. The Platonic vision of man's nature as a radical orientation to the Absolute had been conveyed especially by the omnipresent Augustinianism of the earlier middle ages. Thomas pondered these immutable necessities of the philosophers in the light of the sovereign freedom of the God of Abraham, Isaac, Jacob and Jesus Christ. Thomas shows little sign of doubting that, on the whole, the converging currents of thought fit together.[16]

At the present stage of medieval research, it is impossible to say how original Thomas' personal synthesis was. For one thing, there are the great number of medieval manuscripts that have not yet been edited. Moreover, what comparisons have been made by scholars such as Dom Lottin on the basis of manuscripts, edited and unedited, show numerous medieval antecedents to many of Thomas' statements on moral theology.[17]

Almost as difficult and more important than the question of originality is the question of what Thomas' own thought was behind the formulae he borrowed in synthesizing the Greek and Christian traditions as they had come down to his time.[18] In the medieval world, as in the hellenistic, the extreme respect, or courtesy at least, shown the wisdom of the past makes it dangerous for the historian to base interpretations on isolated statements of a given thinker. The medieval use of sources or "authorities" was to save, whenever possible, the formulae of earlier figures even when the medieval thinker himself meant something different or conflicting. Thomas Aquinas was no exception.[19]

To penetrate behind borrowed formulae to the genuine dynamics of Thomas' synthesis on a given question requires a survey of Thomas' voluminous works, an understanding of the historical development of the question up to his time, and a concentrated theological analysis and reflection on the pertinent texts. I have been unable to find such a study of Thomas' thinking on our question: God's freedom in regard to man and the necessity of moral principles binding men.[20]

The limits of the present investigation, restricted to Thomas' treatment of certain biblical accounts of divine intervention, keep any conclusions from being more than a working hypothesis. The hypothetical nature of the conclusions is increased by the fact that Thomas does not accord a central place to the biblical stories, but deals with them as possible objections to some other truth he is expounding. We will claim to find a unified pattern of thought in Thomas' treatment of the cases. But until further investigation, it will remain hypothetical how seriously Thomas took his own views. Do they reflect his basic moral theology or are they merely *ad hoc* solutions to passing problems that do not fit in at all with the structure of his ethical thought?

Still, a grounded working hypothesis can be a useful beginning. Moreover, the view which emerges from the following study seems a fruitful one for dialogue today. Thomas is no situationist and he does hold the unpopular view of negative moral absolutes. But the study concludes to a way of thinking on the part of Thomas more akin to contemporary ethical reflection than one would gather from today's Thomists.

The contemporary situationist and one who would share this way of thinking of Thomas, when dealing with the question of these absolutes would not disagree as those who cannot comprehend each other and can only trade charges of "legalism" and "moral anarchy." They would differ rather as those who have a remarkably similar vision of man before God, but who, because they have different experiences of man himself, disagree on the concrete realization of the vision. It would appear to be a not unfavorable context for quietly talking to and learning from one another.

In regard to one problem, Thomas consistently presupposes that divine intervention in human morality is possible and justified, but offers no explanation how it can be. To kill oneself is completely wrong.[21] Yet Samson is excused for having killed himself while destroying his enemies. And the holy women are excused for having thrown themselves into the flames in time of persecution. How were they permitted to take such means? Thomas merely appeals to a command or "instinct" given by God or the Holy Spirit.[22] He is not concerned to explain how it can be.

In other contexts, Thomas does attack the question why a particular means that is always evil for man ceases to be so when God commands the man to take it. In one place, however, his answer comes merely to affirming that whatever God wills must be good, simply because he wills it.

> Fornication is said to be a sin inasmuch as it is contrary to right reason. But man's reason is right inasmuch as it is ruled by the divine will, which is the first and highest rule. Consequently, that which a man does at God's will, obeying his command, is not contrary to right reason, although it may seem to be against the common order of right reason—just as what occurs miraculously by divine power is not contrary to nature even though it be contrary to the common course of nature. Therefore, Abraham did not sin in willing to kill his innocent son, because he obeyed God, even though this, looked at in itself, is commonly contrary to right human reason. Thus, too, Hosea did not sin by fornicating on divine command. Nor should such intercourse be properly called fornication, although it is termed fornication in reference to the common course of events.[23]

Thomas appears to be as nominalistic as Joseph Fletcher could desire.[24] To be sins the acts of Abraham and Hosea would have to be contrary to right reason. But human reason is right by following the divine will. The acts of Abraham and Hosea, performed in obedience to God's will, are, therefore, not sins, although, taken by themselves, they normally would be.

But elsewhere Thomas distinguishes his position from any thoroughgoing nominalism. There are things the divine will cannot do, actions it cannot command. As Thomas expounds this on various occasions over the years, his language varies. In two closely parallel passages, he puts it that God can dispense man from precepts of the second tablet of the decalogue, but not from precepts of the first tablet.[25]

In both passages, the limit on God's action is grounded exclusively on the impossibility of his turning men away from himself. Since the precepts of the first tablet simply order men to God, a dispensation in this matter would turn men away from God, for example, a special precept to despair of God or to hate him.[26] The two passages diverge in explaining why it is that God cannot do this. Obviously the reason cannot be any imperfection in God, but must be some transcendent perfection such as his identity with himself or the unconditioned dependence of creatures on him.

The *De Malo* passage, invoking a text of the Second Letter to Timothy, says simply that God cannot deny himself. The *In I Sent.* passage argues that God's power cannot render good, even by way of special dispensation, that which would not be ordered to himself, its final end, just as God's power cannot make a thing exist without the efficient causality of himself, the first cause.

However, both passages justify the dispensations God can give from the precepts of the second tablet by holding simply that the order to be observed between men need not be observed by God. In the *De Malo* passage, dealing with God's command to Hosea, God can dispense from precepts of the second tablet, by which man is ordered directly to his neighbor, because the good of the neighbor, unlike God's goodness, is only a particular good. The *In I Sent.* passage, mentioning the case of Hosea, but making its application to the case of Abraham, complements the explanation.

All goodness in created things has to come from their last end, God. The natural order of one creature to another has its goodness simply because through it the creatures are duly ordered to their last end. The order to the last end is thus the cause of the order between creatures. Just as God, and God alone, can work a miracle and make something exist without using the secondary causality of creatures which normally does it, so he and he alone can make something good without that order to a particular creature which normally would give the thing its goodness. Where the order to the creature was the natural way by which the thing in question was ordered to its last end and received its goodness, now God gives it goodness directly, by giving it, through his command, a direct ordering to its last end.

Both passages come to the same principle. God can do what he wants with men and human relations as long as he is still relating them positively to himself as their final end. The two passages imply by their argumentation that there is no further qualification. Precisely because an order is only to a "particular good" directly, precisely because an order is first to something that is not the final end, God can dispense from it.

Although he employs a different image, Thomas makes a similar implication in the *De Potentia Dei* as he takes up again the case of Abraham and Hosea.[27] A ruler can in the interests of justice, which is the end or purpose of his rule, render virtuous what in itself would be sinful, for example, killing a man. Similarly, God has all things in his disposition to direct to the purpose of his rule, which is his goodness. He can thus, by the purpose he foresees and orders, render meritorious what would itself be sinful, for example, killing an innocent child. The same can be said of God's command to Hosea, since God is the orderer of all human generation.

Thomas' principle, if carried out logically, excludes that there could be some means which, because of its physical nature,

God could not authorize. All things are at his disposition. The sole absolute for him is that the means he authorizes brings his subjects to his goodness. On the other hand, it would go beyond the evidence to claim that Thomas would have been ready to apply to all particular cases the principle he employs in the three passages just considered. Could God authorize a man to practice contraception or commit sodomy? In the passages seen thus far there is no evidence that Thomas has been concerned to think out all the practical implications of that view of the sovereignty of God which he sketches in order to explain the Bible stories.

The fact remains that his view emerges as uncomplicated and, in several respects, close to that of contemporary Christian ethicians. Both they and Thomas find in the God of revelation a free Lord who can bypass any moral order among men and any human good and can authorize any means for man to take on his way to God. The difference is that for Thomas God gives the authorization only by way of exception and miracle. Consequently, it is, practically speaking, not a real possibility for a man to take into account and the generally accepted negative moral prohibitions concerning human relations hold for man as absolutes.

For twentieth-century theologians like Brunner and Thielicke, on the other hand, God has worked the miracle for all men through Jesus Christ and the authorization Thomas speaks of is, for them, just one aspect of the freedom every Christian has. True, the Christian must respect the orders of creation, but it is always up to him to discern whether God's individual command to him in the concrete situation requires that he bypass natural order, as Abraham once did. A dialogue proceeding out of such agreement and disagreement could be stimulating and profitable.

More often, however, Thomas takes a different tack to explain how God can command a man to adopt certain means which would always be sinful for the man by himself. Thomas's language is here closer to that of present-day natural law proponents and it appears to contradict what he has said in the three passages just considered. It does not pertain to our purpose to discuss whether the contradiction is more than verbal. In any case, the folowing analysis should show that there is no profound contradiction and that, as a matter of fact, Thomas's new approach fills in and nuances the one we have already seen.

Thomas sets forth the second approach squarely in two articles in which he is asking, "Do the precepts of the decalogue admit of dispensation?"[28] The answer, surprisingly enough, in the light of the passages previously considered, is a universal negative: none of the precepts of the decalogue allow of dispensation. It is possible that in the formal question of the articles Thomas is inquiring only about the possibility of dispensation by a human being. In any case, dealing with objections, he has to face the question of God's apparent dispensing from the precepts of the decalogue. The occasion once more is God's command to Abraham and Hosea and the Israelites in Egypt.[29]

In the *In III Sent.* article, Thomas merely asserts that "God never commanded anything contrary to the precepts of the decalogue inasmuch as they belong to the decalogue."[30] This suffices to neutralize the objection. He does not assert that God *could not* command such a thing and he does not use the word "dispensation" for what God has never done. I think that by textual analysis one could mount a case that Thomas means to exclude even the possibility of God's "dispensing." But for our purposes a minimal interpretation seems advisable.

In the article of the *Summa,* however, Thomas flatly denies the possibility of God's giving a dispensation in regard to the precepts of the decalogue, though at the same time he is careful to make clear what he means and what it is God could not permit a man to do. "And therefore God cannot give a dispensation in the sense that a man be permitted not to be ordered to God or not to conform to the order of God's justice, even where it is [merely] a case of men being ordered to each other."[31]

It is, of course, in denying God the possibility of the second type of dispensation ("not to conform to the order of God's justice, etc.") that Thomas advances beyond, if he does not abandon, the position taken in the *In I Sent.* and *De Malo* passages. In the present passage, as in those two, the precepts of the second tablet "contain the order itself of justice to be observed among men."[32] But in apparent contradiction to the other two passages, the present one denies that God can dispense in this regard.

What grounds does Thomas offer for his new position? The objection he is replying to argued that God, like any legislator, can dispense from the precepts of the law which he himself has established. Thomas gives the classic metaphysical reply to any such nominalism: God cannot go against himself. He invokes the same text of the Second Letter to Timothy that he did in the *De Malo* passage. But he draws a different conclusion: "as the Apostle says . . . 'God remains faithful, he cannot deny himself.' And he would deny himself, if he removed the order itself of justice; for he is justice itself."[33]

Since even God must always observe the order of justice, the precepts that express it should obviously be termed immutable. "Thus, therefore, the precepts themselves of the decalogue, inasmuch as they contain the quality of justice, are immutable."[34] Is Thomas contradicting not only statements made by himself in other passages, but also the basic position of the twentieth-century Christian ethicians who oppose negative moral absolutes? Is he not saying that there is an immutable order of justice, grounded in the divine essence, and that the negative moral absolutes constituting the order bind God and man? Have we not come to the primal point of separation between Thomistic ethics and that characteristic of the twentieth century? To answer, one must scrutinize more clearly what Thomas means by the order of justice. Does he include in the immutable precepts of justice anything corresponding to "negative moral absolutes" as we defined the term for our problematic?

In the two articles presently being considered, Thomas explicates the immutable order of justice in connection with a famous text of Aristotle: *Nicomachean Ethics,* Book V, 1134[b]–1135[a].[35] Thomas equivalates Aristotle's "natural justice" (*iustum naturale*) with his own "natural law" and the "justice" embodied in the precepts of the decalogue. Aristotle's words, therefore, give rise to an objection. "The precepts of the decalogue belong to the natural law. But natural justice fails to hold in certain cases and is changeable, just as human nature is, as the Philosopher says in the Fifth Book of the Ethics." Therefore, there is place for dispensation.[36]

Thomas meets the objection by an exegesis of Aristotle's meaning of justice in the words quoted. "The Philosopher is not speaking of that natural justice which contains the order itself of justice; for this never fails to hold, that justice should be observed."[36a] The corresponding reply in the *In III Sent.* passage is fuller: "there are two kinds of natural justice . . .: one which is always and everywhere just, as that in which the essence of justice and virtue in general consists, as keeping the mean, observing what is right, etc." But it is the other kind of justice that the Philosopher is talking about, the kind that holds only in the majority of cases, being an application of the first and universal norm.[36b]

In another passage in which the dispensations accorded Abraham, Hosea and the Jews in Egypt are discussed, Thomas raises again the problem of Aristotle's assertion "that nothing is so just among all men that it does not take different forms among some." The solution is similar to that of the other two passages: Aristotle is not talking of the common principles of natural justice, but of certain conclusions derived from them and holding only in the majority of cases.[37]

In all three passages, Thomas merely says that Aristotle is not talking about the one and the same justice that holds everywhere, but is speaking of the relative, mutable kind. But when discussing the Aristotelian text in his commentary on the Nicomachean Ethics, he seems to say that Aristotle himself affirms also the universal, unfailing kind of justice earlier in the passage.

And first of all Aristotle presents natural justice in two ways. One, according to its effect or virtue, when he says: natural

justice is that which has everywhere the same power and
virtue to lead to good and restrain from evil. It happens,
indeed, because nature, the cause of this kind of justice, is
the same everywhere among all men. . . . In the second way
Aristotle explains this justice according to its cause, when
he says that natural justice does not consist in seeming or
not seeming, that is, it does not arise from some human
opinion, but from nature. For just as in speculative matters
. . . , so also in practical matters there are certain naturally
known principles, as it were indemonstrable, and some close
to these, as "evil should be avoided," "no one should be
unjustly harmed," "one should not steal," etc.[38]

Thomas recognizes that Aristotle goes on to assert equally
that *all* human justice is changeable, because everything in a
man, even what is natural, is changeable either *per se* or *per
accidens*.[39] Thomas does not contest Aristotle's assertion and,
as we have seen, accepts Aristotle's presentation of the mutable kind of natural justice. But he adds his own gloss, re-affirm-
ing and further explaining the immutable kind of justice he had
found a few lines earlier in Aristotle's text:

One should note that the essences of changeable things are
immutable and theerfore nothing that is natural to us, belonging as it were to the very essence of man, is changed in any
way, for example, the fact that man is an animal. On the
other hand, the things that follow on nature, for example,
dispositions, actions and movements, do undergo change in
less common cases [in the preceding paragraph Thomas referred to Aristotle's example of men being right-handed].
Similarly, also, those things which belong to the very essence
of justice cannot undergo change in any way, for example
that one should not steal, which is to do something unjust.
But those things which follow on the essence of justice
undergo change in the less common cases.[40]

In grounding natural law and justice on immutable principles, Thomas is certainly adding to, if not contradicting, what
Aristotle himself said about *justum naturale* and ethical

knowledge in general. But in so doing he makes clearer what he, Thomas, means by the immutable order of justice that even God must observe. To return to our question, then, does Thomas include among the immutable principles any principles that fulfil our definition of "negative moral absolutes"?

By the use of the term in our problematic, it will be recalled, are meant principles according to which a specific external action, defined in physical, non-moral terms, may never be used as a means, no matter what the circumstances or end in view. There is no question whether or not Thomas holds negative moral absolutes. He does. But does he identify them with the immutable order of justice, grounded in the divine essence? Or does he see another basis for them? The answer will affect any attempt to make his ethics comprehensible to contemporary ethicians.

In our four passages, there are certain immutable principles that Thomas enunciates explicitly. Others he implies in justifying God's commands to Abraham, Hosea and the Jews in Egypt. The immutable principles he affirms explicitly come to ten. For most of them, the fuller context has been quoted above.

1. Evil should be avoided.[41]
2. What is undue should be done to no one; what is due should be rendered to all.[42]
3. One should not act unjustly.[43]
4. No man should be harmed unduly.[44]
5. No man should be killed unjustly.[45]
6. Justice should be observed.[46]
7. It is always just and virtuous to keep the mean.[47]
8. It is always just and virtuous to observe what is right.[48]
9. It is right and true that one act according to reason.[49]

(In the context, it is fairly clear that Thomas would be willing to formulate this and the preceding two principles as, "One should . . .")

10. One should not steal.[50]

None of the above principles constitute a "negative moral absolute" of our problematic. In the first five, the act which is absolutely condemned is itself expressed in moral terms: evil, what is undue, unjust acting, unjust harming, undue killing. Moreover, the first three are too general to be negative moral absolutes in the sense being discussed, since such absolutes condemn specific actions (as abortion). The following four principles are affirmative, but could be taken as implying a negative one (as condemning acts in which injustice is done, the mean is not kept, what is right is not observed, or in which one does not act according to reason). However, they are still too general to be one of the controverted "negative moral absolutes." One could argue, too, that even in the last three of the four the act which is absolutely condemned is already expressed in moral terms. The prohibition of stealing, the final principle given above, comes closest to being a negative moral absolute. It is negative, takes a specific action, and condemns it absolutely. The question is whether Thomas means by "stealing" something already defined in moral terms. At least in this context he seems to do so: his point seems to be that stealing should not be done because it is, by definition, unjust.[50a] The principle would not, therefore, be a negative moral absolute. The issue, however, need not be urged, since Thomas's understanding of the absolute condemnation of stealing will become clearer in certain passages which will be discussed shortly.

Consequently, none of the immutable principles of morality that Thomas sets down as binding God and man can be said to be negative moral absolutes. We turn now to Thomas' direct justification of God's commands to Abraham, Hosea and the Israelites in Egypt. How does he justify them? He will be seen to presuppose that God always acts according to justice and virtue. Does he imply any negative moral absolutes binding on God? Does his justification of God's commands cast any light on the grounds on which the negative moral absolutes do bind men?

In the matter of taking human life, Thomas sees no negative moral absolutes binding God. True, God is not free to act unjustly, but he can authorize a man to take an innocent life, although it would be unjust and a violation of the natural law for the man to do so on his own.

The command given Abraham to kill his innocent son was not unjust, because God is the author of death and life.[51]

One question arises [concerning the command given Abraham] because the slaying of an innocent person is against the law of nature and thus a sin . . . I reply that he who kills on the command of his superior, if the superior licitly gives the order, he obeys licitly and can carry out his service. But God has authority over life and death . . .

Moreover, when God takes the life of someone, even if he is innocent, he is doing injustice to no one. For this reason, many men, guilty and innocent, die every day by divine disposition. Thus Abraham could licitly carry out God's command.[52]

In two passages in the *Prima Secundae,* Thomas proffers essentially the same explanation why God's command did not authorize injustice or homicide. He adds, as part of the argument, that any divine command to kill merely imposes the penalty due all men because of original sin.[53] In the text of the *De Potentia Dei* seen above, Thomas is envisaging the case of Abraham's decision to slay his son when he says that God has all in his disposition to direct to the end of his rule, that is, his goodness.[54]

Thus in the six passages where Thomas justifies God's command to slay Isaac, he comes from three different points of view to the same effect. The authority and dominion of God over life and death, the guilt of all men because of Adam's sin, the authority of God's rule leading men to his goodness, all prove that God can dispose of man's life without restriction as a means to carry out his good purposes.[55] There are no negative moral absolutes limiting God's activity in this domain. God is not free to act unjustly or authorize homicide even for a good end. But his authority over life and death means that any physical disposition he makes in this regard for his good end will be a just means.

When Thomas comes to justify the taking spoils of the Egyptians he notes that the argument is the same as the one he used in the case of Abraham and Hosea.

Similarly, it was not contrary to justice to command the Jews to take the property of the Egyptians, because all things are God's and he gives them to whom he wills.[56]

And the same argument applies to stealing, which is taking something that belongs to another. For whatever one takes on the command of God, who is Lord of all [*Dominus*], one does not take without the will of the owner [*domini*], which is what stealing is.[57]

God's disposing of property parallels his disposing of human life. There are no negative moral absolutes limiting him in this domain. He is not free to act unjustly, not to steal any more than to kill unjustly. But since all things belong to him, he can dispose of them as he wills. There are no property rights he need respect. Any disposition of property that he makes for his good purposes will be a good and just means.

Even in the question of sexual morality raised by the case of Hosea, Thomas notes that God's action is justified by a reason similar to that which justifies his taking of life and property.

Similarly, also, the command to Hosea to take an adulterous woman was not opposed to chastity, for God himself is the one who orders human generation and that manner of having intercourse with a woman is due which God establishes.[58]

Thomas also develops the theme in a juridical fashion, that is, not in terms of God's general dominion over human generation, but in terms of his authority over the institution of marriage, which he himself established.

And similarly, Hosea, too, going to a fornicating wife or an adulterous woman, did not commit adultery or fornication, because he went to a woman who was his by virtue of the command of God who is the author of the institution of marriage.[59]

Thus also because of the authority of God himself, who is over [*supra*] the law of marriage, that intercourse was not fornication which otherwise would have been fornication . . .[60]

In two other passages, Thomas apparently understands God's authority in a similar way, though his language differs.

> Similarly, too, adultery is intercourse with a wife not one's own; but this one was given to Hosea by a law promulgated by God. Wherefore to whatever woman a man might go on divine command, it is neither adultery nor fornication.[61]
>
> God can remove from an unmarried woman the condition "not his" although she will not become fully his wife. As a result to go to her would not be against the decalogue.[62]

In Distinctio 33 of his commentary on the Fourth Book of the *Sentences,* Thomas describes God's command to Hosea as a dispensation from a primary precept of the natural law.[63] God's capacity to grant dispensations from primary precepts is possibly illustrated also by his granting divorce. Thomas does not hesitate in affirming God's capacity to grant it, but is not sure whether the indissolubility of marriage is a primary or secondary precept of the natural law, nor whether God, in fact, ever authorized divorce.[64]

He affirms without qualification God's power to grant dispensation even from primary precepts of the natural law, though they are, as it were, always in force (*quasi semper existentia*). But he makes no attempt here to explain how the unusual, miraculous intervention is reconcilable with the moral force of the precepts. He does render some explanation of how dispensation from secondary precepts is possible, but since he presents it as essentially different from the dispensation granted Abraham and Hosea, the explanation does not fit into the present stage of our analysis.

It is, therefore, only in the first six passages considered that Thomas explains how the dispensation accorded Hosea can be morally justified.[65] In all six, God's disposing of human generation parallels his disposing of human life and property. In this domain, too, there are no negative moral absolutes limiting his activity.[66] He is not free to authorize fornication or adultery any more than he could homicide or stealing. But since human generation and the institution of marriage are completely subject to him, he can dispose of them as he wills. There is no woman, no matter what her state or situation, with whom God cannot authorize a man to have intercourse, by making her, simply by his fiat, in some sense his wife.

The theological vision of Thomas, within which he places the stories concerning Abraham, Hosea and the Israelites in Egypt, emerges as remarkably unified in text after text. God is free from any negative moral absolutes that would restrict his disposing of human life, property and generation. In these matters, God has authority to take whatever means contribute to his good purposes.

More significant for our problematic is the conclusion Thomas implies for human morality. What is right and wrong for a man in killing, disposing of property, exercising human generation, depends on the extent to which God has shared his authority with man. Any negative moral absolutes that bind man in this area are grounded simply on God's free refusal to grant authorization for using the particular act as a means. He could grant the authorization, but in his wisdom and love chooses not to do so in the normal course of events.

Thomas does not merely imply the general principle that all human morality concerning the disposing of life, property and generation depends on the authority God chooses to grant or not to grant. He explicitly points out that this same principle, which justifies the conduct of Abraham, Hosea and the Israelites, applies analogously to the morality governing the ordinary human situation where no divine intervention has occurred.

The most obvious application is to the disposition of things external to man, which could come into his possession and become his property. The nature of external things is not subject to human power, but to the divine, which all things obey. But, as to their use, man has by God's ordination a natural dominion over all external things to use them for his own benefit. Precisely in sharing his dominion, God has made man to his own image.[67] Similarly, as he explains how God ordered the despoiling of the Egyptians, Thomas twice recalls that this sort of transfer of ownership can be done by human authority, although to a greater extent by divine.

> Not only God, the Lord of all, can do this, but also men with authority can at times transfer property from one person to another for a particular reason.[68]

In the matter of taking a life, too, it is in normal human morality as well as in extraordinary cases such as Abraham's, a question of God's sharing his authority with men. Secular judges who condemn to death according to law are not guilty of homicide, for they do it at God's command and with his authority. "For every law is a command of God."[69] On the other hand, in the next paragraph, Thomas uses exactly the same principle to prove that killing oneself is wrong except in cases like that of Samson and the martyrs.[70] The decisive factor, once more, is that God has not shared his authority over life with most men as he has with Samson and the martyrs.

On the basis of the same reasoning, the killing of a criminal for the sake of the common good is never permitted a private person, but "him alone to whom the care of preserving the community is entrusted . . . ," that is, the rulers possessing public authority. As to those private persons whom God commanded through Moses to slay their neighbors, brothers and friends (*Exodus,* XXXII, 27), they ". . . do not seem to have done this themselves, but rather he, by whose authority they did it, just as the soldier kills the enemy on the authority of the ruler and the executioner kills the thief on the authority of the judge."[71]

In two of the passages considered earlier, Thomas refers to the authority of the judge and ruler to kill criminals and enemies in order to explain the conduct of Abraham and Hosea and the Jews in Egypt. The same principle applies in both cases. Thomas sums up in one general principle the two cases of natural morality and the three cases of divine intervention:

> Consequently, the precepts themselves of the decalogue are immutable inasmuch as they contain the quality of justice.

But inasmuch as they are determined by application to individual acts, namely, that this or that be homicide, stealing or adultery or not, this indeed is mutable. Sometimes the change can take place only on divine authority, namely, in those things which have been established by God alone, as marriage, etc. Sometimes it can take place also on human authority, as in those things which have been entrusted to human jurisdiction. For here men take God's place [*gerunt vicem Dei*], but not in all things.[72]

We may be belaboring the obvious, but so often in current controversy over abortion the natural law defenders speak of the inviolability of human life as if it were an absolute. In the moral theology of Thomas Aquinas, the inviolability of human life is not absolute, but relative to the authority of the one who could take the life. Thomas would condemn all direct abortion performed by men, but only because he believed that it did not fall within the authority God had granted men in the taking of life, such as he had in capital punishment. He denies the State the authority to kill innocent persons (which could be interpreted as the case of abortion), not because of the inviolability of all human life, but because such an authority cannot be justified by the common good.[73]

In the passage just quoted, Thomas included sexual morality under the same principle he had used for the morality of disposing of life and property. Whether an act be adultery or not depends on the decision of the competent authority to authorize it or not. In regard to human generation and marriage, men do not normally share God's authority in as essential a way as they do in regard to property and human life.[74] One can say, it is true, that human generation should be directed to its ends not merely by nature and ecclesiastical authority, but also by civil laws.[75] But whereas God has shared with men some of his authority to take life and transfer property rights, no human authority, but God alone, institutor of marriage, can determine who is whose wife and therefore with whom a man may have sexual intercourse.[76] Still it remains true that the same principle applies to normal morality of human generation as to the case of

Hosea: it depends, not on what eternally has to be, but on what authority has freely determined.

As we said in the introduction, the present study deals with Thomas' views on normal human morality only where he is considering it in the light of the miraculous interventions of God recorded in the Bible. The conclusions we have drawn, however, receive support from the observation of Joseph Fuchs, based on his more extensive survey of all of Thomas' sexual ethics:

> It appears that the boundary between sexual norms of natural law and sexual norms of divine positive law is not precisely observed. In fact, one might ask whether the sexual norms of natural law are not simply placed here on the same level as positive law and treated as such: they are the law that serves the common good and therefore knows no exception.[77]

That certain moral absolutes of sexual morality might be grounded by Thomas rather on principles of positive law than on some intrinsic finality of nature is illustrated by Thomas' refusal to condemn marital intercourse where no child is possible and to permit fornication when the child can be properly reared. In these exceptional cases, Thomas recognizes that the reasons he has given for the natural morality of marital intercourse and the natural immorality of fornication do not apply. Yet he remarks:

> The act of generation [unlike the act of nourishing oneself] is ordered to the good of the species, which is the common good. But the common good is subject to ordering by law. . . .
> [Therefore] to determine of what sort the act of generation should be does not pertain to anyone, but to the legislator, to whom it belongs to order the propagation of children, as the Philosopher also says in the Second Book of the *Politics*. But law does not consider what can occur in a particular case, but what has usually happened suitably. Therefore, although in a particular case, the intention of nature can be saved in an act of fornication in regard to the generation and rearing of the child, still the act is disordered in itself and a mortal sin.[78]

In the passages just considered, the interpretation of natural law morality along lines proper to positive law appears in two contexts. On the one hand, God can grant Hosea an exceptional dispensation from the prescribed form of marriage because he has supreme authority over human generation and marriage. Thomas does not feel it necessary to discuss whether or how the "end" of generation is preserved in Hosea's action. On the other hand, even in exceptional cases where the end of nature and of the legislator would be preserved although the law were not observed, the individual does not have the right to act contrary to the law. Generation concerns the common good and therefore man's use of it is subject to law. But law makes no allowance for exceptional cases; only the legislator can dispense from it.

In the historic thirty-third distinction of his *Commentary on the Fourth Book of the Sentences,* Thomas introduces a third context in which he interprets the natural law morality concerning generation along lines proper to positive law. At one point in this "first treatise of moral theology to have been developed,"[79] the young Thomas Aquinas took up the classic question of the polygamy of the patriarchs and discussed it in the light of Aristotelian ethics. As he saw it, the patriarchs did not have the sort of dispensation accorded Hosea, but neither were they guilty of violating the natural law precept prohibiting polygamy.

> As is clear from what has been said before, a plurality of wives is said to be contrary to the natural law not in regard to the primary precepts, but in regard to the secondary, which are derived as [quasi] conclusions from the primary precepts. But because human acts necessarily vary according to different conditions of persons and times and other circumstances, the aforesaid conclusions do not follow from the primary precepts of the natural law as having force in all cases, but only for the greater part. Such is all the matter of morality, as the Philosopher makes clear in his *Ethics.* Consequently, where the secondary precepts do not have force, they may be licitly set aside. But because it is not easy to determine varia-

tions of the sort, it is reserved to him by whose authority the law does have force to grant permission to 'set aside the law in those cases where the force of the law should not apply. Now the law of having only one wife was instituted by God, not man. It was never communicated by spoken or written word, but impressed on the heart, as was also the rest that pertains in any way to the natural law. Consequently, here God alone can grant the dispensation by internal inspiration. It was done principally to the holy patriarchs and by their example was passed on to others at that time when the said precept of nature needed to be set aside, so that there would be a greater increase of children to be brought up for the worship of God.[80]

Thomas finds a similar dispensation from secondary precepts in the concubinage of the same patriarchs (which he considers a modified form of polygamy) and "probably" in the divorce that Moses permitted.[81]

It has rightly been pointed out that Thomas does not present the distinction between primary and secondary precepts with all desirable clarity and coherence in this first attempt of his to deal with apparent dispensations from the natural law. Nor does he use the distinction again in the way he understands it here.[82] What he does do here and what he will still do years later is not merely to explain the dispensation for polygamy and divorce as the wise and legitimate freedom of the divine legislator, but to justify God's action on more natural grounds than he had the commands to Hosea and Abraham.

As natural inclination is to those things that are for the most part, so law is laid down according to what occurs for the most part. It is not contrary to the reasons given above if in some case it could occur otherwise. For the good of the many should not be passed over for the good of one, since "the good of the many is always more divine than the good of one" [Aristotle, First Book of the *Nicomachean Ethics*, 1094b]. But lest the defect which could occur in some one case should remain completely without remedy, legislators and similar persons have authority to dispense from common statute inasmuch as it is necessary in a particular case. And if indeed it is a human law, men having similar power can grant the dispensation. If the law has been divinely laid down, divine authority can grant the dispensation, as in the Old Law there seems to have been, by way of dispensation, an indult to have more than one wife and concubines and divorce.[83]

In both the thirty-third distinction of the *Commentary on the Fourth Book of Sentences* and the passage from the *Summa Contra Gentiles,* therefore, Thomas outlines a form of dispensation that is neither proper to human authority nor totally supernatural like the commands to Abraham and Hosea, which were justified only by God's supreme authority, choosing to symbolize a divine mystery. The dispensation from the unity and indissolubility of marriage lies in between, proper to God alone, but justified by the natural fact that the natural law in less frequent cases may fail to achieve its own purpose and interfere with a greater good. Thomas compares this kind of dispensation (opposing it to the higher kind accorded Abraham and Hosea) to natural change brought about by chance in the physical world:

Dispensation from precepts, especially those which belong in some way to the natural law, is like change in the course of something in nature. The course can be changed in two ways. One way is by one natural cause preventing another natural cause from its course; this is what occurs occasionally and by chance in nature. But the course that is varied by this way is not that of natural things which are always, but of those which are frequently. . . .

[Analogously] Now the grounds for dispensation from precepts of the natural law can at times be found in lower causes and thus a dispensation can be granted from secondary precepts of the natural law . . . as was said about polygamy and that kind of thing.[84]

It must be left for another inquiry to explore the implications for natural law morality of the natural grounds for dispensation from the natural law. For the purpose of the present investigation, the thirty-third distinction and *Summa Contra*

Gentiles, III, 125, merely illustrate once more how Thomas interprets natural law and exceptions to it not by some absolute qualities of a given act taken by itself, but on an analogy with human law, that is, as the wise judgment of the legislator who has authority to lead men to their final end as he sees fit— whether by laying down a law or dispensing from it. The final end is God himself and this is what determines both the law and the dispensation, whether the dispensation be to symbolize some divine mystery of the supernatural economy or whether it be to adjust a natural law to an exceptional, but natural, situation.

Moreover, the natural basis that Thomas adduces as grounds for the more natural kind of divine dispensation throws into relief, by contrast, the sovereign freedom and authority of God in granting the purely supernatural kind of dispensation he allowed Hosea. Whether or not Thomas continued to understand the latter kind of dispensation in the same way as he did in the thirty-third distinction, the fact remains that Thomas' continuing justification of the dispensation granted Hosea and Abraham never invokes the natural kind of basis he uses for the dispensation for polygamy. He never reconciles the dispensation accorded Hosea and Abraham with natural ends and goods, but merely invokes the supreme dominion and authority of God over all human generation and life.

Let us recapitulate. Our starting point was the current controversy over the possibility of "negative moral absolutes," principles according to which certain means, because of their physical effect, are never justified for a man. To understand the position of the natural law tradition, we turned to the writings of Thomas Aquinas. In order to form a working hypothesis on what was his synthesis of divine freedom and negative moral absolutes, we undertook to analyze in detail his treatment of the incidents in the Bible where God seemed to authorize a violation of the negative moral absolutes Thomas held.

What emerged progressively from the analysis was that the moral center of gravity for Thomas did not lie in the act itself and its physical effect, though these were relevant factors. As long as the acts contributed to some good purpose, the crucial question to decide the legitimacy of a given means was the authority of the person acting: not what was to be done, but who would do it. Abortion and premarital sexual intercourse would be absolutely wrong if the agent had only normal human authority. But God could, by a special initiative, authorize a man to perform the same acts.

Thus in the texts we first considered, Thomas merely said that whatever God willed was good. In other passages God was seen necessarily to will to bring men to himself, but could dispose freely of any created good or order in so doing. Certain other passages, using different terminology, seemed to limit God further. He had to act according to justice and virtue. But Thomas' consistent application to practice showed that justice and virtue never excluded absolutely any particular physical kind of means for divine authorization.

On the contrary, God's universal dominion over external things and life and generation made whatever he chose to do in these areas for his good purpose to be a just and virtuous means. It became progressively clear that a general framework, enunciated several times by Thomas, dominated his methodology throughout. The framework consisted in levels of authority communicable from God to man: the authority naturally belonging to the private individual, that naturally belonging to public officials, that supernaturally granted for what could become good for man by exceptions occurring naturally (like polygamy), that supernaturally granted for *any* use of property or human life or human generation that would serve the divine purpose.

Whether Thomas, in fact, had the framework in mind throughout his entire ethics, and whether, in particular, he would have maintained that God could even authorize acts such as usury or contraception, remains a working hypothesis, requiring further verification. That in a good number of passages he did present the framework and its principles, and that they directly imply God's power to authorize any physical means for a good end, is unquestionable.

In the context we have been considering, therefore, the point of division between Thomas and the more relativistic ethics of the twentieth century lies in a location that is often ignored today. The point of division is not the question whether it is possible that certain means, because of their physical effect, are always wrong. The point of division is the question whether or not God has shared with man the authority and dominion to take certain means when, perhaps by way of exception, they serve the greater good. The question for dialogue, therefore, is how far God has shared his dominion with man.

John de Lugo, writing in the seventeenth century and discussing the question of suicide, pinpointed the question well:

> For some say, first of all, that [suicide] is contrary to justice because man is something belonging to God and therefore cannot be destroyed without the authority of the owner [*absque domini facultate*]. And God is said never to have accorded the authority. But the argument seems weak unless you prove on other grounds that man is not the master [*dominum*] of his life, as he is master of his actions, his reputation, his material resources . . .
>
> One must explain why there is no injustice done to God by dissipating one's reputation or destroying one's house or another's, all of which are things belonging to God, and yet there is injustice in killing oneself. Or one must explain how one concludes in the light of nature that man is not master of his own life as he is of other things.[85]

Few today would accept the cardinal's own solution to the objection: "master" is a relative term, involving the superiority of the master over the person or thing that belongs to the master. Therefore, one cannot be master of oneself, just as one cannot be one's own father or teacher.[86] However, John de Lugo, standing at the entry of the modern era and himself already beginning to think in modern wise, put his finger on a precise area for dialogue today between contemporary thinkers and those who think along the lines of the middle ages. To what extent has God granted each man dominion and authority?

In the dialogue, one would come quickly to a theological question which is perhaps most central as well as most agonizing for Christians today: how can the moral autonomy of the person, which modern man sees so clearly, be one with the theonomy demanded by Christian faith?[87] In this regard, a final remark on the dialogue may also be drawn from words of de Lugo. In the lines immediately preceding the above quotation, he writes of suicide:

> The whole difficulty lies in assigning a reason for this truth [that one may not take one's own life]. For though the evil in question be immediately clear, it is still not easy to find its basis. Consequently, it happens here, as in many other questions, that the conclusion is more certain than the reasons which, being of various kinds, are adduced from different sources to prove the point.[88]

In a dialogue between a Thomas *redivivus* and a contemporary ethician, it might help to recognize that the conclusions on both sides may be more certain than their reasons. To Thomas, living in his particular milieu and sharing its mind, it was "immediately clear" that, let us say, abortion and divorce are always wrong. To many contemporaries today, having the mind of their milieu, it is "immediately clear" that this is not the case. And both Thomas and our contemporaries are less sure when it comes to elucidating the reasons for their positions.

The same may be said of the more profound point of division that the present chapter has tried to bring out. It was immediately clear to Thomas in his times that the hierarchy of authority and law and obedience was the principal factor for good as it brought civilization and morality and religion progressively into the life of the middle ages. Exploiting the Greek philosophical tradition, Thomas naturally conceived moral principles in a framework of authority and law and obedience. The intervening centuries have brought man new perspective and light, centering on his inviolable liberty and personal rights as well as his incredible power over nature and human living.

For twentieth-century man, the place of law and authority

is not so clear, but he sees himself and his companions in the center of the stage, individual persons having "come of age," "condemned to freedom," to the unique solitude of their own moral responsibility and autonomy, as they hold in their hands undreamed of power over nature and other men. He naturally conceives moral principles in a framework of freedom and responsibility for power.[89]

On the deeper level, where the extent of man's dominion and authority under God is in question, the two visions, medieval and contemporary, assuredly differ: man as citizen and man as responsible. But unlike the surface conflicts concerning particular acts such as abortion, the profound difference of vision may not, on the whole, be a black and white contradiction, but rather a shift in perspective where something has been gained and something lost. It is a place for genuine dialogue as Max Müller described it:

> Dialogue and discussion with a great thinker means to work out what his total interpretation of the basic meaning of everything conceals while it is explaining, and to work out what, hitherto unseen and unexplained, the interpretation brings out new while at the same time it forgets other things; for it is, indeed, finite.[90]

Might it not be that one thing new which Thomas Aquinas brought out was the Greek insight into the role of order and authority in the human community and in the cosmos? Might it not be that what he "forgot" was something he never knew because western man had yet to learn it: the extent of man's fantastic power over nature and human life and the extent of his inescapable moral autonomy? And might not the modern vision of the greater dominion and authority that God has shared with men have led Thomas by his own principles to rethink his conclusions on negative moral absolutes? On the other hand, might not his own vision of God as Lord and of the value of law and authority be a valuable reminder to contemporary man of something he tends to forget?

CORNELIUS J. VAN DER POEL

The Principle of Double Effect

The human act is a very complex entity. So often it happens that the same action has a variety of results, some of which we would be inclined to call "good" while others would in our estimation be graded as "evil." But in addition to that, in the performance of the human action we also go through various stages which are not all the object of our will with the same degree of immediacy. Specifically, when we are dealing with actions that carry with them various results, it is easy to speak of the "indirect voluntariness" of the evil results.

In recent writings we read, for example: "A man may offer his own life by risking it to save a friend, and morally nothing could be more acceptable than this. But in such an act he defines what he does in terms of the good at which he aims, and he only *indirectly* wills the possible bad consequence for his own life."[1] I fully agree with the author about the morality of this particular act; I only wonder whether this particular way of approaching it helps us to make a correct judgment about the human act as such. What I mean may become clearer from other examples.

At the present time there is a general agreement among Catholic moralists that surgical intervention is perfectly allowable in cases of ectopic pregnancy. The current agreement, however, is of relatively recent origin. It is not too many years ago that surgical intervention before the tube ruptured was considered immoral. The change in mentality (or approach) came about when the opinion was advanced that the fallopian tube, even before the rupture, is in a *pathological* condition, and that therefore early surgical intervention would be permissible. The life of the mother could now be saved not via that death of the unborn child, but the death of the fetus was the indirectly willed result of the medical action which was directed to the *good* effect alone, namely, the health of the mother.[2]

For our present study the important factor is not *that* this change came about, but *what* has changed in the approach, and *why*. The surgical intervention in the case of an unruptured tubal pregnancy, whether it had taken place before or after this change in understanding, would physically have been completely the same action with the same effect(s)—health of the mother and death of the fetus. The reason why it would have been performed would have been exactly the same, namely, the health of the mother. However, the moral evaluation would have been entirely different. Formerly, it would have been said that the mother was saved *via* the directly intended death of the fetus. This means that via an act which in itself is considered as an evil the positively intended good result of saving the mother was achieved.

Today the moralists would say that the same act (excising the tubal area containing the fetus) is curing a *pathological* condition of the tube, which has two effects. One is good by its nature (taking care of the health) and the other is in itself evil (death of the unborn fetus). This evil effect can be permitted because it is not the *means* to reach the good effect. Only it follows simultaneously but unavoidably from the same action. The good effect is important enough to allow this evil effect to occur.

This is all very good and praiseworthy, but two points in this approach disturb me: first, that ultimately the change in approach seems based exclusively upon the physical condition of the case, so that the physical aspect becomes the ultimate determinant of the morality of the action; second, there seems to exist a strong tendency to view both effects as independent entities rather than as one human action which by its nature is complex.

According to the principle of double effect, an action could not be allowed if the good effect followed as a consequence of the harmful (undesired=evil) effect.[3] If both effects follow simultaneously and independently from the same human act, the action could be allowed if the good effect is proportionately important. It would seem that in this argumentation there is a very great danger that one starts to consider both individual effects as independent entities.

The death of the fetus was seen as one thing, the saving of the mother as another thing. In earlier times the one was weighed against the other, and the conclusion was drawn that one could not take an innocent human life in order to save another (also innocent) human life. Only when science discovered that tubal pregnancy before rupture of the tube was a *pathological* condition was the total action considered morally correct. Thus the *final* determinant for the moral evaluation was then the insight into the *physical* condition of the mother. Without saying so explicitly, many moralists gave the impression that they attribute in a sense a certain moral evaluation to the material effect as such.

Of course, the morality of an act is directly connected with the human will, but the human will is so inseparably connected with the individual (material) result that in practical application the material result became the final determinant of *what* the agent intended by his action. Therefore in fact (though not in theory), the physical aspect became the ultimate determinant of the morality of the action.

Speaking about the principle of double effect, Noldin defines the evil effect as: "the effect which follows from the act in such a way that the act cannot have another effect. When this effect is intended by the agent, either as an end or as a means, he will be responsible for it."[4] Still more explicitly, we find this in Aertnys-Damen when he speaks about "Si agitur de effectu in se malo, ad quem agens," and when he further explains, "talis effectus, quamquam non directe intenditur, tamen est circumstantia actus necessario pertinens ad agentem et a qua abstrahere nequit, cum per positivum influxum ab actione profluat. Et *per se* est circumstantia mala moraliter ideoque facit actum malum." [5]

Thus it would seem to me that there exists a strong tendency (though perhaps not intended as such) to see both effects as independent entities. These entities receive an evaluation based upon their individual reality and they fall *as such* under the human responsibility of the agent, either as an end in themselves or as a means. If we then try to give a moral evaluation of the whole action, there is a real danger that we consider both effects as independent responsibilities, and thus we might give the impression that we have two human activities in one and the same human act. An example of this can be seen in the argumentation of some moralists in the discussion about the liceity of transplantation of living organisms among human beings. According to those moralists, "we have in transplantation to do with a direct mutilation, because we need mutilation as a means to help our fellow-man." [6] It would seem that the connection between physical reality and moral evaluation has been kept too close. Present-day theological thinking makes an effort to avoid these dangers.

THE UNITY AND UNIQUENESS OF HUMAN ACTION

Any study about human activity must by necessity start from a pre-accepted concept of the human being. Moral theology, as we have known this during the last few centuries, was rather strongly based upon the dualism of body and soul as two distinct realities which were somehow brought together in a certain form of unity, though the one could not act independently of the other. Each of these constituents had its own operative faculties, while it was the task of the spiritual faculties to rule over and to direct the often recalcitrant faculties of the bodily element in the human being.

By his intellect and will, as the outstanding spiritual faculties, man accepted the responsibility for his actions, but the determination of the will was not the sole factor in deciding upon the moral value of an action. The material result in itself had already an established value which the act of the will and understanding could not alter, and which entered into the human act through the will of the agent. This comes rather strongly to the foreground when the manuals of moral theology speak about the principle of double effect. Whatever the material result of the action itself may be, this result is willed and intended directly by the human agent.[7]

Today's moral theology, basing itself upon the concepts of contemporary philosophy, tries to avoid this danger of dualism by starting from the reality of human existence. The human person experiences himself as a being-in-this-world[8] and as such he finds himself endowed simultaneously with spiritual and corporeal qualities which are so intimately connected that in every human activity both elements are essentially necessary. The body is human only insofar as it participates in the spiritual mode of being of the soul, and the soul is only human to the extent that it communicates itself to the corporeity.[9] It is therefore not the body nor the soul, not the intellect nor the will which performs the action, but it is the human person as a whole who is ultimately responsible for his activity.

Human action has a uniqueness that makes it incomparable with any other created entity and is therefore essentially different from all other activities in the universe.[10] To a certain degree man determines the shape of his own existence. Knowingly and willingly he determines what he will do in certain circumstances. The proper character of man, his "being human," is not a natural product predetermined in the human organism by birth. This "being human" is given only as a pure potentiality to which man must give an expression in reality by his thoughts and actions in freedom and responsibility. Human existence therefore is not so much a datum as a task and a vocation.[11] But even this vocation is not strictly outlined for him from the very beginning of his existence. As a "being-in-this-world" man must to a large extent find this vocation for himself.

Man is an existence which is searching and inquiring about itself. He must take his life in his own hands, searching for the meaning of it. Living in this world and connected with this world, his life grows to a vision and understanding of this world and life. He discovers values which appeal to him, values by which he is fascinated and for which he judges life worth living.[12]

The human person is aware of the fact that he has the task to become himself, and that he must do so in freedom and through his corporeality, through his knowledge, his inclinations and his emotions. But in this concrete existence he discovers also that he can fulfill this task only by directing himself intentionally toward other persons, toward the society or societies in which he lives, toward the material world, and toward God.[13]

In the immediate contact with other persons of the same quality and with the same rights as he, man discovers himself as a person and as a free subject who is nonetheless in need of others. He knows and experiences that he may not use the others as an object for his own satisfaction, nor can he himself be used by others for this purpose.

Psychological research has abundantly demonstrated that human behavior and activity acquire meaning and value only in relation to a framework of factors operating in a social setting.[14] Proper human devolpment and growth, and consequently proper human satisfaction, occur where he can ask and live these two questions: "What can the other, humanly speaking, expect from me?" and "What can I, humanly speaking, expect from the other?" This human intersubjective exchange and solidarity is the basis for any form of coexistence.

In daily existence man experiences his limitations; in the wider perspective of the society he is able to overcome them partly. The mutual influence of intellectual insight, communal planning, and cooperation are indispensable factors for the awakening and development of those qualities which are specifically human. Through this inter-subjectivity he not only makes the world a better place to live in, but also he himself becomes more *human*. Daily experience also makes it clear to him that he needs the material world. He needs it to stay alive; he needs it to express himself and to have contact with others. It is essential for his whole existence.

In this multiple relationship man is faced with the question of what is the meaning of life. In daily experience he sees this human existence ending in death. The whole human existence, with its constant and conscious striving for growth and self-determination, becomes to man an absurdity unless he accepts that his whole life has a meaning which transcends itself and which finds its final destination in living beyond the present stage of existence. For Christian life this means finding its perfection in the participation of the infinite existence.

Thus human life appears to man not only as a gift of the transcendent God, but also as a task which is to be fulfilled within multiple relationships with the material world, his fellow human beings and society. Then the holy will of God shines through the created reality to the extent that this can be reached by human evaluation. "Human nature itself is ethical. To be man is a commission, an ethical vocation which clarifies itself continuously if we are faithful to its light." [15] The human vocation itself is the law of his existence, but a law which he must discover within himself.

"That this law is the will of God does not mean that God imposes this law upon us from the outside, but it means that God has created man *as man,* namely, as a being which can discover this law within himself as the law of his own existence." [16] Human existence does not find its fulfillment in a self-centered approach to life. Man's full development takes place in relation to others and to the society of which he is member. The totality of the society and its welfare in its proper directedness, that is, as earthly realization of man's journey toward a union with God, is *the* fundamental aspect for moral evaluation.

A moral judgment is made not so much about a human act *in itself* as a separate entity, but rather the individual human act should be evaluated insofar as it contributes to or destroys the building of this society.[17] This social aspect of man seems to be overlooked or at least too much de-emphasized in the application of the principle of double effect. This we see for instance in the difficult question whether or not a fatal (not ectopic) pregnancy may be terminated if it is the only way to save the life of the mother.

In our effort to find a solution we seem to place two moral values in this one act of saving the mother. In such cases it is so easy to speak about the "direct killing" of the child in order to save the mother. But by doing so it would seem that we are giving a full and independent moral evaluation to both the elements of this action. The termination of the pregnancy is seen as a negative value, the saving of the mother as positive. One effect viewed as a completely independent human act in itself seems to be weighed against the other effect, also viewed as a completely independent human act in itself. The "directly intended termination of pregnancy" or the "attack upon an innocent and defenseless human being" [18] seems to be considered as an independent entity with a preconceived moral evaluation, and may never be permitted.

Thus we get the impression that the unity of the human act of saving the mother (which includes the most regrettable but inseparably connected element of the death of the child) is divided into two independent realities. Also the uniqueness of the human act seems to be too much de-emphasized. In view of the human circumstances and of human intention, it seems rash to qualify the death of the child as directly intended and plain murder, as moralists do on many occasions.

It seems to me that we reason more logically in the case of a completely insane attacker who is killed by a person in an act of self-defense. Let us assume that the attacker was irresistibly driven by a psychotic compulsion. He would be completely innocent because he would be the helpless and defenseless object of his irresistible urge or fear. Yet no one would blame the person who defends himself, even if he has to kill the attacker.

This differentiation in judgment cannot be based logically upon the illegitimacy of the attack in the second case. In both cases we have to deal with unfortunate circumstances which result from the physiological and/or psychological structure of the individual. The differentiation seems to be much more the product of the way in which we look at the act, whether we judge the various parts of the total act as independent values, or whether we see the act as a unity in the total perspective of human relationships.

THE PLACE OF THE PHYSICAL EFFECT IN THE HUMAN ACT

A second major difficulty with the traditional application of the principle of double effect is that the present understanding of the principle seems to overemphasize the importance of the *physical* effect in the judgment about the *moral* value of the human action. Some theologians determine what is direct merely by considering the physical structure of the act itself, or the immediate physical causality of the act itself. For example, direct killing is an action which is *per se occisiva;* direct killing is an action whose *finis operis* is killing; direct killing occurs when the destruction of human life is the immediate and *per se* object and effect of the act placed.[19]

The difficulty in considering the direct effect merely in terms of the physical structure of the act became apparent in the controversy among moral theologians on the question of the transplantation of organs. Some moralists condemned transplantation because it involved a direct mutilation. Transplantation calls for the organ to be excised from one individual and grafted on to another person. To excise an organ from one human being (if it is not done because of the pathological condition of the organ itself) involves a direct mutilation no matter what is done with the organ after excision. However, the physical structure of the act of excising cannot be the ultimate determinant of morality. The physical excision of the organ is a part of the total human action of transplantation. The example shows that the physical structure of the act is merely a pre-moral consideration, and not in itself determinant of morality.

The same problem of determining morality on the basis of the physical structure of the action occurs in the various examples used by the manualists to illustrate the problem of direct and indirect killing. For example, a girl may jump to certain death from a very high window to save herself from a brutal attack. Although her death is certain, it is only an indirect effect. The girl "places" the indifferent act of jumping out of the window. From this action two effects follow. She avoids the attack, but she will kill herself in the fall. However, her death is an indirect effect of her indifferent action of jumping. The fact that the window happens to be thirty stories above the pavement is only an accidental circumstance, they say, which does not change the nature of the indifferent act of jumping.

The examples frequently cited by the theologians (for example, the girl jumping out of a window to save her chastity, the kamikaze pilot crashing into an enemy ship, the mountain climber cutting the rope when the man underneath him begins to fall and thus jeopardizes the life of the man on top) illustrate the importance attached to the physical structure of the action itself apart from all the circumstances surrounding the act. In these cases the act itself is the indifferent act of jumping or crashing or cutting a rope. The death in such cases is not direct because the act in its physical structure (the *finis operis* or *per se occisiva*) does not have death as its object.

In line with such reasoning one could almost say that a girl who shoots herself with a pistol to avoid a brutal attack is also killing herself only indirectly. Pulling the trigger would be seen as an indifferent act. It would just be an extrinsic circumstance that her head happened to be the target of the bullet and that the bullet did strike her and bring about death.

When five men are aboard a raft which can safely hold only four, one man may heroically decide to jump off and swim away. He knows with human certitude that he cannot live for long in the swirling seas, but his death is only indirect. However, a prisoner of war who knows the whereabouts of 500 men behind enemy lines is not permitted by some moralists to kill himself to prevent the enemy from brainwashing him and finding out the whereabouts of the others.[20] Such tragic, human situations seem to indicate the fallacy of determining morality merely on the physical structure of the act itself.

The human person is in this world as an *embodied spirit*. Both elements, spirit and body, are so intimately interwoven and interdependent that one cannot exist in this world without the other. Only in the unity of these two does the human person exist. The spirit and body are human because of their interdependence. "But this spirit is spirit in the mode of self-communication to the body which is capable of this humanization. In and through his corporeality man is able to "become-a-person": he assumes the corporeality into the spiritual realm and makes it a *human* corporeality."[21]

The physical and biological aspects of man are seen to have an entirely new meaning exactly because they are part of human existence. The biological structure in itself can never be the basis for establishing human directedness and value, nor can the spirtual aspects alone be this basis. The uniqueness of the human being exists in the self-communication of the spirit to the corporeality and the participation of this corporeality in the human spirit. Therefore, biological nature is not an absolute value or a basis for moral evaluation, it is only co-determinant insofar as it is a *human* corporeality.

As being-in-this-world, human existence is simultaneously a datum and a commission. Every man *is* human but at the same time he must *become* human. He is a dynamism which is expressed simultaneously as a directedness and as an imperative.[22] It is constitutive for the human being to be free and to give actual expression to his own existence in freedom. But his freedom is not unlimited. It is conditioned by his existence in this world with all the relations which this implies.[23] The physiological structure of human activity, therefore, cannot be the ultimate determinant for moral evaluation, nor can the direction of the human mind and will by itself be the ultimate determinant for moral evaulation. It is the relation of the human action toward human existence and dignity in their transcendent relation to God which is decisive for moral good or evil.

This is what we actually practice when we say, for instance, that rhythm can be lawfully used in marriage as often as there is any good reason to limit the number of children, but at the same time it implies that the use of rhythm in marriage can be selfish and sinful if it is used contrary to the commission or task which this particular couple have in their individual situations of life. Not the physical structure of an act, not the intention of the person, but the totality of this particular human existence is the determinant.

The case is the same in transplantation. We can appreciate that in general moralists see no objection against its use, because it is one more way to express charity. But we must carefully avoid viewing the physical harm in the donor as an *independent* disvalue which is to be compared with the other value of charity. If we make this comparison the physiological aspect would easily receive a moral evolution that it does not deserve. The human act *as a whole* is transplantation. The whole act is the "exteriorization" of inter-human relationship. This implies various steps on the physical level—here in particular "excision" and "grafting" are important.

With due respect for the proportion which must exist between the physical harm done to the one and the benefit for the other, these intermediate steps do *not* have an independent moral value. Their moral evaluation can only be seen in the totality of the *human* act, with the full perspective (as far as humanly possible) of man's existence in this world together with its essential relationship to God. Then the so-called mutilation which occurs is not an evil in any moral sense of the word. It is just a physical occurrence (regrettable, no doubt) which receives its *moral* determination from the totality of the human action.[24] We should be careful not to ascribe any moral evaluation to this concomitant, independently of the total act. It is good or evil *only* in relation to the total human action.

This does not mean that we can simply disregard the physical consequences of the intermediate stages of a human action. The material world in which man lives and exists, and of which he is part, is the situation in which he must give concrete expression to his human vocation, in which he must develop as a human being and *become* more *human*. Therefore, the material effects need to be evaluated, not according to their "goodness" or "badness" in themselves but in their relationship to total human existence, namely, insofar as they contribute to it or destroy it, because only in concrete and total activity can they be good or evil.[25]

However, not *any* material effect can be used to obtain a good result; there needs to be a proportionate reason which makes the occurrence of the physical evil acceptable in view of the total human existence. This acceptability does not become clear from the comparison of two physical effects. The human action of surgical intervention, for example, is in its totality directed toward the saving of the mother's life. This is the total intention or reason of the action. This purpose is not something outside the human action, but is exactly the aspect which makes the action *human* and which assumes into itself all the intermediate stages that make this action possible.[26] Then this total human action should be projected against the background of the whole of human existence in this world, to see whether it is contributing to it or destructive in its results. In other words, the morality of the act demands that it be in proportion to the value which is pursued. Within this proportion the intermediate stages share in this morality.[27]

It becomes clear throughout this whole argumentation that we could not stay on the purely physical level. This whole physical or physiological existence and structure of the human being and action is inseparably tied to the intention and purpose of the agent, that is, of the human person through whom and in whom the material existence receives its human meaning. The whole human action is voluntary, although certain parts of the action are willed in themselves while others are willed only in relation to the purpose.

THE INDIRECT VOLUNTARY

The unity and uniqueness of human action do not take away its complexity. That human action is by its essence the result of the concurrent activity of the spiritual and corporeal faculties does not take away the fact that every human action passes through various external stages, which are each individually produced by the human person. Each of these intermediate stages has in its own way an impact upon the totality of the human situation and circumstances, and individually each falls under the responsibility of the human agent.

This presents us with a double question: 1) is each intermediate stage a *separate* product of the human will, that is, is it a separate human action? and, 2) to what degree does each intermediate stage place a responsibility upon the agent.

Turning to the first point, whether the intermediate stages form a separate product of the human will, we come to the problem of the indirect voluntary.[28] The person who loves nature and beauty may want to see the wonderful panorama of the country from the highest mountain peak in the area. The climb to the mountaintop may be long, fatiguing, and perhaps dangerous. The fatigue and the risk are inseparably connected with his ultimate goal.

The climbing of the mountain is a *human* activity, yet it is not willed for its *own* value, but only insofar as it is part of the total action of the agent. What the agent wills are not two different things—the fatigue and danger (which he might resent) and the view of the panorama—but in one and the same act of the will he wants this total goal, the view from that mountain peak. In willing so he has made an evaluation of the hardship of the trip and of the dangers involved, he has taken into account the height and gradient of the mountainside and also his own ability and strength. Based upon this information he has made his decision. The trip and the view are both included in the same act of the will. The *totality* is the end of the human action.

> The end is merely a series of acts viewed at a remote stage: and the means is merely the series viewed at an earlier one. The distinction of means and end arises in surveying the *course* of the proposed *line* of action, a connected series in time. The end is the last act thought of; the means are the

acts to be performed prior to it in time. Means and end are two names for the same reality. The terms denote not a division in reality but a distinction in judgment.[29]

There is no doubt that the mountain climber accepts the fatigue and the dangers, and therefore he wills them. But as we said earlier, he wills them not as a value in themselves— only *as leading to the final goal*. He wants the means or the intermediate stages only insofar as the final goal *is contained in these means*.

This was sharply outlined by St. Thomas Aquinas[30] where he says that the means to the end are not goods in themselves nor are they willed for their own sake, but in relation to the end. Consequently, the will is directed to them only insofar as it is directed to the end. Therefore, what the will seeks in them is the end. So it would seem that the will (the act of the will) is related to the goal, not to the means, except insofar as the goal is already contained in the means. In that case, *in the means* the act of the will is concerned with the goal.[31]

The fatigue and the danger of the mountain climb are not willed for themselves,[32] but only insofar as the satisfaction of the vision of the landscape is contained in it. It seems, therefore, to be incorrect to speak of a double object of the will, the climbing and the vision. There is only one object, the vision, which communicates its meaning to all the intermediate stages of the one *human* act. As soon as we start to consider the climbing with its fatigue and dangers as an independent entity we are not honest and fair anymore, because then we take away from it the specific *human* determination and values which it has in this individual case. This would mean that we ascribe a human value to an abstract physical entity.

It would seem that similar reasoning can be applied to those human actions which have a double effect. The amputation of a leg may be an absolute requirement for the life and health of a person. In such case the act of the will directs itself not to two different actions of amputation and cure, but the one action of curing includes the amputation unavoidably, and defines the *human* meaning of the amputation itself.

The same reasoning applies to many other situations: for instance, in transplantation of living organisms among human beings. Here also the implantation and cure are contained in the *human* action of the excision of the organism in the donor. This excision is not willed independently from the implantation,[33] but only insofar as the implantation is "contained" in it, or depends on it. It would be incorrect to consider it in terms of its *own* value as a human action.

Exactly the same approach is to be used in actions which we consider immoral, for instance, the abortion of a pregnancy that is simply unwanted. Here also the abortion may not be considered on its *own* value, but the ultimate goal (in this case, avoidance of shame or burden) enters into the act of terminating the pregnancy. It is this goal, therefore, that determines the human meaning of it.

This now brings up the second question that we asked: To what extent does the intermediate stage place a responsibility upon the agent, or how do we judge the morality of this kind of actions. I have already indicated that the physical effect may never be the ultimate norm for the moral judgment of the human action. But, on the other hand, the physical effect may not be disregarded as if it had no value, since it is the condition and environment within which the human action expresses itself visibly in this world.

At the risk of repeating myself, I must stress again the importance of the totality of human existence. Man is responsible for his own actions. But here we must take "man" not in the isolated existence of an individual human being, but in the totality of relationships with the surrounding world, including men and things. Man has his responsibility before God, but this same responsibility receives a concrete shape in his human activity. This includes all his relations to other persons and to things.

The relationship and responsibility to God penetrates every

aspect of this human activity, and does not exist apart from this human activity which in its turn is essentially related to other persons and human society. "The human action is not the material reality as such, but the inter-human reality."[34] This is because " 'to be man' is not a datum but a vocation. Vocation means being called by someone. This someone is another person. Every person is 'calling' the other. 'To what' one is called is the community with others. . . ."[35] The human being "becomes himself" in his relations with others. Here he experiences the fact that his growth and development are not possible unless he contributes to others and permits others to contribute to him.

This relationship is not just accidental, but exactly these relations constitute him as an "incarnate person," and form an integral part of the essential definition of "being human."[36] But if the human person has this essential relationship, then the human activity (which is the intended expression of the personality) must also have the same relationship. When Thomas Aquinas calls the voluntary act an *agere propter finem,* then this "acting for a purpose" cannot be related to the individual and isolated act alone, but in and through this individual act it is related to the totality of human existence.

The specifically *human* aspect of man's activity lies not only in the fact that every specifically human action has a purpose for which it is performed, but also, and perhaps primarily, in the fact that in some way or other it has a relation to the totality of human existence. It has an intersubjectivity in which the individual human shares, and to which he actively contributes.[37] In every action the human person participates in intersubjectivity and he himself acts intersubjectively.

By focusing upon this human totality we may give to some readers the impression of overlooking man's relationship to God. This, however, is not true at all. It is precisely in human existence, in his discovery of freedom and responsibility, that man becomes aware of the transcendent values of his being and acting. The experience of self-insufficiency, of the limitations of his social relationships, and of the finality of his whole being in this world, brings man to the acceptance of a transcendent power which is present in every aspect of his being and acting, and which simultaneously is the cause of it.

This transcendent reality is experienced as being contained and present in every aspect of human life, and still the totality of it always escapes the grasp of human understanding. This transcendent value, which is the reason and the source for human action, always goes beyond the action itself. This power drives us irresistibly to the activity, and still it is not totally contained in the action itself. It manifests itself in human activity but is not human activity. It manifests itself in a specific way in human intersubjectivity, but itself is not this human intersubjectivity. Yet simultaneously it is the source and the norm of the demands which this same intersubjectivity makes upon the individual.

But "if God manifests his presence to us only in an action in which he is the source of our existence, and if he remains transcendent even in this action of being-our-source-of-existence, then this means that he is not there because we exist, although we know his divine existence only through (by means of) our existence. It means that we exist because of him."[38] So man discovers in the completeness of his existence these two realities: the worldly human reality and the divine reality. These two are interrelated in such a manner that the worldly reality is there because of the divine reality and the divine reality manifests itself in worldly existence which, however, it surpasses in every aspect; it is simultaneously totally immanent and totally transcendent.

> The world of nature and of history in which the "religious" man lives becomes a part of the dialogue in which man encounters God. It becomes the theme of the divine commissions to man, and simultaneously the visible expression of the response of God to human prayers and efforts.[39]

Now the *agere propter finem* receives a new dimension. It not only includes the direction of the human person in relation to *worldly* human existence, but this whole existence has an intrinsic relationship to God. The *agere propter finem* becomes an "acting for the sake of God," but this acting expresses itself by necessity in the worldly sphere in which and through which it expresses the divine presence and transcendence as its source and goal. On the other hand, however, the divine expresses itself, or makes itself known, in the form of human reality in which human persons search for their proper destiny and determination.

The absolute greatness and power of God is not a reality which is merely outside human existence. It is as much immanent as it is transcendent, and his transcendence can be known to men only to the extent that they know his immanence. Thus human expression of the relationship to God and the person-to-person encounter with the divine can only take place when a human being lives his earthly life to the best of his abilities in faith and acceptance of the transcendent reality which is the continual source and reason of his existence.

This should give us an indication of the peculiar place and condition of the human person. He has the experience of being responsible to the transcendent God in his activity, but simultaneously this responsibility is fulfilled only in a social setting. This means that man fulfills his responsibility to God through and in his responsibility to the totality of his surroundings.[40] Thus "the task which man has in relation to the world exists in creating the conditions which are favorable for the personalistic *and* community-building life of everyone."[41]

From this point of view it becomes more clear that individual human action, precisely in its *human* aspects, may not be divided into independent parts each with an independent moral value. The means to the end may have in themselves a merely physical effect which may, precisely in its isolated physical condition, seem harmful to a certain aspect of life, but in the totality of the *human* quality of the total action it may be community-building, and not destructive. So it is possible that the same physical act and effect may have an entirely different *human* value because of the total environment (if you wish, call it the circumstances) in which the act is performed. The same material act of shooting a person to death may be an act of justice, it may be self-defense, or it may be plain murder— the same material act and effect, but three totally different *human* acts.

We may call the *material* effect "evil" in all these cases, but as soon as this material effect enters into the realm of *morality* by becoming part of the *human* action it then shares in the value of the totality of human action. Then there is not anymore the effect, which in itself is an evil, but which can be "permitted" because of good reasons. There is only *one* moral value, which is either good or evil. Even the killing of a person considered in itself constitutes a different act *secundum speciem moralitatis* in each individual case.[42]

We do not say here that the end justifies the means, but what we do say is that the end *determines the human meaning* of the means. If the end is social justice or self-defense or plain revenge, the killing of the person shares in the same human meaning, and we do not merely permit an evil effect for a pro- portionate reason. This does not imply that *any* reason is pro- portionate and acceptable for *any* means. There must be a due proportion between the means and the end. But the end itself must not be judged *only* according to its individual material re- sult. This end needs to be considered in the totality of its re- lationship to man-in-this-world and his transcendent destina- tion.[43] The material effects, or results, have no moral value in themselves.

Morality enters the field only where these material results become the visible expression of *human* activity in the strict sense of the word. Human activity is always communication with others or the frustration of this communication,[44] and as a con- sequence it is good or evil accordingly. Man has no other way of acting than through his material existence. Therefore if the purpose of man's existence is the service of God, that is, a mani- festation of God in creation, then this too is only possible through human activity and in human activity. "For how can he who does not love his brother whom he sees, love God whom he does not see?" (Jn 4:20). Therefore, "community with God cannot exist without human inter-subjective communication, and inter-human communication includes in fact community with God, whether this is recognized and accepted or not."[45] This does not mean that inter-human communication is the same as community with God, because the human does not comprehend God, but God is present and manifests himself in human existence.

In this approach to his *total* existence, man recognizes his responsibility. "Creation is placed in the hands of man and is entrusted to his decisions, because it is in his power to bring it to perfection or to counteract it."[46] Here arises the obligation "which is nothing else than the creation insofar as this is experienced and understood by the creature who has achieved the use of his intellect."[47]

This total human existence becomes the final and ultimate norm of morality, because this is what is intended by human intentionality. The means as the intermediate stage of the final result of human action, as well as the "side-effects" which are more or less essentially connected with the result, derive their proper meaning and moral value from this total structure. The ultimate norm, therefore, is not the individual human being and his personal individualistic interests, nor is it the society as human community in itself, but rather the totality of the inter-human relationship which on all its levels is penetrated by and directed to the transcendent greatness of God.

On one hand, this includes by necessity a continuous development and change, since human society changes as it develops and progresses, but on the other hand it has the continuous, stable, and never-changing element of the divine majesty. The history of ethical and religious development gives numerous examples of this. For instance, the polygamy of the patriarchs was not justified by a special "permission." It was simply an expression of contemporary development.[48]

The approach to morality which we have here considered employs a different method for the solution of moral problems. We accept very readily the fact that the agent is responsible for all the intermediate stages of his action; but we may never make an intermediate stage the final determinant of the total action, just as we may not make the physical structure of the act the final determinant. Methodologically, we must see human action in the multiple structure and implications of a human being in-this-world. Human action in its totality is, as we have said, community building or destroying. As soon as we start focusing our attention (and consequently our moral evaluation) on one specific stage in the total action, then we do an injustice to the human being who by nature goes beyond any form of isolated existence.

The question of abortion can serve as an illustration of this newer methodology. The traditional approach condemns direct abortion, with the notion of "direct" defined in physical terms and concentrating on just one stage of the total human action. It is well to note, however, that Catholic theology traditionally did not condemn all abortion. Indirect abortion has been permitted. Thus the older methodology tries to come to grips with conflict situations through an application of the notion of direct and indirect killing. However, our proposal rejects such a methodology. The ultimate moral criterion is the community building or destroying aspect of the action.

There are many factual problems connected with abortion which are beyond our present scope. Is the genetic package human life in the same sense as human life outside the womb? If not, what are the differences? Is there a definite point at which human life begins or is there only a continuum in process? I would conclude that at least the genetic package is in direct continuity with human life. As a Christian one must show great reverence for human life. The Christian does not base his respect for human life on what the human life contributes to society or to others, but rather on the gift of life received from God.

However, conflict situations will arise in which the moralist must weigh the different values involved. For example, when the life of the mother is certainly threatened by the fetus, the moralist (following the community building criterion) can conclude to the taking of the life of the fetus in these circumstances.

In fact, the moralist employing such a criterion cannot *a priori* exclude the possibility of taking the life of the fetus in other circumstances. I would strongly oppose abortion just for the convenience of the mother, but there might be some circumstances in which the moralist just does not know what is the community building alternative.

One may object that by this reasoning we reject all absolute norms. This seems to me not to be true. The one and absolute norm: God and the directedness of creation to him, remains unchanged; but this absolute norm can only find a relative expression in the human world, because man himself— in whom this norm is expressed—is subject to continuous change. What we in our human way of speaking accept as general norms are often in fact *not* general norms, but rather "ethical imperatives." This means ethical norms in which a certain situation is already incorporated.

The strict prohibition during earlier centuries against demanding interest on loans incorporated the contemporary understanding of the value of money in medieval society. This general norm was valid at that time but cannot be maintained at the present.[49] Often we make a mistake which is worse when we apply a specific ethical value to the performance of a certain material act and we make this value so inherent to it that we basically stick to the same evaluation even when this act has a totality different value. This we do easily when we call the excision of a healthy organism in the donor (in transplantation) a mutilation. This is true in certain "types" of causing bodily harm, but in many other cases it might have an entirely different value. In doing so we "identify" moral value with the material result, and then we are often obliged to twist our logic and reasoning in order to "justify" another human action which in its totality is morally good.

Again it must be said that the individual human being is not the ultimate norm, but it is the individual who must make a personal decision. In doing so he may not disregard the generally accepted ethical norms as they exist in his society *and* as he knows that they are sanctioned by the Church. The Church on its part has the task of explaining and teaching the specific God-related aspects of human values, but in doing this it cannot remain aloof from human society.

It is understandable that during periods when changes in human society are more pronounced, the individual conscience may find itself in severe conflict about the steps to be taken. This problem is treated in another chapter of this book. For our purpose here it suffices to state that legislation and conscience, law and love, regulation and faith will never perfectly coincide during the earthly pilgrimage of the people of God.[50]

The individual must make the choice of the means which are apt to assist him in the fulfillment of his individual action in relation to his overall task in this world. In this choice, however, he must remember that the means for a particular action may never be so grave that the total result of the whole action would be damaging for the community. In the variety of choices which he might be able to make, he must generously make those choices that make the total action the most beneficial for the progress of proper human development, as understood and sanctioned in his contemporary environment.

Although it was used in a different context, we may perhaps apply here the words of Schillebeeckx:

> Our sole aim is to stress on the one hand the real existence of absolute ethical norms, and on the other the fact that moral norms are only operative in terms of ethical commands. These depend for their obligatory character, however, on the historically shaped vision of man and the world. In this I am rejecting "situation ethics," which states that moral norms should sometimes yield to circumstances. We are at present concerned with absolute norms, valid in all circumstances. But given the necessary historicity of human experience, these only exist in terms of ethical commands depending on the actual conception of man and the world. And therefore, in fact, they themselves evolve on account of the evolution of this concept.[51]

If I were to go into any further detail concerning this topic I would enter the field of other contributors. I only point to examples where the principles of indirect voluntary action and double effect are used in practice. It would seem that it does not make any essential difference whether we speak of "indirect voluntary" or "voluntary in cause", or whether we call the means to the end *voluntarium in se sed non propter se* in contradistinction to the end itself which is *voluntarius in se et propter se*. These qualifications do not indicate separate voluntary actions of the person, but rather describe *how* they receive their moral value from the overall human purpose of this individual action. They indicate simultaneously that they play a distinct role in the moral evaluation of the individual action, but this role is not based upon their *own* material result independent of the totality of the action.

We do not weigh the independent value of the human life of the unlawful attacker against the independent value of the life of the person who legitimately defends himself against the attack. We place the total action in the social setting of human existence, and we call the whole action morally good provided that this was the only way to defend himself. If proper self-defense could effectively be achieved in a way which involves the social structure less seriously, then this act of killing the attacker would have been evil. Not *only* because of the comparison between the partial and material aspects of the action, but rather because of the combination of the partial aspects and their relations to the *total* end of the action.

On the one hand it would seem that we take away many "absolutes" and that we "relativize," but on the other, it would seem that the only existing absolute, which is God manifesting himself to us in creation,[52] does not lose any aspect of his majesty and importance. The human being, however, seems to become more personally responsible for his task of becoming "the master of the earth."[53] In a fuller sense, man will become "the image and likeness of God," his Creator.

DENNIS DOHERTY

Consummation and
the Indissolubility of Marriage

The prohibition of divorce, a prohibition long considered in Catholic teaching to be absolute, is currently the subject of much and necessary discussion. While the Catholic Church does not acknowledge the validity of divorces granted by civil authority, in Catholic teaching the absolute prohibition of divorce is restricted to the instance of a sacramental consummated marriage. It is precisely this absolute prohibition that is being controverted today by Catholic theologians and canonists.[1]

Although at present there would seem to be more reasons for acknowledging papal power to dissolve every marriage than there are for denying it, this growing controversy is not our interest here. Rather, our purpose in this chapter is to suggest a wider framework within which those marriages still regarded as absolutely indissoluble might be seen as able to be dissolved.

The fundamental reason that prompts the approach we are suggesting is radically the same as that which motivates those intent upon showing that the Church can dissolve any marriage: namely, to apply Christ's gospel of love in an effort to relieve the unnecessary suffering that exists because of tragic marriages —marriages that should never have been entered into and which show no reasonable hope of success.[2] At the same time we are interested in making manifest a more dynamic understanding of what should constitute a dissoluble or indissoluble

211

Christian marriage. But we are upholding the absolute indissolubility of a sacramental consummated marriage. Accordingly,
we hope to determine what such a marriage implies.

Since dissolution is already an established practice on the
basis of physical non-consummation (as well as non-sacramen-
tality), the present restricted notion of absolute indissolubility
can remain both restricted and absolute, but it may be further
refined. For there are reasons to believe that the notion of consummation as presently understood in the Catholic Church need
not be regarded as absolute, and that an expanded understanding would make possible dissolutions that should be granted.

Before attempting to establish a qualitatively wider basis
for dissolution, it will be not only helpful but also necessary to
give a brief summary of indissolubility and dissolubility in
Catholic doctrine. The treatment of indissolubility in the *De
Matrimonio* tract in any standard manual of moral theology is
usually a summary statement of traditional, that is to say, natural law, argumentation. Accordingly, it may be recalled here
that the dissolubility of the marital bond, as Catholic authors insist, is seen to be evil for several reasons.

First of all, it is detrimental to the rearing of offspring;
children, it is clear, need both parents. Second, the stability of
any marriage would be jeopardized if one could entertain the
thought of divorce in view of difficult circumstances, a thought
that would doubtless even lead one to bring about such circumstances in order to have certain grounds for divorce. Third,
the spouses themselves need each other, a need felt especially
by the wife once she becomes older and less attractive physically; if her husband could lawfully abandon her in this condition, this would be a grave injustice to her, one proscribed
by natural law. Moreover, a wife needs her husband for the security which he provides for her. Finally, the practice of divorce
is destructive of morals and therefore the good of society is
endangered.[3]

The bishops at Vatican II, after referring to the "plague
of divorce"[4] and certain mistaken notions of human love and
sexuality, sum up the traditional position by asserting:

The intimate partnership of married life and love has been established by the Creator and qualified by his laws. It is rooted in the conjugal covenant of irrevocable personal consent. Hence, by that human act whereby spouses mutually bestow and accept each other, a relationship arises which by divine will and in the eyes of society too is a lasting one. For the good of the spouses and their offspring, as well as of society, the existence of this sacred bond no longer depends on human decisions alone.[5]

Emphasizing that marriage is not instituted solely for procreation, the bishops again stress the indissolubility even of childless marriages:

its very nature as an unbreakable compact between persons, and the welfare of the children, both demand that the mutual love of the spouses, too, be embodied in a rightly ordered manner, that it grow and ripen. Therefore, marriage persists as a whole manner and communion of life, and maintains its value and indissolubility, even when offspring are lacking—despite, rather often, the very intense desire of the couple.[6]

Understandably, more is said about marriage in "Schema 13," the Pastoral Constitution on the Church in the Modern World, than in other of the conciliar statements. But in the Decree on the Apostolate of the Laity, for example, Christian couples are reminded that today more than ever "it is the supreme task of their apostolate to manifest and prove by their own way of life the unbreakable and sacred character of the marriage bond."[7]

In the passages excerpted above from "Schema 13" marriage is not specified as Christian; it is a question simply of marriage as instituted by the Author of nature and the indissoluble bond that comes into existence through the exchange of consent. It is interesting to note that the unbreakable bond of marriage is reasserted in terms of a threefold good accruing to the offspring, to the spouses themselves and to society. These goods, in other words, are seen to be consequent upon the preservation of indissolubility.

In view of all this, it should perhaps seem more than curious that the Catholic Church would dissolve any marriage. After all, not even a divine dispensation can take away consequences which are *per se* evil. In point of fact, however, the Church does dissolve valid marriages—and this with a view to the good consequences that obtain: namely, the supreme law, the salvation of souls. As the eminent Dominican canonist Antoninus Abate notes so aptly: "In practice, circumstances can arise in which the salvation of souls cannot be envisaged unless man's normal obligation of obeying the divine law be suspended."[8]

The circumstances in question, however, are those which have to do with conversion to the Catholic faith. This is explained by another canonist as a just cause for the pope "to judge that God would want him to grant an exception. There are cases in which conversion to the true faith, and consequently the way of eternal salvation, would be too difficult if dissolution were not possible. In such instances the pope intervenes *in favorem fidei* to sever a bond which lacks the indissolubility of a consummated marriage between the baptized."[9]

One may recall, for example, the constitution *Populis* (Jan. 25, 1585) in which Pope Gregory XIII permitted converts the liberty to contract new marriages in order that the danger of incontinence might be averted if the new converts were to persevere more resolutely in their faith and set good example for others.[10] To facilitate the way of eternal salvation is surely reasonable; indeed, the actual practice of dissolution and the reason which prompts it appear to be more reasonable than the reason commonly adduced by canonists (and moralists) to justify the practice—namely, "the proof that the pope has this power rests upon the use which has been made of it."[11]

To say that because a pope does or has done something he therefore has the requisite authority is not to say that when he acts contrary now to what had been commonly thought, he acts without reason. Nor is it sufficient to say that he acts simply because he has a just cause. The just cause—for example, *in favorem fidei*—is seen more fully to be just because of theological and anthropological insights. Ideally, the Church must reflect in its positive formulations the good news of salvation.

The determination that a marriage between Christians which has been sexually consummated is absolutely indissoluble was arrived at only after many centuries. It is a refinement in theological thinking and, in legislative consequence, in canonical formulation. But further refinement is still possible. The Christian understanding of the complex reality that is marriage is not based exclusively on Revelation. In the words of the prominent Dutch theologian, Edward Schillebeeckx: "It is important to bear in mind that, although Christ declared that marriage was indissoluble, he did not tell us where the element that constituted marriage was situated—what in fact made a marriage a marriage, what made it the reality which he called absolutely indissoluble. This is a problem of anthropology, since it is concerned with the human reality, the essence of which man must try to clarify in its historical context."[12]

In view of man's historical development it would seem most unwise to assert that in this "ultramodern" era we have conclusively (that is, absolutely) determined the nature of marriage whether natural or Christian. Indeed, in their conciliar deliberations the bishops at Vatican II directed the attention of all to a consideration of marriage, among other "particularly urgent" problems, "in the light of the gospel and of human experience."[13] Our own purpose now is to view consummation in this same light.

The code of canon law succinctly states the Catholic position when it declares that in the case of a Christian marriage indissolubility obtains a special firmness by reason of the sacrament[14] and that death alone dissolves a valid marriage that is sacramental and consummated.[15] The special firmness is seen to be completely solidified by reason of consummation which itself is seen to be the decisive factor according to the reasoning of theologians.

Cardinal Cajetan nicely summarizes the scholastic (and subsequently traditional) teaching in this regard. He distinguishes the four conditions that attach to matrimony: the *sacramentum tantum*, the *res et sacramentum*, the *res tantum significata et contenta* and the *res tantum significata et non contenta*. The *sacramentum tantum* is said to be those sensible acts whereby marriage is contracted, not absolutely however since this same obtains considering marriage as an *officium naturae;* rather, it is these acts considered as both significative and causative of invisible grace by reason of divine institution. The *res et sacramentum* is called the very bond of marriage, but again not absolutely for the same reason; rather, because as divinely instituted it signifies something sacred and disposes one to grace. The *res tantum significata et contenta* is the *gratia gratum faciens* which the sacrament of matrimony affords enabling spouses to live their marriage holily.

The *res tantum significata et non contenta* admits of a threefold distinction: namely, the spiritual conjunction through charity between God and the soul, the conjunction through charity between Christ and his Church, and the conjunction through personal union between the Word and human nature; this last is the actual conformity of Christ to his Church. With this in mind, Cajetan can pinpoint precisely where sacramental indissolubility obtains, for only where dispensability is seen to be incompatible is indissolubility to be found.

He determines that the indissolubility of marriage stems from the *res tantum significata et non contenta* and, more precisely, under the aspect of its being a sign of the union between Christ and his Church. Moreover, he draws on the actual practice of the Church to confirm the doctrine of St. Thomas that only a consummated marriage is thus significative; a *matrimonium ratum* but *non consummatum* signifies the union between God and the soul through charity.[16] The indissolubility of marriage therefore is seen to be rooted in its sacramentality and is effected finally (absolutely) through the (first) physical act of true sexual intercourse.

That the first act of marital coitus should be regarded as effective of absolute indissolubility was not always the case; indeed, in point of historical fact the development of this idea is long and involved.[17] The concept involved may be considered both theologically and legally. Theologically, to cite an earlier and respected author:

> The ultimate reason for this inflexibility may be found in the mystical signification of Christian marriage. According to St. Paul (Ephesians 5:32), marriage between Christians reproduces the perfect union which exists forever between Christ and his Church. Now this reproduction is achieved in its perfection in marriage between baptized persons which has been consummated. Common sense teaches us that by the use of the conjugal right marriage receives a sort of completion; something irreparable has taken place; the affective and verbal self-surrender has been supplemented by an actual physical one which justifies the expression, very significant of itself, of *consummated marriage*. It is consummated in the physical order, and it is also consummated in the symbolical and mystical order, in which it represents the indefectible union between Christ and his Church.[18]

The appeal to "common sense" is most interesting. From the standpoint of terminology, as far as we can determine, Gratian is the first to speak of a marriage as *consummatum*.[19] Legally, conjugal coitus is defined "according to its physiological elements as the penetration of the vagina by the male organ and the emission of true semen within it. If any of these elements is wanting there is no consummation."[20] (There is further discussion too regarding the nature of true semen.) Moreover:

> 2. If conjugal intercourse has been had only with the use of contraceptive instruments several cases may be distinguished: if the instrument was used by the man, there is no consummation; if it was used by the woman the case would be doubtful.

> 3. If birth prevention has taken the form of onanism in the strict sense, it may be admitted that the act is not a consummation of the marriage; but if this fact appears in the course of proceedings for a dispensation from the bond, the dispensation will not be granted, even though it be proved that the marriage was not consummated.[21]

This view of consummation, by way of interpreting canon 1119, is not only "according to its physiological elements"; it is exclusively physiological. If law looks to the external and minimal, further casuistic considerations make even more precise how consummation is to be understood. A marriage is regarded as consummated and hence absolutely indissoluble even if coitus is accomplished by force or fraud.[22] Still more remarkably, in a reply to the query whether an actual human act of intercourse in contrast to a mere animal act (or rape) is required for the consummation of a marriage the Congregation of the Sacraments answered in the negative.[23] All that is required, therefore, regardless of any other consideration, is vaginal penetration with seminal emission.

While it is proper to canon law to specify what constitutes consummation, the law nonetheless remains open to reformulation in view of insights which theology provides, insights borrowed in part from other disciplines. Although it may be objected that the consent (to each other's body) once given perdures because never revoked, nonetheless one might reasonably hope that, since sexual intercourse supplements the "affective and verbal self-surrender," the law would exclude any physical act that is merely animal. "Common sense" might also be appealed to here.

Admittedly the first act of conjugal intercourse adds a new dimension to the marriage. Thereby marriage does receive a "sort of completion; something irreparable *has* taken place." According to present teaching, the exchange of consent is now completed in a special way; the bond that has been called into existence by the consent of the spouses is, by reason of this initial sexual experience, permanent and the consent or commitment effected by the consent is therefore irrevocable. But this is so essentially because consummation in the physical order represents consummation in the "symbolical and mystical order." However, just as there are different degrees of indissolubility (according to whether a marriage is sacramental or not, sexually consummated or not), it would seem that the concept of consummation should admit of further distinction, of different levels or degrees which have a bearing on dissolubility. And hence on this basis it should be possible to dissolve a "non-consummated" marriage, namely, a marriage that is not sufficiently consummated.

Consummation is a forceful word. It is a conclusive word. Since in question is a conclusion or completion of a sort, it would be more true to say that sexual intercourse consummates the promise of marriage or engagement, now legally recognized by the formal and public exchange of consent. In this sense the understanding of consummation must be physiological. But it would seem that this whole approach reflects more the Church's traditional insistence on the primary purpose of marriage, namely the procreation (and education) of children,[24] rather than the relationship of Christ to his Church.

Love, as will be pointed out in a moment, is not required for a valid marriage. Consequently, one may legitimately wonder how in the symbolical and mystical order a genitally consummated but loveless marriage represents the "indefectible union between Christ and his Church." The emphasis on the primary purpose of marriage is clear also from the determination that if the first act of conjugal coitus is to be a consummating one it must be *per se* apt for generation. Similarly, the canonical stipulation of age regarding marriage—sixteen years of age for males, fourteen for females[25]—looks to procreation. Before the code the age was fixed at fourteen for males, twelve for females; moreover, whereas present legislation is not directly concerned with puberty, the attainment of puberty even before the specified canonical ages brought with it the capacity to marry.

Although it is true that the code takes into account local customs in this regard,[26] it is clear that the ability to place procreative acts is the decisive element and that the emphasis is on human physiology—which, as reproductive, is not specifically human. This same emphasis is clear also from a consideration of the minimal amount of knowledge required to contract marriage validly; the couple need have only some knowledge of procreation and permanence.[27]

It is fifty years since the code appeared. Even in this short time the whole cultural and social picture, at least in the West, has changed drastically. Accordingly, if the concept of consummation is not to be restricted to an exclusively biological understanding, then these minimal determinations, though perhaps sufficient for validity, must be seen as too minimal to effect absolute indissolubility. Moreover, since at Vatican II the bishops chose not to specify any end of marriage as "primary," then for this reason too the concept of consummation may be re-evaluated.

We are suggesting then that since a sacramental marriage is regarded as indissoluble under the aspect of the *res tantum significata et non contenta,* most precisely as significative of the spiritual union through charity between Christ and his Church, so too the idea of consummation itself might be made more precise. The objection is an obvious one that, "since this seems to be impossible, it is difficult to see how this proposal can lead to a solution of the divorce-remarriage problem."[28]

More precisely, it is objected that "the condition of spiritual union would have to be determined in such a way that its presence or absence could objectively be established in every marriage, independently of the partners' wish to dissolve it or not" and that, as in the case of fear, "it seems impossible to delineate the condition of validity satisfactorily to a point which would enable the ecclesiastical judge to apply it to marriage failures."[29] But it is exactly this lack of legal precision which makes possible a certain leeway. (Many dissolutions and invalidations are on the basis of "force and fear.") Legally fixed limits admit of latitude within those limits. A legally recognized open-ended view admits, clearly, of greater latitude— a latitude to be used, of course, with great discretion.

Regardless of the emphasis on the importance of love in marriage and the moral obligation of the spouses to show their love for each other, from a strictly juridical standpoint love is not regarded as essential to (the validity of) marriage.[30] It is seen to be necessary, but nonetheless of no decisive importance. This juridical view of marriage, according to which the marital bond exists by reason of the free and mutual exchange of consent and is independent in its own right, is certainly valid if both the intention and the ability to place procreative acts are the most important (primary) considerations.

However, since love is clearly essential for a successful and happy marriage the ability to love—with a love normally considered proper to human marriage—should also be a legal requisite just as it is a moral one. But actual ability is determinable only in the concrete—as is evidenced, for example, in the case of sexual impotence that is relative; this will also be pointed out in the instance of certain sexual anomalies. (The objection is not valid that conjugal unions would then be simply "trial marriages" for there is the publicly vowed intention of permanence, and dissolution is not left to the whim of the partners.)

The oneness brought about by love is by reason of the mutual modification of the wills of the lovers. Just as in physiological consummation which is expressive of this oneness the sexual organs must be proportionate, so too psychologically or psychosexually "the union which is achieved in the actual mutual modification of the wills of the lovers presupposes the suitability, fitness and adaptability of this mutual modification."[31]

It can be objected that just as subsequent sexual impotence in no way affects the integrity of the marriage bond, neither does the subsequent inability to love one's spouse make the bond dissoluble. Although one may be unable to express his love sexually he can still (and in fact must) be a loving spouse. However, to deny that one need be able to love or that he must love, that the ability to love plays an essential part in establishing the decisive element of consummation, is to maintain a static notion of what constitutes consummation, a notion that is not consonant with the dignity of the human person. Suitability and adaptability and the actual and constant mutual modification all bespeak something dynamic.

The marriage bond called into existence by the mutual consent of the spouses and specially strengthened by sexual consummation is a reality loaded with potential or perfectibility. We may agree that the "first act of sexual union does not 'complete' the marriage contract in the sense of executing that contract once and for all: the contracted obligation, though fulfilled in each act, is yet never 'fulfilled' until the death of either partner breaks the very bond itself."[32] But it is the degree to which this potential has been actualized that must constitute our understanding of consummation as that which effects absolute indissolubility.

Consummation is clearly a process culminating finally with the death of either partner. But it happens at times that this very process ceases long before the death of either partner. For some the process can resume; for others it is impossible of resumption. As something dynamic marriage is meant to help spouses and their children achieve a certain fulness of life. Indeed, spouses must be able not only to place acts said to be *per se* apt for the begetting of children; they must be able to vivify each other, to communicate life to one another and to their offspring on as many levels as possible and as fully as possible on each of those levels. This is what consummation is all about. It is consummation thus understood that should be decisive in the determination of what constitutes an absolutely indissoluble bond.

Although of its nature love cannot be legally defined nor the degree of existing love between a couple legally delineated, legal recognition could be given to a prudential establishing of whether marital love, by which we understand psychological or psychosexual consummation (or spiritual union), really exists and whether it exists to a degree sufficient to determine that dissolution is no longer possible. Since the ability to love and to love in a way proportionate to the demands of marriage is something that can be determined only in the framework of an existing marriage (in a given culture), its presence or absence can be objectively established by prudent men in terms of situations that arise and perdure. We think here of several such situations which could be judged to be sufficiently indicative of the absence of consummation to the degree effecting absolute indissolubility.

There is, first of all, the situation of the spouse who has been deserted (and perhaps successfully but unjustly has been sued for divorce). Desertion can effectively remove the ability—if indeed it ever existed, and more will be said of this in the context of sexual aberrations—to consummate a marriage. From a human standpoint, to insist that the couple are still "two in one" can ordinarily have only crippling results. That is, the potential of the deserted spouse to love can no longer be actualized in the way proper to marriage. Sublimation may indeed solve the problem but this presupposes the ability to sublimate. The law could determine, with a certain amount of flexibility (lest the year and day be rigidly specified), within how much time after a marriage desertion would be regarded as such grounds, or the length of time before which desertion would be regarded as legal grounds. Both the law and its application require a human prudent judgment. (Is it not this that is meant by "common sense"?)

Sexual perversion, secondly, strikes at the very heart of the conjugal relationship. This relationship is thoroughly sexual but male-female complementarity is not exclusively genital. And it is precisely for this reason, as we have tried to indicate, that the concept of consummation must be broadened. Even though consummation as canonically understood can take place, sexual perversity clearly dehumanizes marriage. The whole gamut of such perversity need not be discussed here although it may be helpful to illustrate it with the instance of homosexuality, which has occasioned a good bit of discussion.[33] In this regard the conditions attaching to error regarding the quality of the person, for example, as a basis of invalidity are formidable.[34] On the other hand, dissolution of a still dissoluble bond, according to prudent judgment, readily and reasonably obviates otherwise legally complex considerations.

Thirdly, and closely allied to the situation suggested above, is the matter of promiscuous adultery. It is a type of sexual perversion, although in traditional moral terminology adultery is not regarded as an unnatural act. Adultery, promiscuous or infrequent, however, does militate directly against the nature of marriage. In 1957 for the first time the Rota granted a decree of nullity to a marriage involving a nymphomaniac for the reason that nymphomania has "the juridical figure of a diriment impediment and is quite similar to the impediment of impotence."[35] Although it is a question here of invalidity, of declaring a marriage null instead of dissolving an existing bond, it is important to note that the "impotence" in question, the inability to assume the obligations of the contract, was determined, as suggested above regarding the ability to love, within the context of a given union.

In view of advances in the past half century in the fields of psychology and psychiatry, the code understandably has no specific legislation concerning psychic impotence and in consequence cases must be adjudicated. To speak of promiscuous adultery is not to define it; indeed, it cannot be defined since promiscuity has a relative connotation. But it can be determined in the practical order by the judgment of reasonable men, a determination that could permit the dissolution of a valid (or doubtfully valid) but non-consummated marriage.

Also frustrative of the perfectibility of marriage are the matters of addiction to alcohol or drugs, abuse of the other spouse (whether physical or emotional), and certain psychological disorders other than those of a sexual nature. Here again definition of terms is not possible, but the matters in question are undeniable in their effects. And, therefore, the absence of sufficient consummation in a given marriage could be established according to a prudential judgment with dissolution as the solution.

While these various possibilities are not recounted in any order of importance since they are virtually all destructive of the potential of marriage, there is, further, the matter of apostasy. While the good example of the believing spouse may indeed win over the unbelieving one (cf. 1 Pet 3: 1f.), often enough rejection of the faith by one spouse is most harmful to the one who is striving to remain faithful and to any children as well. The unbeliever becomes a real *scandalum* in the true sense of the word, and thereby effectively prevents a dynamic two-in-oneness. (Present ecclesiastical privileges which dissolve valid marriages do so *in favorem fidei*. In fact, one such ecclesiastical privilege has been extended to a non-Catholic spouse in a Fresno case in which, moreover, the "praevia conversione" clause was dispensed from.[36])

And finally, we would suggest the matter of voluntary sterilization or the repeated practice of contraception without the consent of the other spouse. Just as the intention to exclude children vitiates the marital contract from the start, so too the prevention of conception as we have qualified it should be regarded as such an injustice to the unwilling spouse, and therefore such an obstacle to genuine love that dissolution of the bond can still be considered possible.

Each of these several possibilities is certainly grounds for separation and all are encompassed by the all too familiar expression "incompatibility."[37] In fact, some of these same ones are regarded among the Eastern Orthodox as just causes for divorce with the right to remarry.[38]

We have emphasized the matter of prudential judgment. Who is to make that judgment? The clerical members of ecclesiastical marriage tribunals are assigned on the basis of both their knowledge of Church law and practice and their prudence in applying that law. The presence of psychiatrists, psychologists and professionally trained marriage counselors, preferably married themselves, as well as other select married couples on those tribunals, is equally essential if the consummation of a marriage in question is to be judged in a competent human way. That these persons are all prudent is a legitimate presumption. Their consensus could easily be accepted as a prudential judgment.

The natural law argumentation which we summarized at the beginning would have to be taken into account but would not have to be regarded as absolute—just as in the case of ecclesiastical privileges whereby marriages are now dissolved. Privileges, as we have already noted, do not remove *per se* consequences; a privilege is justified in practice when it has been determined that *per accidens* those consequences will not ensue. Moreover, the potential for the eventual success of a marriage would also have to be prudently evaluated. To ensure the greatest equity the same judicial system of appeals should be retained.

The excellent and conscientious attempts of canonists, on the one hand, to make more precise the essential conditions of psychic ability (inability) to contract a valid marriage appear doomed to failure. We have accepted their own admission that the whole area is too nebulous to admit of definition.[39] Even if legal definitions could be formulated, determining when they applied would still be a matter of prudential judgment. On the other hand, the suggestion that the sword of divorce is the only realistic remedy, instead of other attempts to unravel the Gordian knot,[40] is not likely to be effective either—at least for some time to come, even though it may be conclusively shown that the Church does in fact have this power.

For these reasons and others, dissolution on the basis of non-consummation appears presently to be the *via media* through the impasse. First of all, dissolubility and validity are not incompatible; valid marriages are dissolved. Neither, secondly, is sacramentality incompatible with dissolubility. Thirdly, the common teaching, even though it is not *de fide*, regarding the indissolubility of a sacramental consummated marriage is respected and, in fact, is enhanced because the dynamic quality of human nature is further recognized, a recognition that is seen to preserve and promote the dignity of the human person. And finally, the ability to love as demonstrated concretely would seem to represent better the indissoluble relationship of Christ to his Church.

It is not a question of a fixed concept here of the object of consent, or of a multiplicity of distinctions, but of the historically conditioned reality that is marriage.[41] This attempt to resolve the dilemma of reconciling justice and mercy is not a "tortuously devious means"[42]; it is neither tortuous nor devious. On the contrary, it is as direct as the suggestion that divorce is the only remedy. Dissolution on the basis of non-consummation understood more broadly is equivalent to divorce in the same sense that dissolutions presently granted are so regarded, namely the severance of a bond that is still dissoluble.

The power to legislate impediments to marriage is exercised with a view to protecting the sacredness of the bond and the persons who enter marriage. One would hope that the very perfectibility of the spouses would be better protected—a protection afforded by a legally recognized but legally undefined broader concept of consummation. Nor is this a legal fiction as is, for example, a *sanatio in radice*. Further, even if a given couple should not want to petition for dissolution on the grounds of non-consummation, the validity of their marriage can still be recognized. Indeed, validity itself may be overlooked in given instances (when, namely, knowledge thereof would give rise to grave inconveniences, when professional secrecy would be violated, etc.).[43]

The suggestion that non-consummation be declared in cases of sterility is a positive attempt to enlarge the concept of consummation but it is unreal.[44] If actual procreation is the determinant of a consummated marriage, then the *una caro* of marriage, the *duo in carne una* (Gen 2:24; Mt 19:5), would be impossible of realization in childless marriages. But this is not the case.[45]

There was some dispute among the scholastics on the precise meaning of *una caro*. Physiologically, sexual intercourse is merely the juxtaposition of two bodies; husband and wife still retain their individual identity. It is not his body and her body but their body, yet there are still two bodies involved. To suggest that the couple become two in one flesh in the flesh of their offspring is to deny, as mentioned above, that *una caro* is possible where conception is impossible. Rather, *una caro* bespeaks— that is, signifies and strengthens—the *unio animorum*,[46] a union which we may rightly call psychological consummation or spiritual union. The above suggestion, however, does prompt us to observe that generation is a factor to be considered. That is, the welfare of the children of a marriage being contested as non-consummated must surely be taken into account as was done, for example, in the Fresno cases.[47]

A comparison with another matter may be helpful. When moralists speak of *irritatio votorum*, one of the reasons adduced is the *jus tertii* which must be respected. Offence to the rights of a third party is a justifiable basis for relaxing the obligation of the vow.[48] The vow, however, is said to be annuled (although strictly speaking it was originally valid), and this in virtue of the power which one in authority has either over the person who made the vow or over the matter of the vow. The Catholic Church, it is clear, has this power and there is no reason why the power of the keys may not be extended to dissolution for non-consummation otherwise understood.

In this same regard, according to canon 1311, a vow ceases to bind if, among other reasons, there is a substantial change in the matter promised. Moralists explain that this obtains if the existing situation is impeditive of a greater good or is impossible or useless: "in fact, a vow ceases also if an accidental but notable circumstance occurs which, had it been foreseen, would have kept one from making the vow, for this change is rightly equated with a substantial change—unless the common good *ipso facto* stands in the way of cessation."[49] Since the non-permanence of marriage is regarded as contrary to the common good, in canonical jurisprudence (which must remain distinct from moral theology) the above explanation of the meaning of substantial change has not been applied to the marriage contract.

Examples are legion of marriages that would never have been contracted had one spouse known beforehand that the other was promiscuously or perversely inclined, or an alcoholic, etc. Indeed, even when outright deception has actually been the case the legal interpretation of error regarding the quality of the person opts for the validity of the marriage. However, since the notion of the common good does not stand in the way of the dissolution of marriages by Pauline or papal privilege, it can hardly be appealed to as an objection to dissolution for non-consummation understood in the sense of genuinely human marital union which has become impossible, or when the existing situation is impeditive of a greater good and is useless.

One further comparison may also add something to an understanding of the strength of a marital bond. In order to emphasize the firmness of a relationship between a person and his duty or state in life the Church uses terminology (and therefore concepts) proper to the conjugal state. A bishop is said to be wedded to his see[50] and a religious is said to be espoused to Christ. Although this may be some kind of a mystical union, whatever its origin it is clear that the union is dissoluble. Bishops can resign and be transferred, and religious can be dispensed from their vows. (Moreover, it is not clear what "consummates" such a union.)

At this point additional reasons, if only as arguments *ad hominem,* may perhaps be suggested as sufficient to warrant at least a reconsideration of the nature of (non-)consummation with a view toward dissolubility. Among them: the situation today of so many who are living in invalid second marriages[51]; the pastoral plea that something be done for those who married in haste[52]; the reason adduced by Pope Gregory in *Populis,* namely the danger of loss of faith and incontinence; the fact that the necessary natural disposition for the grace of the sacrament to be operative is at times impossible to bring about; instances when the invalidity of given marriages is factually clear or can be reasonably presumed but cannot be legally established (for example, when one spouse will not cooperate or cannot be reached for cooperation[53]); the popular notion that, in the instance of a second marriage, the law favors the unbaptized and those who though bound to the Catholic form chose in the first instance not to observe it. All of these reasons bolster the conviction that something must be done to help those whose marital status has become for them a real obstacle to happiness and holiness of life.

We have endeavored to show that the present understanding of consummation is a legal one (based on traditional theological understanding) but not an immutable or absolute one. The ability to effect such a consummation is required for the validity of a marriage. The concept of validity itself is a legal one and as such is narrow and minimal; it could, however, be enlarged. But the more this concept would be enlarged, the more restricted would become the natural right to marry; at the same time, of course, the basis for dissolution (annulment) by declaring marriages invalid would thereby be wider. All acknowledge that the right to marry is clearly not an unrestricted right and most would doubtless agree that because of the demands which marriage makes today, at least in certain societies, the right to marry should be somewhat more restricted than it presently is—for example, in terms of age and understanding. Our own concern, however, has been to expand the concept of consummation.

Since in Roman Catholic teaching a more firmly indissoluble bond obtains by reason of sacramentality, and an absolutely indissoluble one by reason of genital consummation, this latter factor is seen to confer the fulness (in a certain sense) of sacramental signification. Moreover, since man and woman can and should complement each other on all levels of their personality, a fact of life more appreciated in our own day, for our own part we think it reasonable to postulate a dynamic understanding of consummation as effective of indissolubility, of consummation understood in the sense of the *unio animorum* of the couple as made concrete in their *communio vitae*—to postulate, in a word, that the spouses themselves have something decisive to say about the consummation of their marriage, something expressed by their actual manner of life.

Admittedly, carnal consummation does bring about a "sort of completion" which death makes to be final. We are submitting, therefore, that consummation as effecting absolute indissolubility should be viewed in terms of a dynamic love relationship that obtains between husband and wife, more precisely between *this* husband and *this* wife, and that somewhere between the initial completion and final completion the fact of consummation be determined. The practical problem lies in determining precisely how and where this should obtain before a marriage might be regarded as still dissoluble because non-consummated or declared indissoluble. (One could perhaps speak of *consummatio tantum* or the first physical act of marital coitus, the *res et consummatio* or the union itself signified and effected by that act, and the *res tantum* both *significata sed non perfecta* in the sense of *non adequate perfecta* and hence dissoluble and *significata et perfecta* and therefore indissoluble.)

We have suggested that, the doctrine of the indissolubility of a sacramental consummated marriage remaining intact, this be resolved by a prudential judgment, for this appears to be the only realistic way to deal with the contingencies to which marriage is subjected in a changing world, a way which both preserves and enhances the dignity of marriage and of those who elect to serve God in the conjugal state.

MARTIN NOLAN

The Principle of Totality
in Moral Theology

THE NATURE OF TOTALITY

On the 13th of September, 1952, Pope Pius XII addressed the
First International Congress on the Histopathology of the Nervous System in the following words:

> The principle of totality affirms that the part exists for the
> whole, and that, consequently, the good of the part remains
> subordinate to the good of the whole; that the good of the
> whole is the determining factor in regard to the part, and
> can dispose of the part in its own interest. The principle
> flows from the essence of notions and things, and must, for
> that reason, have an absolute value.[1]

The principle is self-evident, and has a-prioristic force, whether
in the learned sayings of the philosopher[2] or for the simple peas-
ant band who listened to Christ.[3] It is woven into the fabric
of theology and philosophy through the centuries,[4] and can be
seen at play in the gigantic efforts of the great minds towards
synthesis. With the full backing of tradition, then, Pius XII
could assert that the principle has absolute value. What, however, he immediately adds by way of explanation, is as important as the understanding of the principle itself:

> In regard to the principle of totality in itself: in order to be
> able to apply it correctly, it is always necessary, first of all,

to explain certain presuppositions. The first presupposition is the clarification of the *quaestio facti,* the question of fact: are the objects to which the principle is applied in relation to one another as whole to part? A second presupposition: the clarification of the nature, the extent and the strict nature of this relationship. Is it on the level of essence, or only on that of action, or on both levels? Is it applied to the part under a determined aspect or under every aspect? And in the field of application, does the whole completely absorb the part, or does it leave it a limited finality of its own, a limited independence? The answer to these questions can never be inferred from the principle of totality itself: this would resemble a vicious circle. It must be drawn from other facts and other knowledge.[5]

While the principle, then, is absolute and self-evident, its application calls for previous investigation and ascertainment of the case in hand. Preoccupation with the psycho-physical totality, man, and the moral totality, society, and their mutual relationships as whole and part, called forth Pius' teaching on the principle. A brief review of the case-work will provide a field for interpretation.

1. TOTALITIES

The foregoing exposition on the principle of totality was given by the pope in the course of dealing with "the interests of the community as a justification for new medical methods of research and cure."[6] In answer to the question whether the public authority could really limit or suppress the right of the individual to this body and life, to corporal and psychological integrity in the interests of society, the pope expounded the Church doctrine on the relationship that exists between the individual and society in regard to personal rights. He then went on to develop the same doctrine in the light of the principle of totality.

The course of theological debate on the principle of totality over the past decades centered on the physical totality of man. Yet this physical whole was considered under two aspects: first, in its relations to the social totality and second, insofar as it is itself an ordered totality. On this double aspect the pope's oft-repeated teaching dwelt.[7]

During the Third Reich claims were made by the State to the life and integrity of the citizens in virtue of an application of the principle of totality, which was, however, unwarranted. Adolf Hitler did not expressly make the State the end of the individual. The State was a means to attain the end, namely, to preserve those primordial elements of the Aryan stock, the superior race. To this end, the State took it upon itself to limit man's natural right to life and integrity.[8] On July 14, 1933, was promulgated the "law for the prevention of hereditarily diseased offspring." The law provided for the use of police action and physical force for the carrying out of its provisions.[9] Already by December 31, 1934, 56,244 people were ordered to be sterilized. Not only was the physical integrity of man encroached upon, but claims were made on his very life for the common good.[10]

Here the good of the whole, the preservation of the pure strains in the race, was considered as ample justification for the disposal of the members who, in the eyes of the State, were not suitable to its end. The members were utterly subordinate to the good of the whole to which they belonged. Had not St. Thomas used the principle similarly to justify capital punishment?

> Every part is naturally for the whole. Every individual person is compared to the whole community as a part to the whole. And therefore if any man is dangerous to the community and a corrupter of it on account of some sin, it is praiseworthy and healthy to kill him.[11]

Had not a stream of moralists followed him in this argument?[12] Nevertheless, some theologians such as James of Viterbo,[13] John Duns Scotus,[14] Nicholas of Occam,[15] Layman,[16] and others, took exception to the simplistic application that emerges from a first reading of St. Thomas.

The teachings of Pius XII were a vehement reaction to the

extremes of application to which the totalitarian states brought the principle. He complained that it was characteristic of totalitarian states to show little regard for the means they make use of in pursuit of their aims.[17] Even in the case of capital punishment, he was at pains to preclude the principle of totality as its justification.[18] It was not that the principle itself was disputed—rather, the conditions for applying it were unverified.[19]

The pontiff underscored the difference between a totality on the level of being and one merely on the level of action, that is, one constituted by the combined activity of the members. In the former, each little part depended for its very existence on its being a member of this whole, such as a hand in the body. Thus the good of the body, in which the good of the part was totally absorbed, could in some circumstances demand the suppression of the part. When the State however laid claims without more ado to the physical existence of the members comprising it, it was simply overlooking the question of fact, namely, that it in no way possessed a physical entity, with its members depending on it for their very being.[20]

Medical science, in the meantime, was making vast strides. Experimentation always, and often failure, are the necessary first steps in the development of new treatments and cures. What eventually turns to the immense benefit of mankind has often behind it a long history of trial and error, and a list of funerals. When experimentation is but the last desperate measure to save a life already doomed, then the intervention is really for the good of the whole person. If one submits to experiments, not for one's own health, but to benefit others and eventually the whole of mankind, the principle of totality once more points out the directions of morality. In reaction to the pretensions of the totalitarian states Pius XII asserted:

> The physical organism of living beings, plants, animals and man have a unity existing on its own: each of the members, for example, the hand, the foot, the heart, the eye is an integral part, destined in its whole being to be inserted into the totality of the organism. Outside the organism, on account

of its very nature, it possesses no meaning, no finality; it is entirely absorbed by the totality of the organism to which it is tied.[21]

Although a rigid application of the stated norms would seem to eliminate any possibility of a person's submitting to interventions for the sake of another or of mankind in general, Pius XII nevertheless saw the necessity of some experimentation. To avoid risks altogether would be beyond human capabilities, and in fact paralyze research.[22] That it was permissible to experiment, within certain limits, despite the oft-repeated doctrine on totality, was the opinion of most moralists, of whom notable examples are Shinners,[23] Tesson,[24] Kelly[25] and Ford.[26]

On the liceity of organic transplantation among living people a protracted and often hot debate took place. Pius XII spoke on the subject, but was at pains to make it clear that his object was not to condemn the practice in itself, but only insofar as its lawfulness was based on the application of the principle of totality to the moral whole, society. In other words, one could not justify the donation of a kidney to another person on the grounds that, being members of the same social body, the organs of one member had a finality in the body of another.[27]

A further important question presents itself: has organic transplantation, that is, the transplant of an organ or part thereof from a live and healthy person to another in need, been excluded by the principles Pius XII repeatedly insisted upon, and in particular, by the principle of totality as applied to man? Yes, definitely, has been the answer of Fathers Bender, Borg, Tabone, Zalba, McFadden, Madden, Sölch, Perico, Iorio, Hürth and others.[28] Man, they say as Pius said, is usufructuary, not proprietor of his being and its parts, and so may not dispose of them except insofar as he serves the good of that being.[29]

On the other side are ranged Fathers Kelly, Scremin, Bongiovanni, Babbini, Simeone, Groner, Guzzetti, Palazzini, Gunningham and others.[30] The present question was not envisioned, they assert, and provided the function was left intact though an organ or part of it removed, the perfection of the person through charity would justify such an operation. A person could donate a kidney, since a person can lead a normal healthy life on one kidney.

If the principle of totality is absolute in the material sense of the word, then it seems to exclude both experimentation and transplantation under any circumstances. If bodily and psychic integrity is something given by God to be used, but never diminished, except insofar as this is demanded by prudent administration of what is God's, not man's, then it is difficult to see any possible escape from the conclusion just quoted. Did the pontiff have such a material outlook on the content and application of the principle?

2. INTERPRETATION

One of the most pregnant and yet least-spoken-of statements Pius XII made on the principle of totality is the following:

> To the subordination however of the particular organs to the organism and its own finality, one must add the subordination of the organism to the spiritual finality of the person himself. Some medical experiments of a physical or psychical nature can, on the one hand, entail certain injury to organs or functions, but, on the other, it may be that they are perfectly licit, because they are in keeping with the good of the person and do not transgress the limits placed by the Creator on man's right to dispose of himself.[31]

If the totality of man is conceived as a limited area of space closed off from all its surroundings, into which it is the person's freedom to fit himself, then problems such as that of experimentation for the sake of others and transplantation offer no reasoned solution. Since the principle is all pervading, the advocates of this altruism must officiously ignore its logical conclusions or deny outright its validity in this case. Totality in man is not, however, a line enclosing a limited space like the circumference of a circle. Nor are the various levels of physical, physiological, psychological and spiritual concentric but self-excluding bands in this circle, so that it is impossible to infringe on the one, say, the physical organism, to the advantage of the other, say, spiritual part. "Physicism" in moral theology tends to trace finality in terms of man's physical make-up, and soon ends up in a theological *cul-de-sac*.

Totality can no longer be considered a fixed system into which man chooses to insert himself to be perfect. This is to render God's creation brutally material. His body is not the dictator of laws and limits to him. Rather it is his presence to God and to others in which he unfolds his response. A singular pursuit of bodily health to the neglect of the spirit receives the seal of frustration in death. An unbalanced scramble for spiritual heights to the neglect of the body is a denial of man's own nature, and of the incarnation. The human person, who is this live body, must in it give himself to God and to others to reach fulfilment. The total good to which each single part is subordinate is not that of the body, nor that of the spirit, but that of the whole person.[32] The total good of the whole person however is achieved in actuating oneself in one's innermost reality which is relationship to God and to others.

Whatever exists that is not God is totally relative. The innermost core of all creaturehood is utter relationship. It is cushioned in existence by the cradling hand of God, without which it would lapse into the abysmal nothingness from which it was evoked by God's creative call. To imagine a creature standing apart from God, over against him on its own little independent island of existence, is metaphysical non-sense. To render creaturehood absolute is to relegate it to a fictional existence of the mind. The deeper one penetrates into nature's heart, the more one lights on the sustaining hand of God.

Inanimate nature reflects back to God at its own inanimate level, as, for instance, the overhanging fern is reflected back to the sky in the unseeing eye of the lake. With the emergence of life, the universe related back to God at that level, in the instincts and survival fight of the animal kingdom. With the advent of man, however, the narrow bonds of inanimate or animal relationship were snapped and between God and his universe arose an interpersonal dialogue. The person of man overflows the narrow limits of material existence and inborn drives and reaches out in freedom and love to God. He embodies the response he is called on to make in his domination of nature. He delves into its inner springs to change its course. Its energies he channels and multiplies to his own use. He spans the earth and has begun to conquer the stars. He sheds the shackles inherited from a former age by using what is specifically his as human: his knowledge, to break the bonds of matter that anchor him to the dust of his origins; and his freedom, to elect and create the future into which he wishes himself and his posterity to be ushered.

The human person is, then, relationship, a vast emptiness to be filled—or, in Augustine's words, a restlessness to be quelled only by God.[33] St. Thomas says that man, by his intellect and will, is a potency to all truth and good.[34] This vast emptiness is alone filled by charity which unites him, as a person, with the person of God and of others. This is how the relationship which he is, is actuated. The teaching of Christ is that charity is the basis of the whole law and the prophets[35] and Paul re-echoes this by stating that charity is the fullness of the law.[36]

The total good of the whole person is not discoverable in terms of the person himself—yet it is more intimate to the person than he is to himself.[37] The total good of the whole person is God, who by his graciousness evokes from him an openness to receive and a positive surrender to the gift of fulfilment. Man does not perfect himself by conserving but by giving away. He does not store up but empties himself of self to receive. His perfection is not what he achieves for God but what God achieves for him.

Totality, then, is not in terms of subordination to a self-enclosed whole, but in terms of how one might give himself to the larger perfecting reality in every member and function that he himself is. He gives himself, however, as a whole person to be fulfilled, not to be eliminated.

When wholeness or perfection is considered as a possession of the person almost apart from others, then totality is a cage or network already existing in God's mind, a blueprint to which each person must comply. The universe would then be an established totality into which all its parts, man included, must fully fit to be perfect. Man's freedom would be that of choosing the established order as his own, and making his peace with it. A static view of creation emerges. The contemporary theological view is that of the universe *in via*, in pilgrimage, as something-to-be-achieved by responding to God's continual call. It is not yet perfect, but needs man to dominate its unruly torrents of energy and make of it something new. Man makes of it something utterly new, not simply by his own labor, but by embodying in his own labor his response to God. He gathers up beauty, which he shares with inanimate creation, and the life that he shares with the animal kingdom into his own answer of love. In this answer he opens himself, and the universe of which he is the crown, in surrender to receive from God the immortalizing gift which is the fruit of communion.

If the total good of the whole person, achieved in self-gift, is considered, vast new possibilities arise. Experimentation for the good of another becomes a moral possibility, perhaps at times a demand. Yet the present teaching of the Church is that one may not deliberately run into serious danger of death, nor may one maim oneself either physically or psychically.[38] Should it not seem otherwise: that the more one loves, the more one is prepared to give for another even to the point of life itself?[39] Does not this run counter to all that has been stated?

In the Christian view, life is the continual gift of God to which we open ourselves in receptive surrender. This receptive surrender culminates in death, in which we shed mortality to make place for the unrestrained gift of eternal life. Always, however, it is God's gift, when and howsoever he wishes to bestow it. The present, provisional, "anticipated" life is accepted in which to unfold oneself to God and man. It cannot therefore arbitrarily be discarded as if it were not at each moment received in gift.

Is the bodily organism the untouchable gift of God, already constituted by him in an unchangeable nature? Are all its faculties, functions, organs unalterably marked with a specific finality? While there are unending disputes over particulars, there is general agreement that man has physically and culturally evolved to a vast degree since his appearance on the earth.[40] From the biological point of view, man's organism, like that of the animals, adapted to environment and was modified by it. As he pervaded this universe with his thought, he gradually liberated himself from the limitations of his physical inheritance, and made himself, body-soul, more and more the "dominator" he was called to be.[41] His psychocultural evolution saw him gradually modifying the very environment into which he had been born.[42] He laid hands on space and time, and even reached into the future, pervading it with his thought and planning it out, creating it with God.[43] In this way he unfolds his response to God's word to him: "Be fruitful, multiply, fill the earth and conquer it. Be masters. . . ."[44]

The finalities man finds in his own members converge on the total good of his own person. They are not therefore to be disposed of arbitrarily. He is this body and soul to give himself fully to God and to others, and thus find his fulfilment. The particular finalities, then, do not finish in the physical good of the whole, but point upwards to the person, and through the person, in the free gift of himself in response, to God and to others. It is the person, however, that must remain in the gift of himself: should he deliberately give over in suicide the life that he holds in gift from God, or diminish his possibilities for self-giving by maiming himself, he is acting contrary to his own personhood and thus too contrary to God's law.

Applied to society, the principle of totality shares the relativity of society's function. Any human society is geared at providing a common good—an optimum of condition so that the people comprising the society can come to fulfilment.[45] The optimum conditions will change as fast as time and circumstances do, and so laws need continual adaptation.

Community, on the other hand, reaches beyond the narrow limits of society. Community is welded in love, society is framed in law. Society provides the conditions in which community can, possibly, emerge. As a totality, society is made up of the combined activity of the members striving to establish the conditions called the common good. Since these conditions are themselves measured by their usefulness to the members in the pursuit of their fulfilment, society is extremely limited in the demands it can juridically make on the members. It can make none at all on their physical being, since this in no way makes up the totality of society. Only such actions as are conducive to the conditions called the common good are claimed by society, for it is only of such that it is comprised.

What the juridical totality, "society," cannot demand of its "parts," can indeed be asked of the person by the "community." Only by reaching out of one's own little cell in self-gift to others and to God is perfection achieved. This free, creative outpouring, without which there is no personal fulfilment, overflows the narrow juridical claims that the state can make on a person. The gift of self in transplantation or experimentation is far beyond what the state is entitled to demand in virtue of the principle of totality. The person himself, whom society serves, may well run counter to his own opprtunities for fulfilment if he forecloses himself once and for all against all self-donation of this nature.

Yet, should he give himself in this way, the "totality" to which he subordinates the good of the part is the totality of perfection to which he is called—and which can only be achieved in self-donation to form a community. The community is quite different from a framed society into which man chooses to fit himself. Community is the flowering of love freely given and received. This totality is that without which man is alone and unfulfilled.

Here, then, the seeming enigma finds arrows pointing towards a solution. Man is physical but man is free. The laws in his physique seem fetters to his freedom.[46] If the laws in his physique point to his personal fulfilment, which in turn can only be had by his free self-gift to form a community, they no longer shackle him. His physical and psychical wholeness is his presence, in space and time, to God and to others. Most fundamentally, the human person is relationship, which is perfected by being actuated under God's grace. But it is actuated at the level of personhood, in freedom and love. Man's island existence is also his insulation against fulfilment. His self-gift is what makes him perfect.

On the negative side, no inferior totality or grouping, such as the State, can subordinate the person to itself or make the least demand on what constitutes the person. To do so would not indeed be in virtue of the principle, but rather to the splintering of the wholeness to which the human person is called in community. Society is concerned with conditions: community is the consummate end.

Again on the negative side, one may not reject one's life which is God's gift. Nor may one eliminate the possibility of giving oneself as a person even if it involve maiming oneself, for example, by giving both eyes. The "extent" of physical or psychical self-gift in experimentation or transplantation is no longer to be measured in terms of what is merely physical or psychical integrity. Both the one and the other are coordinated in the human person, and their finality exhausted in the total good of that person. The total good of the person is achieved in self-outpouring in community.

Will this enlarged understanding of the principle point out different solutions to the old problems of mutilation, transplantation, experimentation, sterilization? In the long debate theologians were apt to find themselves in the embarrassing predicament of bartering charity to totality, or *vice versa*, depending on the position they were committed to holding. The "conservative" held that totality confined charity, while the "liberal" saw the hard edge of totality softened in the surge of charity. Yet the only course left open to consistency is to retain both principles to the theological end.

Self-contained physical or psychical integrity and perfection is not to be equated with the perfection of the person; in fact, its exclusive pursuit is to the damage of the whole person. If the person is a relationship to be actuated in self-giving then his perfection is to be thought of in terms of the larger reality to which he opens himself to be filled when he gives. Totality, in the sense explained, makes provision for self-giving, even physically, since the human person is a flesh-and-blood relationship, yet all the while indicating that it must always be self-giving and not self-elimination.

It is no longer a question of physical measurement, but of delicate moral judgment. In a case of mutilation, perhaps even on occasion of sterilization, the discussion is not confined to the organs in question, whether they are directly or indirectly a danger to the whole organism, whether their removal or suppression is compensated by the corresponding benefit to the whole physique, and so on. The good of the whole person is taken into account, and therefore, perforce, his relationship to his family, community and the larger society. While, therefore, exceptional circumstances might call for more drastic procedures in individual cases, the new directions of totality also provide more fundamental reasons for a respect for personal integrity, both psychical and physical.

3. ABSOLUTENESS

In what sense, then, is the principle of totality an absolute in moral theology? It flows from the essence and notion of things, answers Pius XII, and must, for that reason, be considered absolute.[17] The deepest essence and notion of things is relativity to the Absolute who is God. Everything created is in its innermost depths in an all-pervading creaturely relationship or response to the Creator. This is not a static reflection, but a living dialogue. The universe is in movement, with man at its head to express its yearnings. Not alone does each moment of time immediately surrender to the next in a continued stream, but the person of man must at each moment hold himself open to receive the creative Word from God and to respond. God is absolute, unchanging, never withholding himself; while the universe, through the response of man, is being gradually gathered up, possessed, and laid open to receive God's immortalizing gift.

The final, perfect totality is not yet achieved. Man's freedom has its utterly important part to play, as the perfection God plans for his creation is more than material orderliness. It is a communion of people, freely given to each other and together open in positive surrender to God's self-gift. This is how man actuates his potentialities, which are summed up in relationship. His perfection is not something he can have on his own, any more than grace can be conceived as something held apart from God.

The principle is absolute in that it makes the position, progress and direction of all "parts," of everything less than whole towards the consummation of all in communion. The vast cosmic totality envisioned by St. Thomas in his *Summa contra gentiles*[48] is as absolute as its sharing the Creator's gift of himself in existence. The cosmos has the person of man as its crown who, in his personal response, sums up the rest of creaturehood so that Creator and creature are welded in a bond of transforming love. In this all else converges, and since God's love is unrestrained, the creature who, under his grace, opens himself to be pervaded by it, shares most fully in its absoluteness. But always however one is *in via,* marching through the dark of time towards the dawn of a vaster totality.

In the practical order of acts here and now to be performed, one must beware of giving absolute value to what is as passing as time. Often enough the rigidity of material laws seems to hamper the spirit in its flight. Fixed patterns of behavior, taken as good or bad, lay a heavy hand on freedom. Applying the principle of totality to the physical whole, the wider urges of a generous spirit might seem to be kept in check by the laws found written into the flesh. There is, however, no external mode of behavior that is, inevitably, moral or immoral. What is enacted in time and space can embody hate or love, or by remaining indifferent simply fail to rise to the level of human activity. Christ insisted more on what the act contained than on the extrinsic value of the widow's mite,[49] and warned men not to judge.[50] Paul re-echoes his teaching: no matter how impressive one's external activity, without charity it counts for nothing.[51]

Nevertheless, a relative stability of value is to be attributed to certain kinds of actions. Establishing as central the love that fulfils, and spreading out in ever-widening circles to embrace the different human activities, one can state that what fails to be irradiated from that central love is not moral. What opposes love of God or neighbor runs counter to the fundamental direction in each person's heart. It precludes, at least partially, the totality of communion to which all are called.

Are there actions, or norms governing exterior actions, so intimately joined with the precept of love that the one cannot be infringed upon without involving the other? Does the need to love, to be whole, inevitably claim certain similar or identical external actions in which to be expressed and, by the same token, exclude others? External actions are, as a rule, good because they have become the accepted modes of expressing love for God and one's fellowman, and their absence would denote love's absence. At the center, they flow almost immediately from the basic urge, attitudes and acts of charity: reverence for each person, his life, his integrity, be it psychical, physical, social or cultural. The actions themselves are, however, time- and culture-bound. History and cultural anthropology often alarm the moralist and upset his neat patterns: they show that what is abhorred in one area as an insult to God and men, such as, for example, burying the dead instead of burning them, is an act of reverence and love in an adjacent area, while cremating the dead would be offensive in the extreme. They remain modes of expressing what is most stable and enduring in the human person: the yearning to love and be loved, and in this way come to fulfilment.

Similarly, the principle of totality points, in the large picture, to the ultimate wholeness of communion that is achieved by love alone. Every act along the way that "incarnates" that direction is moral. Every thwarting of it is a lapse. Every incarnation of that fundamental direction in the heart of man belongs to the community on their common pilgrimage. For this reason it will fit into patterns of activity which embody respect and love in each for the other. Activity can for this reason be legislated. The ten commandments are a good example. Without love, however, they are nothing. With love they are not commandments. A person who refrains from killing merely because he is commanded from without has not yet risen to his true stature. If he loves, he needs no commandment to keep him from killing.

In the smaller picture of each person along his way, the principle of totality points up the subordination of part to whole. It precludes the minimizing of the person's value, even in his physical integrity. Each person is a totally unique creation by God, in immediate response to him. No inferior grouping can claim him as its part. Everything in him converges in his person, or, in Pius' words, in the "spiritual finality of the person."[52] As person, he flowers in freedom that is self-donating. Body-soul, the whole person, unfolds to God and men to come to his fulfilment. When, as a whole person, he is utterly given over in positive surrender to God and men, then is he perfected.

4. THE CHRISTIAN FULNESS

Moral theology is about God creatively addressing man, and the response this call evokes from man in his daily life. In the Christian economy, the emptiness of man without God is filled up with the gift of the Spirit who fuses people into the Word's response. The Word was addressed to mankind in flesh and blood taken from the Virgin, so that at last there would walk the earth a Man totally open and given over to the master-designs of God. ". . . and this is what he said, on coming into the world: 'God, here I am! I am coming to obey your will.' "[53] At last there was a Person unfolding his total relationship to the Father in flesh and blood. This was embodied in the service of his fellowman, which came to its climax in the full outpouring of himself on the Cross.[54] The point of this outpouring was to "draw all men to himself."[55] The end of all was the fulness of joy[56] that would be fruit of their being perfectly one as he and the Father were,[57] that is, drawn together in perfect interpersonal communion which left nothing of self that was not totally given over.

Such a magnificent vision would of course have been beyond the capabilities of any human person. So the Spirit was pledged[58] and sent[59] to establish the wavering disciples in power and weld them together from within as the mystical person of Christ. The welding power is of course, charity, poured abundantly into the hearts of men by the gift of the Spirit.[60] This charity pervades the person to carry it beyond the narrow bounds of mortality[61] into the eternal communion prayed for by Christ. This is the rimless totality that fulfils. People are drawn from their own little cells of existence by the beauty of God's countenance revealed to them in Christ now incarnate in his people, and soon to be seen "as he is."

Like Christ, people embody their response by making of their persons a living oblation,[62] a continual outpouring of self to their fellowmen. Everything else is subordinated to this supreme end. The human person himself is a "part" to be completed by giving himself, under grace, to that fulfilling communion prayed for by Christ. In relation to this absolute, all else is relative. To delay along the way by erecting as absolutes what will crumble with time is to remain stunted morally. The will of God that perfects is larger than the still-imperfect man who obeys it. He must refuse the temptation to reduce it to his size in neat and tidy patterns. He must instead follow his vocation, which is to rise at each moment to its grandeur, to find himself larger than he was before, and ultimately be fulfilled by it.

KIERAN NOLAN

The Problem of Care for the Dying

The purpose of this chapter is to consider some of the medico-moral problems related to the preservation of life and the prolongation of death. Precisely because of the success of medical science in overcoming many obstacles to man's life and health, many problems of a medico-moral nature have arisen which never existed before. Today it is possible to give a patient medical assistance which provides neither a cure nor a basic improvement, but simply the preservation of life. There is question about whether the medical assistance provided to some patients is really helping to preserve life or rather aiding to prolong death. While speaking of the right of the living to life, is it not also possible to speak of the right of the dying to death?[1]

At the very outset it is important to state some basic Christian axioms with regard to the human person. The documents of the Second Vatican Council repeatedly stress the deep Christian respect for the integrity of the individual and the obligation of society to support and protect each of its members. The Christian concern must be to provide for human survival, and not for mere biological preservation.

Another axiom is the reality of death and its deep Christian significance. The universality of death is a biological necessity. The Christian sees death in the light of sin and the call to enduring life in Christ Jesus.[2] Failure to think through the positive aspects of death for the Christian can only lead to a rather morbid view of sickness, suffering, the act of dying and death itself. A proper understanding of Christian death as the finalization of what was initiated in baptism engenders that hope, joy and peace which only the Christian gospel is capable of providing.

Fortunately, recent studies have served to focus greater attention on the death-resurrection theme of the gospels,[3] and even at the present time such studies are bearing fruit in the various liturgical reforms. Our intention at this point is not to engage in a long discussion on the theology of death, but merely to stress that all Christian moral reflections regarding life and death must spring from divine revelation and man's reflections on human experience.

The problems we here wish to consider spring from the technological and medical advances which some in the medical profession use unintentionally, at times, to the disadvantage of the dying.[4] In 1957, addressing the South Carolina Chapter of the American College of Surgeons, Dr. John Farrell, Professor of the Department of Surgery at the University of Miami School of Medicine, remarked, "I submit that the death bed scenes I witness are not particularly dignified. The family is shoved out into the corridor by the physical presence of intravenous stands, suction machines, oxygen tanks and tubes emanating from every natural and several surgically induced orifices. The last words, if the patient has not been comatose for the past forty-eight hours, are lost behind an oxygen mask. I discuss this, not because I have an answer to the problem but because it is a very real problem which all of us must face. . . ."[5]

In 1961, Dr. Edward Rynearson, emeritus consultant in internal medicine at the Mayo Clinic, Rochester, Minnesota, observed: "There are too many instances, in my opinion, in which patients . . . are kept alive indefinitely by means of tubes inserted into their stomachs, or into their veins, or into their bladders, or into their rectums—and the whole sad scene thus created is encompassed with a cocoon of oxygen which is the next thing to a shroud."[6] In 1963 Dr. John Cavanaugh argued against useless interference medically with the dying process and advocated the right of the patient to die with dignity.[7]

On April 6, 1967, Dr. Rynearson underlined another medico-moral problem when he urged that doctors "should not try to keep 'dead' people alive."[8] He related the case of a woman kept in a Rochester nursing home in an unconscious state for five years at the cost of $50,000 to her family and the county polio fund. When he became aware of the situation Rynearson counseled a relative to see her religious advisor. The result was that they agreed to the doctor's removing the tubes that were keeping the woman alive. Through an autopsy it was discovered that the woman "had no brain." Rynearson urged hospital chaplains and clergymen to help make decisions in such cases.

Despite their sincerest desire to provide good guidance, the fact is that when faced with the complex problems of modern medicine many priests find themselves unable to be as helpful as they would like to be to doctors, patients and their families. Dr. George Hanzel explains: "This situation arises because medicine and moral theology are moving at different rates of speed. A gap has arisen where it would be desirable to have a closer association between these two disciplines."[9]

The general advice which priests recall from their moral theology manuals and which is presently found in the *Directives for Catholic Hospitals* is that, while there is no obligation to make use of extraordinary means to preserve a person's life, neglect of ordinary means is regarded as euthanasia.[10] But it is by no means clear what exactly constitutes ordinary or extraordinary means since, with the advance of science, the extraordinary means of past years become the ordinary means of today.

After making a rather thorough examination of the traditional moral theologians from St. Alphonsus to Aertnys-Damen, Genicot-Salsmans, Jone, Merkelbach, Noldin-Schmitt, Prümmer and Vermeersch, Father Gerald Kelly reports that most of these writers say very little on the subject of ordinary and extraordinary means.[11] The distinction is determined by those things which can be obtained and used without great difficulty, and those which involve excessive difficulty by reason of physical pain, repugnance or expense. With the advent of modern medicine the general distinction appeared less and less helpful. Some authors regarded as extraordinary any artificial means and as ordinary any natural means such as eating, drinking and sleeping. But then it was argued quite clearly that this type of distinction would be of no practical use and that the distinction would be better made between uncommon and common usage.

Whether the particular means is artificial or natural, if it is commonly used it can be regarded as ordinary.[12] The beginnings of this awareness are apparent at the start of the century when moral theologians only very gradually approved the use of surgery. In 1882 Capellmann was encouraging theologians to modify their opinions about the danger of major operations.[13] With the advance in medicine in every decade, the problem areas increased for the moralists to such an extent that in 1960 one author wrote, "When the real question arises: namely, are the advances of modern medicine in general to be classified as ordinary or extraordinary means; and in particular, what is to be said of modern surgery, X-ray treatment, Wangensteen tubes, oxygen tents, iron lungs and intravenous feeding, the moderns go riding madly off in all directions."[14]

It is important to bear in mind that neither ordinary nor extraordinary means are obligatory unless there is reasonable hope of checking or curing the disease. This is the general teaching of all authors either implicitly or explicitly, as Kelly has pointed out.[15] In recent years this general teaching has been subject to some rather severe testing. The question arises whether intravenous feeding should be provided a dying man. In 1949, Father Donavan wrote that since intravenous feeding is an ordinary means (artificial but nevertheless commonly uesd) to stop it would be equivalent to mercy killing.[16]

Father Kelly objected to this view and pointed out that one may not immediately conclude, simply because intravenous feeding is an ordinary means, that it is obligatory. He remarked,

"To me the mere prolongation of life in the given circumstance seems to be relatively useless, and I see no sound reason for saying that the patient is obliged to submit to it."[17] Father Joseph Sullivan wrote on this subject, "Although intravenous feeding is an ordinary means in itself, circumstances of great pain can make it extraordinary and it may be discontinued. Its use depends very much on the condition of the patients."[18]

Intravenous feeding may be called an ordinary means only in a very limited sense. The present cost of an average American hospital room, at least $30 per day, added to the cost of intravenous feeding for one day (another $30), plus other possible medication and doctor's fees, does not total a sum which is easily within the means of most American families. Besides the case of intravenous feeding there are the problems regarding the use of incubators, blood transfusions, oxygen tents, masks, iron lungs, highly technical operations, insulin, etc. How does a doctor deal with a person suffering from a case of advanced carcinoma, or with an infant who has hydrocephalus and develops a pneumonia which could cause death in a short time?

O'Donnell suggests that the word "relative" is perhaps the key word to the whole problem.[19] Were all the means of preserving and prolonging life to be regarded as ordinary, it would still be difficult to justify using such means for all cases. For in the case of dying persons such means would not be aids to life but rather prolongations of the dying process.

The dying process has been defined as that time in the course of an irreversible illness when treatment will no longer influence it and death is therefore inevitable.[20] The act of dying is regarded as the last agony itself. While these are convenient definitions, they do not cover all cases. At present it is practically impossible for the physician to determine the dying process, in its initial stages, in the case of young or previously healthy patients. What needs to be stressed repeatedly, and in the final analysis this may prove to be the one general positive guideline from the past that will remain, is that the use of any means should be based on what is commonly termed a "reasonable hope of success," and this can only be established by considering all the variable combinations of factors that call for evaluation.[21]

Referring to the present situation, Karl Rahner has written:

> The real situation in which the Christian of today has to make his moral decisions is in any case such that in very many and very important instances, the decision can no longer be the simple and obvious application of the principles concerning essences, even if he respects these as absolutely and universally valid. Even on this basis the Catholic nowadays is very often, and in the most important questions, in a situation which in practice resembles the one assumed to be always and necessarily present by those who advocate Christian situation ethics. Of course Catholic moral theology has always known that there are concrete moral situations in which the application of universal principles leads to no certain, generally accepted and theoretically unambiguous results . . .
>
> What is decisive in the present connection, however, is that the number of such cases has increased in a way that we might almost say involves a change of kind. As a result, the scope for freedom and responsibility which the moral principles of the Church and Catholic moral theology, based on essences, must concede to the moral conscience of the individual (even if they did not in fact wish to do so) has become considerably greater. Even for the Catholic the road from the general principles of Christian ethics to concrete decision has become considerably longer than formerly, even when he is determined unconditionally to respect all those principles, and for a good part of the way, in the last decisive states of the formation of the concrete moral imperative, he is therefore inevitably left by the Church's teaching and pastoral authority more than formerly to his own conscience, to form the concrete decision independently on his own responsibility.[22]

Those who would exhort the physician to make use of all means in his power to sustain life, applying any remedy that offers any hope (even the slightest) of cure or relief, should also be willing to support a physician's professional judgment that a particular patient is actually dying and that therefore to provide further medical assistance is actually to prolong the dying process. A case in point is the patient dying of cancer who is in great pain. Death is certain and inevitable. A stimulating drug may prolong life for another hour or two. Presupposing the physician has the expressed or implied consent of the patient or relatives to act in the patient's best interest, and assuming the patient is aware of his condition and disposed for death, the physician may withhold administering such a drug.[23] Further, he may apply another drug, an anesthetic for the purpose of relieving pain even though such a drug will induce unconsciousness and indirectly hasten death.[24]

Another example is that already cited by Dr. Rynearson, namely the use of oxygen or intravenous feeding to sustain life in so-called "hopeless" cases. Such hopeless cases are those where a firm diagnosis of a relatively chronic condition has been established which may be expected to terminate fatally because curative treatment is either not known or not applicable. The use of oxygen or intravenous feeding in these cases does not have as its goal a reasonable hope of success, that is, effecting a cure. Hence there is no obligation for the patient to use these things. Still another example is that of a diabetic patient who has contracted cancer that is incurable and painful. In such a case the use of insulin need not be considered as a necessary medicine since it would not sustain life but rather lengthen the number of days the patient must spend on his deathbed.[25]

If and when the physician can ascertain that the patient has begun what is called the dying process, many problems regarding the prolongation of life can be rather easily settled. There remains however the problem of death itself. With modern medical technology old definitions lose their value to assist the physician in this area. Dr. Hanzel reports: "Until 1960 death was thought of as a cessation of respiration and of heartbeat. . . . Today that definition no longer pertains. Now we speak of 'cerebral death,' that is, death of the brain cells after approximately four minutes of absolute oxygen lack."[26] It is possible that an individual patient may have undergone "cerebral death" and yet through artificial means continue to register "life" through heartbeat and respiration. Is it then unreasonable to declare a person dead despite heartbeat and respiration, once cerebral death has been clearly established? Further assistance seems difficult to justify as assistance at all, since the patient has ceased to function as a human person capable of cognition and human response.[27]

Living man has a right to life. Yet quite different is the case of positively interfering to prolong what is only apparent life. But what in fact is actually the dying process? Can we not say that the dying man has a right to death, and only for the most exceptional reason should this death be artificially prolonged? Physicians and theologians should be willing to investigate how much and to what extent their duties and responsibilities to the living differ from those which they have to the dying.

The dominion of God must be acknowledged and respected in both areas, but it seems to me this must be done in different ways. One does not give much help to the living sick by treating him as though he were about to die. Neither does one honestly provide the dying with the assistance he requires by treating him as though he were going to get well. Provided the dying man is aware of his condition and prepared in a Christian manner for death, other preparations in keeping with death as a most decisive event should also be made. The following guidelines by Dr. Rynearson reflect some of the concern of a Christian caring for the dying patient.

1. The dying patient should die with dignity, respect and humanity.

2. He should die with minimal pain.

3. He should have the opportunity to recall the love and benefits of a lifetime of sharing; he and his family and friends should visit together, if the patient so wishes.

4. He should be able to clarify relationships—to express wishes—to share sentiments.

5. The patient and relatives should plan intelligently for the changes which death imposes upon the living.

6. The patient should die in familiar surroundings, if possible; if not, then quietus should take place in surroundings made as near homelike as possible.

7. Finally, but importantly, there should be concern for the feelings of the living.

Leaving the details of biology and chemistry aside, Dr. Rynearson summarizes: "If these two things are certain: first, that the patient is dying of a malignant process for which there can be no treatment, and second, that the patient, his relatives and his spiritual advisor are aware of the situation, then what I am suggesting is that the physician should do all he can to alleviate the patient's suffering and make no effort to prolong his life."[28]

Nowhere in the life of man is the possibility of physical or mental suffering completely eliminated. Like death, it is not something that is of itself desirable, but like death it can serve as a reminder to man on his pilgrimage through this world that the present condition of man is not what it ought to be.[29] Christ did not remove all suffering. Indeed the attempt to alleviate such sufferings is demanded of us by the Gospel. Suffering of itself can in no sense be considered a good. For a particular person, due to a number of factors, it can be instrumental in effecting a deeper awareness of relationships and thus intensify the love of God in that person's life. However, it is also quite possible for sickness to be an occasion in a person's life for him to revolt against God. It is difficult to remove the impression of an underlying "Christian masochism" in that mentality which deliberately advocates physical suffering as a sure means to "sharing in the sufferings of Christ."

I should like to make clear that what is advocated here is a sincere Christian acknowledgement of the fact that a person is actually dying and then a desire to act in a Christian manner in accord with that fact. The continued use of any means in the cases we are speaking about is only forestalling an inevitable process which has already begun. The patient's decision to discontinue such means cannot justly be called suicide since it is no more than discontinuing means which are only functional where there is reasonable hope of success.

There is admittedly the very complex problem of establishing generally accepted norms for determining the dying process. The present definition is not very helpful in this regard. Defining the dying process as "that time in the course of an irreversible illness when treatment will no longer influence it" can be misread to include all irreversible illnesses from the time such illnesses are declared irreversible. Even when better guidelines are established there will still have to be modifications in the course of time, as recent history has demonstrated. And this possibility of change leads us to another concrete problem in the practical order.

Discontinuing ordinary and extraordinary means in the case of the dying becomes increasingly difficult when through scientific discovery, perhaps in the near future, some cure may be discovered. Such a course of reasoning, however, avoids the issue to be settled at the present moment. Prudent judgment regarding the present situation must be made in the light of information now available, and not what might perhaps be available at some future date.

There is no doubt that the distinction between the process of living and the process of dying is a very complex and tenuous one. The decision therefore whether this particular suffering patient is actually living or dying is equally complex and tenuous, and yet such a decision must be made with every individual in need of attention and care. Once it is established that a person is dying, it is at least somewhat easier to proceed to the decision of not using or discontinuing the use of artificial means which prolong the process of dying.

Is there anything more that can be done to assist the suffering dying? Dr. Dwight Ingle, a professor of physiology at the University of Chicago, in describing the problem of the right to death remarked that today, "The physician must take every known means to prolong the life of the patient. Although there is also an obligation to ease suffering, this is not always possible, and life is to be extended nevertheless. One rationalization of this ethic is that during the prolongation of life a cure for the apparently hopeless disease may be discovered. Cases occur in which hope is justified, but others are truly hopeless. What are the rights of the individual to die with dignity, to escape pain and hopelessness, and to spare anguish and expense to the family? Is this not a needed freedom?"[30]

If to use expensive means to add a few hours of life to a terminal patient is not in keeping with Christian charity, is it in keeping with Christian charity to allow a terminal patient to continue for months in such a condition without providing some positive assistance to the dying process? There is, for example, the person dying of bone cancer who is in great pain. The doctor relieves the pain by periodic injections of a drug which leaves the patient in a state of heavy sedation. This method of assistance continues until the person finally dies. Could the doctor act in another manner?

Is it possible for him to consider it a definite act of Christian service to the dying to administer a larger dose of such a drug? Perhaps the question may be better stated by asking whether a doctor is obliged to limit the quantity of a particular drug at any one time "to preserve life," although he is very well aware that such a dying person is prepared for death and yet may linger for months in pain under heavy sedation before finally expiring. Can the doctor increase the quantity of a particular drug or in any other way positively assist and accelerate the dying process?

Dr. Laforet speaks of the unconscionable prolongations of vital functions by means of the latest technological methods. When such methods are employed there are cases where "one is dealing not with a living human being but with a functioning human heart-lung preparation."[31] Is it possible to speak of the unconscionable prolongation of dying by a refusal to recognize the reality of the death process and all its implications? The discussion about "quantity versus quality of life"[32] may be of great help in eventually making somewhat clearer how positive assistance to the suffering-*dying* is a matter quite different from euthanasia as the merciful relief of suffering when one is not dying.[33] Can man not positively interfere through some means to hasten the dying process? Positive assistance to the dying process definitely seems to be encompassed in the reasonable understanding of the Christian and human right to die. What this positive assistance to the dying means will have to be determined from person to person and not from "case" to "case."

Two questions may serve to crystallize the issues. The first question is: when is a person actually dying? The second question is: how may the doctor assist the patient in the dying process?

These questions are admittedly very disturbing and not capable of flat, simple answers. They are nevertheless questions which demand serious study and discussion as the problems of medicine and morality continue to grow. Answers will be found in the results of continuous research and discussion on the part of scholars in all related fields, enabling priests and physicians to make still greater contributions in their mutual ministry to the dying.[34]

Notes

INTRODUCTION

1. Roger Aubert, *Le pontificat de Pie IX (1846-1878)*, Vol. 21 in the series, *Histoire de L'Église* (Paris: Bloud et Gay, 1952), pp. 257-259.

2. Pius Augustin, O.S.B., *Religious Freedom in Church and State* (Baltimore: Helicon, 1967), especially pp. 215-218; Pope Leo XIII, "Libertas Praestantissimum," in *The Church Speaks to the Modern World*, ed. Etienne Gilson (New York: Doubleday-Image, 1954), p. 77, 80.

3. John Kenneth Galbraith, *The Affluent Society* (New York: Mentor, 1963), p. 15.

4. Bernard J. F. Lonergan, S.J., *Insight: A Study of Human Understanding* (New York and London: Longmans, Green, and Co., 1957), p. 733.

5. These historical generalizations are based on the writings of Louis Vereecke, C.SS.R. See Vereecke, "Moral Theology, History of (700 to Vatican Council I)," *New Catholic Encyclopedia*, Vol. 9 (New York: McGraw-Hill, 1967), 1119-1122; Vereecke, "Le Conceil de Trente et l'enseignement de la Théologie Morale," *Divinitas*, 5 (1961), 361-374; Bernard Häring and Louis Vereecke, "La Théologie Morale de S. Thomas d'Aquin à S. Alphonse de Liguori," *Nouvelle Revue Théologique*, 77 (1955), 673-692. Also Bernard Häring, C.SS.R., *The Law of Christ*, Vol. I (Westminster, Md.: Newman, 1961), pp. 3-33.

6. *DS* refers to *Enchiridion Symbolorum*, ed. Henricus Denzinger, Adolfus Schoenmetzer, *et al.*, 32nd ed. (Barcilona: Herder, 1963).

7. For an acclaimed history of the Catholic Church in the

nineteenth century, see Aubert, especially pp. 224-261, and the bibliographical references mentioned by him.

8. The Code of Canon Law, in the official footnote to canon 1366 § 2, lists 14 papal documents and other decrees of curial congregations issued between 1879 and 1916 which call for Catholic philosophy and theology to follow the teaching of Thomas Aquinas. Later papal documents include Pope Pius XI, "Studiorum ducem," *AAS*, 15 (1923), 323ff.; Pope Pius XII, "Humani generis," *DS*, 3894; also other allocutions of Pius XII: *AAS*, 31 (1939), 246ff.; 38 (1946), 387ff.; 45 (1953), 684ff. Pope Paul VI has continued "to recommend the works of St. Thomas as a sure norm for sacred teaching" ("Address to the Thomistic Congress," *New Scholasticism,* 40 [January 1966], 82).

9. For the best examples of such renewal in moral theology, see Häring, *The Law of Christ* and Häring's many other published works.

10. A more complete consideration of the gravity of masturbation can be found in my article, "Masturbation and Objectively Grave Matter: An Exploratory Discussion," *Proceedings of the Catholic Theological Society of America,* 21 (1966), 95-112.

11. Harold Speert, *Obstetric and Gynecologic Milestones* (New York: Macmillan, 1958). On the homunculus in the spermatozoa, see Richard A. Leonardo, *A History of Gynecology* (New York: Forben Press, 1944), p. 202.

ROBERT H. SPRINGER

1. W. Abbott, S.J., ed., *The Documents of Vatican II* (New York, 1966). "Constitution on the Church in the Modern World," n. 62 (*Gaudium et Spes*).

2. *Ibid.*, n. 7.

3. A further weakness has been the multiplicity of rules in code morality. The maturity of the people of God recognized by Vatican II calls for simplification in this regard.

4. *Op. cit.*, nn. 16-17. Other passages develop the theme of these sections.

5. *Loc. cit.*, n. 16.

6. Declaration on Religious Freedom, n. 14.

7. The Church in the Modern World, n. 16; Decree on Priestly Formation, n. 11, footnote 140.

8. Too often, one suspects, the voices objecting were from those who had grasped neither the ethics of the person and sub-

jectivity nor the metaphysics on which the ethics is based. It is thus possible to use such terms as "interpersonal" and "ethic of love" without adequately knowing their objective content.

9. Cf. the classic article, "Conscience," by Carpentier in *DTC*.

10. *Gaudium et Spes*, n. 16.

11. N. 3; cf. also the Constitution on the Church, n. 12.

12. Pruemmer, *Manuale Theologiae Moralis*, II, n. 112; cf. Noldin, *Summa Theologiae Moralis*, II, n. 326.

13. Cf. de Finance, *Ethica Generalis*, n. 192.

14. Cf. his *Theological Investigations*, II (Baltimore: Helicon, 1963), and elsewhere in his writings.

15. *Gaudium et Spes*, n. 16.

16. *Loc. cit.*, n. 35.

17. Decree on Priestly Formation, n. 19.

18. "The Declaration on Religious Freedom," *America*, April 23, 1966.

19. *Gaudium et Spes*, nn. 15-16.

20. The reader is referred to the council's own description of change in the world, *Gaudium et Spes*, nn. 4-10.

21. N. 36; it is rewarding to reread this whole section on the autonomy of science together with n. 44, "The Help Which the Church Receives from the Modern World."

22. Cf., for example, the works of Erik Erikson; and Roger Brown, *Social Psychology* (New York: Free Press, 1965).

23. See the chapter by Cornelius van der Poel.

24. Constitution on Divine Revelation, n. 8 (emphasis added).

25. Unpublished paper prepared for the *International Encyclopedia of the Social Sciences*.

26. *Gaudium et Spes*, n. 44.

27. St. Thomas had the same dedication to truth when rediscovered Aristotelianism challenged the philosophy and theology of the times. He, too, tasted opposition from within the Church.

28. This is not new for the theologian. John Courtney Murray subjected official teaching on Church and State to the test of the empiric evidence of history. This culminated in the Declaration on Religious Freedom.

29. Cf. Peter Berger, *The Noise of Solemn Assemblies* (Garden City: Doubleday, 1961).

30. Peter Berger, "A Sociological View of the Secularization of Theology," *Journal for the Scientific Study of Religion*, 6 (Spring, 1967), 3-16.

31. *Gaudium et Spes*, n. 44.

32. Judging by the norms of the sociology of change, Berger sees the forces for change in the Catholic community as assured

of their goals, beyond the power of the defenders of the *status quo* to contain.

33. *Gaudium et Spes*, n. 7.

34. Unpublished manuscripts from the Interreligious Conference on the Role of Conscience, Boston, May 7-8, 1967.

35. *The Moral Judgment of the Child* (New York: Harcourt-Brace, 1932).

36. Roger Brown, *op. cit.*, pp. 403-404.

37. Robert White, *The Abnormal Personality*, 3rd. ed., p. 177. His reference to Murray is: *Explorations in Personality* (New York: Oxford University Press), pp. 136, 190.

38. *The Abnormal Personality*, pp. 177-178.

39. *Loc. cit.*

40. *The Impact of the Social Sciences* (Rutgers University Press, 1966), p. 92.

41. *Ibid.*, pp. 80-81.

42. In addition to his *Noise of Solemn Assemblies*, cf. his *The Precarious Vision* (Garden City: Doubleday, 1961).

43. Unfortunately the encyclical does not recognize the great American economic experience, unique in economic history for its internal viability and its aid to other nations, as well as the economic philosophy behind this experience.

44. *The Noise of Solemn Assemblies*, p. 132.

45. Cf. the moral manuals of the recent past, for example, *Noldin-Heinzel*, I, nn. 4-5. These sources were aware of the contribution of the social sciences to moral. Noldin explicitates this service in part as effecting "that . . . the concepts and opinions of moral which are false or obsolete may be corrected . . . ," *loc. cit.*

46. *The Modes and Morals of Psychotherapy* (New York: Holt, Rinehart & Winston, 1964), p. 164.

47. *Ibid.*, p. 180; cf. also pp. 181-184.

48. Cf. Abraham Edel, *Ethical Judgment, the Use of Science in Ethics* (Free Press of Glencoe, 1955).

DANIEL C. MAGUIRE

1. Carroll Stuhlmueller, C.P., *The Revival of the Liturgy*, ed. Frederick McManus (New York: Herder and Herder, 1963), pp. 15-32; Gregory Baum, "The Magisterium in a Changing Church," *Concilium*, Vol. 21, pp. 71-75.

2. It must not be presumed that the role of hierarchical figures in the early Church is the perfect paradigm for heirarchical functioning in all subsequent ages. In the process of societalization

the early Christian community was inescapably influenced by the societal forms of the day.

3. Paul Hinnebusch, O.P., "Christian Fellowship in the Epistle to the Philippians," *The Bible Today*, 12 (April, 1964), 793-798; G. Ricciotti, *The Acts of the Apostles* (Milwaukee: Bruce, 1958), pp. 77-78; Nicholas Crotty, "Biblical Perspectives in Moral Theology," *Theological Studies*, 26 (1965), 587-589.

4. Cf. *Epistle to the Trallians* 13, 1, Ancient Christian Writers 1 (Westminster, Md.: Newman, 1946), p. 79; cf. also J. S. Romanides, "The Ecclesiology of St. Ignatius of Antioch," *Greek Orthodox Theological Review*, 7 (1961-62), 53-77.

5. Oscar Cullmann, *The Earliest Christian Confessions* (London: Lutterworth Press, 1949).

6. Johannes Quasten, *Patrology*, Vol. 1 (Utrecht-Brussels: Spectrum Publishers, 1949), pp. 23-29, 150-153.

7. Piet Fransen, "The Authority of the Councils," *Cross Currents* (1961), 357-374.

8. *Adversus Haereses*, 3,3,3, *Sources Chrétiennes* (Paris: Editions du Cerf, 1952), Liure III, p. 106. Cf. *Handbook of Church History*, Vol I (New York: Herder and Herder; 1965), ed. Hubert Jedin and John Dolan, pp. 356-357. "Irenaeus' line of thought is, plainly, as follows: The apostolic tradition is found with certainty in the communities which rest on a directly apostolic foundation; there are several of these and each of them has a stronger power, grounded in its apostolic origin, for the ascertaining of truth. . . . One of these churches is the Roman church; which is even in a particularly favorable position for establishing the apostolic tradition, but not exclusively so."

9. Epistle 9, *PL* 62:66.

10. Cyprian, "Life of Caesarius," *PL* 67:1021.

11. Cyrille Vogel, *La Discipline penitentielle en Gaule des origines à la fin du VII siècle* (Paris: Letouzey et Ané, 1952), p. 85.

12. Bernhard Poschmann, *Penance and the Anointing of the Sick* (New York: Herder and Herder, 1964), pp. 124-138.

13. The moral and dogmatic magisterium do, of course, face many common problems. Both face the problem of the fallibility of language and the tendency for meaning to slip fluidly from under propositional formulae so that only a new proposition could express the original meaning. Special challenges arise for the dogmatic theologian as he takes modern biblical exegesis and insights and faces formal magisterial pronouncements of the past on questions of original sin, the preternatural gifts, the knowledge of Christ, the eternity of hell, and similar points.

13a. For a fuller treatment of the Christian reaction to war and peace see my essay, "Modern War and Christian Conscience," *On the Other Side* (Englewood Cliffs, N.J.: Prentice-Hall, 1968).

14. *Contra Celsum VIII*, 68-69, *Die griechischen Christlichen Schriftsteller*, II (Leipzig: Heinrichs, 1889), 285.

15. *Ibid.*, 73.

16. Roland H. Bainton, *Christian Attitudes Toward War and Peace* (Nashville: Abingdon Press, 1960), pp. 66-84; *Dictionnaire de Théologie Catholique*, 6, col. 1916; Ruinart, *Acta Martyrum* (Ratisbon, 1859), pp. 341-342.

17. Bainton, *op. cit.*, pp. 72-73, 77-84; Stanley Windass, *Christianity Versus Violence* (London: Sheed and Ward, 1964), pp. 3-20.

18. Eusebius, *Historia ecclesiastica* X, IX, 6-8, *SC*, 1958; *Vita Constantini* 2, 19, *GCS*, 1902; *Handbook of Church History*, pp. 405-432.

19. Bainton, *op. cit.*, pp. 85-89.

20. *Theodosiani Libri* XVI; cf. Bainton, *op. cit.*, p. 88.

21. *De libero arbitrio*, Vol. 12, *PL*, XXXXII, 1227; *Quaest. hept.*, IV, 44, *CSEL*, XXVIII, 2, p. 353.

22. *Contra Faustum*, *PL*, XXXXII, 448-449; cf. Windass, *op. cit.*, pp. 20-35.

23. Bainton, *op. cit.*, p. 109.

24. Windass, *op. cit.*, p. 43.

25. Bainton, *op. cit.*, pp. 101-121; Windass, *op. cit.*, pp. 36-53; Steven Runciman, *A History of the Crusades*, Vol. I (Cambridge, Eng., 1951), ch. I, "Holy Peace and Holy War."

26. Poschmann, *op. cit.*, p. 218.

27. Bainton, *op. cit.*, p. 112.

28. *Historia Francorum*, tr. Frederick Duncalf and August C. Krey, *Parallel Source Problems in Medieval History* (New York: Newper & Brothers, 1912); quoted with permission by Bainton, *op. cit.*, pp. 112-113.

29. Philip Hughes, *History of the Church*, Vol. II (New York: Sheed and Ward, 1952), pp. 299-300.

30. Bainton, *op. cit.*, p. 115.

31. *Decretum Gratiani*, pars II, caus. XXIII, q. V, c. 46.

32. E. Schillebeeckx, O.P., *Marriage, Human Reality and Saving Mystery* (New York: Sheed and Ward, 1965); Helmut Thielicke, *The Ethics of Sex* (New York: Harper and Row, 1964).

33. The slight amount of casuistry which does appear in the New Testament must be critically appreciated. In reading Paul's remarks to the Corinthians, for example, one must consider the known cultic aspects of much Corinthian fornication as well as Paul's eschatological expectations. Only then could one decide how relevant his remarks are to modern debates.

34. *Diog. Laer.*, VII, 110.

35. Ocellus Lucanus, *The Nature of the Universe,* text and commentary by Richard Harder (Berlin, 1926), sec. 44.

36. John T. Noonan, Jr., *Contraception* (Cambridge, Mass.: Harvard University Press, 1965), pp. 46-49, 56-91.

37. *Stromata* 3.7.57, *GCS*, 15:222.

38. Noonan, *op. cit.,* p. 126-131.

39. "Concupiscence" is normally used by Augustine in a bad sense: "This custom of speaking obtains that if avarice or concupiscence is spoken of and no modification is added, it cannot be understood except in an evil meaning" (*The City of God,* 14.7.2., *CSEL* 40:14); cf. Noonan, *op. cit.,* p. 134.

40. Ironically, Augustine, whose authority has been much cited in the Church's condemnation of contraception, vigorously attacked the contraceptive use of the sterile period (*The Morals of the Manichees,* 18.65, *PL* 32:1373), the one method approved by the extraordinary magisterium.

41. "No land could give lawful fruit which in a single year was frequently sowed. Why does one do in his own body what he would not do in his own field?" (Sermons 44.3-6, *CC* 103; 196-199).

42. Noonan, *op. cit.,* p. 78.

43. *On the Seven Penitential Psalms* 4, *PL* 217:1058-1059; cf. Noonan, *op. cit.,* p. 197.

44. *Le Prediche volgari,* ed. Piero Bargellini (Milan, 1936), p. 400.

45. Cf. above, p. 12 and note 42.

46. Noonan, *op. cit.,* p. 248.

47. Thomas, *On the Sentences* 4.32.1.2.2.; Raymond, *Summa* 4.2.6; Scotus, *On the Sentences,* Oxford Report, 4.32.

48. Session 24, November 11, 1563, Johannes Dominicus Mansi, Sacrorum Conciliorum Nova et Amplissima Collectio, ed. by H. Welter (Paris-Leipzig, 1903), 33:150.

49. Leo XIII, "Arcanum Divinae Sapientiae," *AAS* 12:385-402.

50. *The Documents of Vatican II,* Walter M. Abbott, S.J., General Editor (New York: Herder and Herder, 1966), "The Pastoral Constitution on the Church in the Modern World," no. 49, p. 253.

51. *Ibid.,* p. 254.

52. John T. Noonan, Jr., *The Scholastic Analysis of Usury* (Cambridge: Harvard University Press, 1957); "Authority, Usury and Contraception," *Cross Currents,* Vol. 16 (1966), 55-79.

53. "Authority, Usury and Contraception," 55-56.

54. Mansi 21:529-530, 22:231; *Clementine Constitutions,* 5.5., *Corpus juris canonici.*

55. "Authority, Usury and Contraception," 62-63.

56. *The Scholastic Analysis of Usury,* p. 346.

57. *Ibid.,* pp. 283-285, 289.

58. Patrick Granfield, O.S.B., "The Right to Silence," *Theological Studies,* 26 (1965), 280-298.

59. *PL* 119, 1010.

60. Patrick Granfield, O.S.B., "The Right to Silence: Magisterial Development," *Theological Studies,* 27 (1966), 404.

61. *Bullarum, diplomatum at privilegiorum sanctorum Romanorum pontificum Taurinensis,* editio 3 (Turin, 1858), p. 556.

62. Benedict XIV, *Bullarii Romani continuatio* (Florence, 1846), tom 3, pars prima, 13-17, n. 6.

63. *Regulae servandae in iudiciis apud* S.R. Rotae Tribunal, Aug. 4, 1910, *AAS* 2, 1910, 783-850.

64. "The Right to Silence," 417.

65. "Declaration on Religious Freedom," *The Documents of Vatican II,* p. 679.

66. Space permitting, a useful study could be done on the development of thought in the Church on questions of ecumenism and church-state relations; cf. Edward H. Flannery, *The Anguish of the Jews* (New York: Macmillan, 1965); George H. Tavard, *Two Centuries of Ecumenism* (New York: Mentor Omega, 1962); John Courtney Murray, S.J., "The Problem of Religious Freedom, *Woodstock Papers,* No. 7 (1965); and Pius Augustin, O.S.B., *Religious Freedom in Church and State* (Baltimore: Helicon, 1966).

67. Louis Bouyer, *Dictionary of Theology* (New York: Desclee Co., 1965), p. 237.

68. Trans. Cuthbert Butler, *The Vatican Council,* Vol. II, (London: Longmans, Green and Co., 1930), p. 295; cf. Denz. 1838-1840.

69. "Constitution on Divine Revelation," n. 12, *The Documents of Vatican II,* p. 120.

70. Mansi 52:1204. This occurs at the beginning of the *Relatio* of Bishop Gasser. The reference is to Isaiah 33:7.

71. Cf. Butler, *op.cit.,* vol II, chap. XIX; cf. also Hans Küng, *The Council, Reform and Reunion* (New York: Sheed and Ward, 1962), p. 161.

72. Mansi 51:1026B.

73. Mansi 52:761.

74. Mansi 52:764. "Idem Spiritus sanctus qui per charisma infallibilitatis adsistit papae et episcopis docentibus, idem dat fidelibus edoctis gratiam fidei, qua magisterio ecclesiae credunt."

75. *Ibid.* ". . . quoniam assistentia non est nova revelatio, sed manifestatio veritatis quae in deposito revelationis iam continetur, sanctus Spiritus agit et adiuvat papam ad veritatis con-

quisitionem ex fontibus divinae revelationis, quae in sacris Scripturis et traditione continetur."

76. *Ibid.* Quare neque diligentiam neque curas potest omittere, quae necessario ad cognoscendam veritatem praerequirentur. Idcirco papa inquisitionem instituit sive cum clero et theologis ecclesiae Romanae, sive cum formali synodo romana, ut inquirat quid in subiecta fidei et morum materia teneat ecclesia Romana, in qua immaculata semper est servata apostolica doctrina; unde mater et magistra ominum vocatur et est. Addit etiam aliquando inquisitionem cum episcopis sive seorsum, sive in conciliis provincialibus, et quoties opportunum in Domino iudicaverit, solemniorem etiam inquisitionem instituit, convocatis simul totius orbis episcopis. . . ."

77. Mansi 52:1212.

78. Mansi 52:1213. "Sed ideo non separamus pontificem ab ordinatissima coniunctione cum ecclesia. Papa enim solummodo tunc est infallibilis, quando omnium christianorum doctoris munere fungens, ergo universalem ecclesiam repraesentans, iudicat et definit quid ab omnibus credendum vel reiiciendum. Ab ecclesia universali tam separari non potest, quam fundamentum ab aedificio cui portando destinatum est. Non separamus porro papam infallibiliter definientem a cooperatione et concursu ecclesiae, saltem id est in eo sensu, quod hanc cooperationem et hunc concursum ecclesiae non excludimus."

79. Mansi 52:1213-1214. ". . . quia infallibilitas pontificis Romani non per modum inspirationis vel revelationis, sed per modum divinae assistentiae ipsi obvenit. Hinc papa pro officio suo et rei gravitate tenetur media apta adhibere ad veritatem rite indagandam et apte enuntiandam; et eiusmodi media sunt concilia vel etiam consilia episcoporum, cardinalium, theologorum etc. . . ." "Sed nonnulli ex reverendissimis patribus, his non contenti, ulterius progrediuntur, et volunt etiam in hanc constitutionem dogmaticam inducere conditiones, quae in tractatibus theologicis diversae in diversis inveniuntur, et quae bonam fidem et deligentiam pontificis in veritate indaganda et enuntianda concernunt; quae proinde, cum non relationem pontificis, sed conscientiam ipsius ligent, ordini potius morali quam dogmatico accensendae sunt."

80. *Ibid.* "Demum papam non separamus, et vel minime separamus a consensu ecclesiae, dummodo consensus iste non ponatur ut conditio, sive sit consensus antecedens sive sit consequens. Non possumus separare papam a consensu ecclesiae, quia hic consensus nunquam ipsi deesse potest."

81. Mansi 52:12.7. "Sed hoc systema aut est prorsus arbitrarium aut totius infallibilitatis pontificiae eversivum. Est arbitrarium si requireretur maioris vel minoris partis episcoporum assensus.

Nam quis statuet illorum numerum? Quis faciet delectum, cum episcopi inter se sub hoc respectu sint omnino pares, et assensus quorumdam assensui et iudicio aliorum non possit praeiudicare?"
    82. Cf. Mansi 52:1216-1217.
    83. Mansi 52:1226. "Iam vero cum de infallibilitate summi pontificis in definiendis veritatibus idem omnino dicendum sit, quod de infallibilitate definientis ecclesiae; eadem oritur quaestio de extensione infallibilitatis pontificiae ad huiusmodi veritates in se non revelatas, pertinentes tamen ad custodiam depositi: quaestio, inquam, oritur utrum infallibilitas pontificia in his veritatibus definiendis non solum sit theologice certa, sed sit fidei dogma eodem prorsus modo sicut dictum est de infallabilitate ecclesiae. Cum autem patribus Deputationis unanimi consensione visum sit hanc quaestionem nunc saltem non definiendam, sed relinquendam esse in eo statu in quo est: . . ."
    84. Mansi 52:1227. "In illis autem in quibus theologice quidem certum, non tamen hactenus certum de fide est ecclesiam esse infallibilem, etiam infallibilitas pontificis hoc decreto sacri concilii non definitur tanquam de fide credenda."
    85. "Constitution on Revelation," n. 8, *The Documents of Vatican II*, p. 116.
    86. "Constitution on the Church," n. 12 and n. 15, *The Documents of Vatican II*, p. 29 and pp. 33-34.
    87. Noonan, *op. cit.*, p. 395.
    88. Edgar Hocedez, *Histoire de la théologie au XIXᵉ siècle*, Vol. I (Brussels, 1947-1952), pp. 67-69; 132.
    89. Rudolph Schnachenburg, *The Moral Teaching of the New Testament* (New York: Herder and Herder, 1965), p. 122.
    90. Schillebeeckx, *op. cit.*, p. 389.
    91. Schnackenburg, *op. cit.*, p. 249.
    92. Mansi 52:1235. "Verba doctrinam de moribus insinuant, Romanum pontificem ab errore immunem non esse, quando de honestate vel pravitate alicuius actionis in concreto spectatae decernit; puta de latrocinio temporalis dominii sanctae sedis a gubernio Italico perpetrato."
    93. Pius XII, Allocution "Magnificate Dominum," Nov. 2, 1954; *AAS* 46 (1950), p. 561.
    94. John XXIII, Encyclical *Pacem in terris*, Apr. 11, 1963; *AAS*, 55 (1963), p. 301.
    95. Gregory Baum, O.S.A., "The Christian Adventure--Risk and Renewal," *Critic* 23 (1965), 44.
    96. John J. Reed, S.J., "Natural Law, Theology, and the Church," *Theological Studies* 26 (1965), 55.
    97. Richard A. McCormick, S.J., "Notes on Moral Theology," *Theological Studies*, 26 (1965), 614.

98. Even the strong stand of Trent on marriage and divorce is not seen today as prohibiting the growing debate concerning those matters.

99. For St. Thomas' appreciation of the essential role of circumstances, cf. I^a II^{ae}, q.18, a.10; *ibid.*, q.73, a.7; *Sent.* 4 d.16, q.3, a.2; *De malo* q.2, a.6, 7.

100. Karl Rahner, S.J., *Nature and Grace* (New York: Sheed and Ward, 1964), p. 41.

101. Fransen, *art. cit.*, p. 366.

102. Jan H. Walgrave, O.P., "Is Morality Static or Dynamic?" *Concilium* V (London: Paulist, 1965), p. 20.

103. Alfred North Whitehead, *Process and Reality* (New York: Harper Torchbooks, 1960), p. 297.

104. *Ibid.*, p. 298.

105. John Macquarrie, *God-Talk: An Examination of the Language and Logic of Theology* (London: S.C.M. Press Ltd., 1967), p. 127.

106. Butler, *op. cit.*, I, 101; II, 215-216; Rondet, *op. cit.*, p. 126.

107. Mansi 52:1133-1134; 1226-1228.

108. Richard A. McCormick, S.J., *art. cit.*, 615.

109. *Ibid.*, 612.

110. *Ibid.*, 615.

111. Gregory Baum, O.S.A., *art. cit.*, 52.

112. Decree on Ecumenism, n. 11, *The Documents of Vatican II*, p. 354.

113. Constitution on the Church, n. 25, *The Documents of Vatican II*, p. 48.

114. Encyclical *Mater et magistra*, no. 239: *AAS*, 53 (1961), p. 457.

115. Reed, *art. cit.*, 59. For a similar interpretation and citations from other authors, cf. Ford and Kelly, *Contemporary Moral Theology*, Vol. I (Westminster, Md.: Newman, 1963), pp. 19-41.

115a. Y. Congar, "La primaute des quatre premiers conciles oecumeniques. Origine, destin, sens et portée d'un theme traditionnel," *Le Concile et les Conciles* (Paris: Editions de Chevetogne, 1960), pp. 76-80; cf., Hans Küng, *Structures of the Church* (Camden, N.J.: Nelson, 1963), pp. 52-64.

116. Augustine, *Retractationes*, lib.2., c.18; *PL*, 32, 637 f.

117. *Summa Theologica*, III, q.8, a.3, ad 2.

118. Karl Rahner, S.J., "The Church of Sinners," *Cross Currents*, I (1951), 68.

119. Church in the Modern World, n. 5, *Documents of Vatican II*, p. 204. My frequent use of the documents of Vatican II in

this development is not without recognition that this council, perhaps more than most others, contains the fruit of many theologies and does not represent a synthesis of these theologies. I think it important, however, that philosophical and theological theories that support my analysis did find a place in the council.

120. *Ibid.,* n. 54, p. 260.

121. Declaration on Christian Education, n. 1, *Documents,* p. 640.

122. The Church in the Modern World, n. 43, *Documents,* p. 244.

123. *Ibid.,* n. 5, *Documents,* pp. 203-204; n. 53-62, pp. 259-270; and passim.

124. *Ibid.,* n. 61, p. 267.

125. Reed, *art. cit.,* 59. From here on, references to this article will be given in the text.

126. McCormick, *art. cit.,* 613. Hereafter reference to this article will be made in the text.

127. *AAS,* 42 (1950), 568.

128. Ford and Kelly, *op. cit.,* p. 32.

129. Reed, *art. cit.,* 57.

130. *Ibid.,* note 30.

131. Ford and Kelly. *op. cit.,* vol. I, p. 314.

132. *Ibid.,* p. 315.

133. Cyprian, Ep. 55, 9; cf. *Handbook of Church History,* p. 380.

134. *Handbook of Church History,* p. 427.

135. Cf. Y. Congar, *Chrétiens en Dialogue* (Paris: Editions du Cerf, 1964).

136. Constitution on the Church, n. 12, *The Documents of Vatican II,* p. 29.

CHARLES E. CURRAN

1. E.g., Joseph Fletcher, *Situation Ethics: The New Morality* (Philadelphia: Westminster Press, 1966), p. 21; Edward LeRoy Long, Jr., *A Survey of Christian Ethics* (New York: Oxford University Press, 1967), pp. 167-185.

2. General discussions of medical ethics by American Catholic authors in the last two decades include: B. J. Ficarra, *Newer Medical Problems in Ethics and Surgery* (Westminster, Md.: Newman Press, 1949); Frederick L. Good and Otis F. Kelly, *Marriage, Morals, and Medical Ethics* (New York: P. J. Kenedy, 1951); Edwin F. Healy, S.J., *Medical Ethics* (Chicago: Loyola University Press, 1956); Gerald Kelly, S.J., *Medico-Moral Problems* (St.

Louis: The Catholic Hospital Association, 1958); John P. Kenny, O.P., *Principles of Medical Ethics,* 2nd ed. (Westminster, Md.: Newman Press, 1961); Charles J. McFadden, O.S.A., *Medical Ethics,* 4th ed. (Philadelphia: F. A. Davis, 1958); Timothy O'Connell, *Morality in Medicine* (Paterson: St. Anthony Press, 1953); Thomas G. O'Donnell, S.J., *Morals in Medicine,* 2nd ed. (Westminster, Md.: Newman Press, 1959). Also there are a number of Catholic journals devoted to morality and medicine: England: *Catholic Medical Quarterly;* France: *Cahiers Laënnec* (five volumes of articles from *Cahiers Laënnec* have been published in the United States by Newman Press under the title *New Problems in Medical Ethics,* ed. Dom Peter Flood, O.S.B.); Belgium: *Saint-Luc Médical;* U.S.A.: *Linacre Quarterly.*

3. The textbooks mentioned in note 2 give the pertinent references to papal teachings and other magisterial pronouncements.

4. *National Catholic Reporter,* April, 19, 1967.

5. John Marshall, *Catholics, Marriage, and Contraception* (Baltimore: Helicon, 1965), pp. 96-98; Richard A. McCormick, S.J., "Practical and Theoretical Considerations," in *The Problem of Population,* Vol. III (Notre Dame: University of Notre Dame Press, 1965), pp. 61-67. The minority report of the Papal Commission admitted that the natural law arguments against artificial contraception are not entirely convincing; thus, "men need the help of the teaching of the Church, explained and applied under the leadership of the magisterium, so that they can with certitude and security embrace the way, the truth, and the life."

6. Healy, p. 171. In his allocation to the Italian Catholic Union of Midwives (*AAS,* 43 (1951), 835-854), Pius XII stated: "Direct sterilization, that which aims at making procreation impossible both as means and end, is a grave violation of the moral law, and therefore illicit" (N.C.W.C. translation). Cf. "Casti Connubii," *AAS,* 22 (1930), 564, 565; and also the decree of the Holy Office of February 22, 1940, *AAS,* 32 (1940), 73.

7. John C. Ford, S.J., and Gerald Kelly, S.J., *Contemporary Moral Theology: Marriage Questions* (Westminster, Md.: Newman Press, 1963), pp. 315-337.

8. Pope Pius XII, Address to the Hematologists, *AAS,* 50 (1958), 734 ff.

9. For a complete bibliography, see Ambrogio Valsecchi, "La discussione morale sui progestativi," *La Scuola Cattolica,* 93 (1965), supplemento 2, 157*-216*. A word of caution is in order. Many of the authors mentioned in Valsecchi's article have since changed their opinions about the morality of contraception. Likewise, some of the authors cited in the present chapter have changed the opinions recorded here.

10. The Ethical Directives of the Catholic Hospital Association are included as appendices by Healy, McFadden and O'Donnell.

11. Pope Pius XII, Address to the Second World Congress of Fertility and Sterility, May 19, 1956, *AAS*, 48 (1956), 472; Address to Italian Urologists, October 8, 1953, *AAS*, 45 (1953), 678; Decree of the Holy Office, August 2, 1929, *AAS*, 21 (1929), 490.

12. Bernard Häring, C.SS.R., proposed such an opinion as probable at a course for professors and others interested in moral theology at Regis College, Toronto, Canada, July, 1963. See L. M. Weber, "Onanismus," *Lexicon für Theologie und Kirche* (Freiburg: Herder, 1962), Vol. 7, 1157-1158.

13. Pope Pius XII, Address to the Fourth World Congress of Catholic Doctors, Rome, September 29, 1949, *AAS*, 41 (1949), 560; also in later addresses, *AAS*, 43 (1951), 850; *AAS*, 48 (1956), 469-471.

14. Kelly, p. 242.

15. P. Kanuer, S.J., "La détermination du bien et du mal morale par le principe du double effet," *Nouvelle Revue Théologique*, 87 (1965), 356-376; W. van der Marck, O.P., *Love and Fertility* (London: Sheed and Ward, 1965), pp. 35-63.

16. T. Lincoln Bouscaren, S.J., *Ethics of Ectopic Operations*, 2nd ed. (Milwaukee: Bruce Publishing Co., 1944); Kelly, pp. 105-110.

17. van der Marck, p. 59, 60.

18. Bert J. Cunningham, C.M., *The Morality of Organic Transplantation* (Washington: The Catholic University of America Press, 1944); O'Donnell, pp. 122-131. For a fine summary of the controversy and pertinent bibliography, see Kelly, pp. 245-252.

19. Archbishop Denis E. Hurley, "A New Moral Principle," *The Furrow*, 17 (1966), 621.

20. The specific question of the double effect and its relation to abortion are considered extensively also in the chapter by Cornelius van der Poel. They are mentioned here as illustrations of the dissatisfaction in certain areas of medical morality.

21. Jean Marie Aubert, "Le Droit Naturel: ses avatars historiques et son avenir," *Supplément de la Vie Spirituelle*, 81 (1967), especially 298 ff.

22. *The Digest* or *Pandects of Justinian*, Book 1, t. 1, n. 1-4.

23. Odon Lottin, *Le Droit Naturel chez Saint Thomas d'Aquin et ses prédécesseurs*, 2nd ed. (Bruges: Charles Beyaert, 1931), p. 62.

24. *In IV Sent.* d. 33, q.1, a.1, ad 4.

25. *In V Ethic.*, lect. 12.

26. *I-II*, q.90, a.1, ob.3; q.96, a.5, ob.3; q.97, a.2; *II-II*, q.57, a.3, ob.1 and *in corp.*

27. *I-II*, q.95, a.4

28. *II-II*, q.57, a.3

29. E.g., H. Noldin et al., *Summa Theologiae Moralis: De Castitate*, 36th ed. (Oeniponte: F. Rauch, 1958), pp. 21-43.

30. Decree of the Holy Office on the ends of marriage, April 1, 1944, *AAS*, 36 (1944), 103. Also various addresses of Pius XII: *AAS*, 33 (1941), 422; 43 (1951), 835-854.

31. Regis Araud, S.J., "Évolution de la Théologie du Marriage," *Cahiers Laënnec*, 27 (1967), 56-71; W. van der Marck, O.P., "De recente ontwikkelingen in de theologie van het huwelijk," *Tijdschrift voor Theologie*, 7 (1967), 127-140. English summary on page 140.

32. Gerard Watson, "The Early History of Natural Law," *The Irish Theological Quarterly*, 33 (1966), 65-74.

33. John L. Russell, S.J., "The Concept of Natural Law," *The Heythrop Journal*, 6 (1965), 434-438; Pierre Colin, "Ambiguïtés du mot nature," *Supplément de la Vie Spirituelle*, 81 (1967), 253-255.

34. Charles E. Curran, "Masturbation and Objectively Grave Matter: An Exploratory Discussion," *Proceedings of the Catholic Theological Society of America*, 21 (1966), 95-109.

35. H. Noldin et al., *Summa Theologiae Moralis*, Vol. II: *De Praeceptis* (Oeniponte: F. Rauch, 1959), pp. 553-560; E. F. Regatillo, S.J., and M. Zalba, S.J., *Theologiae Moralis Summa*, Vol. II (Matriti: Biblioteca de Autores Cristianos, 1953), 1000-1018.

36. J. A. Dorszynski, *Catholic Teaching about the Morality of Falsehood* (Washington: Catholic University of America Press, 1949); Francis J. Connell, C.SS.R., *More Answers to Today's Moral Problems*, ed. Eugene J. Weitzel, C.S.V. (Washington: Catholic University of America Press, 1965), p. 123, 124. Augustine had at one time accepted the distinction between falsehood and lying, but he later changed his opinion.

37. Bernard Lonergan, S.J., *Collection* (New York: Herder and Herder, 1967), pp. 252-267; Lonergan, "A Transition from a Classicist Worldview to Historical Mindedness," in *Law for Liberty: The Role of Law in the Church Today*, ed. James E. Biecher (Baltimore: Helicon Press, 1967). Lonergan along with other theologians such as Marechal, Rahner, and Metz maintains that although Thomas Aquinas reflected a classical worldview, the followers of Thomas distorted his teaching especially in such areas as the emphasis on a deductive methodology and a non-relational understanding of being.

38. John Courtney Murray, S.J., "The Declaration on Reli-

gious Freedom," *Concilium: Moral Theology,* Vol. 5, n. 2 (May 1966), 3-10.

39. Eulalio R. Baltazar, *Teilhard and the Supernatural* (Baltimore: Helicon Press, 1966); Leslie Dewart, *The Future of Belief* (New York: Herder and Herder, 1966). Lonergan espouses historical mindedness but strenuously opposes the approach of Dewart. See Lonergan, "The Dehellenization of Dogma," *Theological Studies,* 28 (1967), 336-351.

40. Murray, *Concilium,* 7-10.

41. John Courtney Murray, S.J., *The Problem of Religious Freedom* (Westminster, Md.: Newman, 1965).

42. John Courtney Murray, S.J., "Freedom, Authority, Community," *America* (December 3, 1966), 735.

43. *Gaudium et Spes* (The Pastoral Constitution on the Church in the Modern World), n. 44. For a competent one-volume translation of the documents of Vatican II, see *The Documents of Vatican II,* ed. Walter M. Abbot, S.J. (New York: America Press and Association Press, 1966).

44. Karl Rahner, S.J., *The Dynamic Element in the Church* (New York: Herder and Herder, 1964).

45. See the chapter by Daniel C. Maguire.

46. Herbert Butterfield, *The Origins of Modern Science, 1300-1800* (New York: Macmillan, 1951); Lonergan, *Collection,* p. 259 ff.

47. Andreas van Melsen, "Natural Law and Evolution," *Concilium: Church and World,* Vol. 6, n. 3 (June, 1967), 24-29.

48. *Law for Liberty: The Role of Law in the Church Today, passim.*

49. *Documents of Vatican II,* p. 686, n. 20. The footnote on the role of civil law was written by John Courtney Murray.

50. Thomas B. McDonough, "Distribution of Contraceptives by the Welfare Department: A Catholic Response," in *The Problem of Population,* Vol. II (Notre Dame: University of Notre Dame Press, 1964), pp. 94-118.

51. Douglas Sturm, "Naturalism, Historicism, and Christian Ethics: Toward a Christian Doctrine of Natural Law," *The Journal of Religion,* 44 (1964), 40-51. Note again that some Catholic thinkers see in the excessive emphasis on *res in se* apart from any relational consideration a distortion of the understanding of St. Thomas.

52. Russell, *The Heythrop Journal,* 6 (1965), 434-438.

53. Karl Rahner, S.J., "Theology and Anthropology," in *The Word in History,* ed. T. Patrick Burke (New York: Sheed and Ward, 1966), pp. 1-23; Rahner, "Naturrecht," *Lexikon für Theologie und Kirche,* Vol. 7, 827-828.

54. Lonergan, "Dimensions of Meaning," *Collection,* pp. 252-267.

55. Lonergan, *Collection,* pp. 221-239; *Theological Studies,* 28 (1967), 337-351.

56. Philippe Delhaye, *Permanence du Droit Naturel* (Louvain: Editions Nauwelaerts, 1960); Heinrich A. Rommen, *The Natural Law* (St. Louis: B. Herder, 1947); Yves R. Simon, *The Tradition of Natural Law* (New York: Fordham University Press, 1965); Lottin, *Le Droit Naturel chez Saint Thomas d'Aquin et ses Prédécesseurs;* Pierre Colin, *Supplément de la Vie Spirituelle,* 81 (1967), 251-268; Jean Marie Aubert, *Supplément de la Vie Spirituelle,* 81 (1967), 282-324.

57. Russell, *The Heythrop Journal,* 6 (1965), 434-446.

58. Watson, *The Irish Theological Quarterly,* 33 (1966), 65-74.

59. For a summary of the different exegetical opinions, see Stanislaus Lyonnet, S.J., "Lex naturalis et justificatio Gentilium," *Verbum Domini,* 41 (1963), 238-242.

60. Delhaye, 44-53; *Decretum Gratiani,* p.I, d.1.

61. John T. Noonan, Jr., *Contraception: A History of its Treatment by the Catholic Theologians and Canonists* (Cambridge: Harvard University Press, 1965), pp. 56-107.

62. V. Vangheluwe, "De Intrinseca et Gravi Malitia Pollutionis," *Collationes Brugenses,* 48 (1952), 108-115.

63. *II-II,* q.154, a.2.

64. The relationship between natural law theory and the magisterial teaching of the Catholic Church as well as a detailed explanation of the "non-absolute" character of natural law may be found in my essay, "Absolute Norms in Moral Theology," in *Norm and Context in Christian Ethics,* ed. Paul Ramsey and Gene Outka (New York: Charles Scribner's Sons, 1968).

65. This paragraph will also summarize the conclusions of the essay mentioned in note 64. The chapter by John G. Milhaven, S.J., in the present volume develops in detail St. Thomas' considerations of the exceptions to natural law as mentioned in the Old Testament. See also John Milhaven's chapter in this volume.

66. *I-II,* q.94, a.4

67. *In I. Sent.,* d.47, a.4. Also *De Malo,* q.3, a.1 ad17; *Quodlibetum,* I a.18.

68. Paul Elmen, Presidential Address to the American Society of Christian Ethics, 1966. Law indicates what is generally true, but miracle shows the need for exceptions to the general law.

69. Jacques Jullien, "Nature et culture: Droit naturel ou droit culturel?" *Supplément de la Vie Spirituelle,* 78 (1966), 482-502.

70. Columba Ryan, O.P., "The Traditional Concept of Natural Law: An Interpretation," in *Light on the Natural Law,* ed. Illtud Evans, O.P., (Baltimore: Helicon Press, 1965), p. 33.

71. R. Paniker, *El concepto de naturaleza: Analysis historico y metafisico di un concepto* (Madrid: Instituto Luis Vives de Filosofia, 1951); Delhaye, pp. 9-21; *Supplément de la Vie Spirituelle,* 81 (1967); 251-268; 282-322.

72. Thomas E. Davitt, S.J., *The Nature of Law* (St. Louis: B. Herder, 1951); Edouard Hamel, S.J., "La vertu d'epikie," *Sciences Ecclésiastiques,* 13 (1961), 35-56; Joseph Fuchs, S.J., "Auctoritas Dei in auctoritate civili," *Periodica de Re Morali, Canonica, Liturgica,* 52 (1963), 3-18; Gregory Stevens, O.S.B., "Moral Obligation in St. Thomas," *The Modern Schoolman,* 40 (1962-63), 1-21; M. Huftier, "La loi ecclésiastique: Sa valeur et son obligation," *L'Ami du Clergé,* 74 (1964), 375-382.

73. Such an admission is made even by the respected Thomistic scholar Jacques Maritain in *The Rights of Man and Natural Law* (New York: Charles Scribner's Sons, 1943), p. 62.

74. John C. Bennett, "Capitalism and Ethics," *Catholic Mind,* 65 (May, 1967), 44. "Though there are some differences of methodology, I am aware of no distinctive Protestant position now that can be contrasted with the economic ethics reflected in the social encylicals of Pope Pius XI and Pope John XXIII."

75. Emil Brunner, *The Divine Imperative* (Philadelphia: Westminster Press, 1947), pp. 291-562.

76. Dietrich Bonhoeffer, *Ethics* (New York: Macmillan, 1962), pp. 73-140.

77. Reinhold Niebuhr, *An Interpretation of Christian Ethics* (New York: Harper, 1935); *The Nature and Destiny of Man,* Volumes I and II (New York: Charles Scribner's Sons, original editions 1941 and 1943; paperback editions 1963); *Christian Realism and Political Problems* (New York: Charles Scribner's Sons, 1953), especially chapter 10 on "Love and Law in Protestantism and Catholicism."

78. John C. Bennett, *Christian Ethics and Social Policy* (New York: Charles Scribner's Sons, 1950), especially pp. 116-124; Bennett, "Principles and the Context," in *Storm over Ethics* (No plave given: United Church Press, 1967), 1-25; Bennett, *Christian Social Ethics in a Changing World,* ed. John C. Bennett (New York: Association Press, 1966), pp. 369-381.

79. Paul Ramsey, *Nine Modern Moralists* (Englewood Cliffs, New Jersey: Prentice-Hall, 1962), pp. 1-8; Ramsey, *Deeds and Rules in Christian Ethics* (New York: Charles Scribner's Sons, 1967), especially p. 121, 122.

80. James M. Gustafson, "Context versus Principles: A Mis-

placed Debate in Christian Ethics," *Harvard Theological Review,* 58 (1965), 171-202.

81. Unfortunately, I was unable to consult the following works in the preparation of this chapter: *Das Naturrecht im Disput,* ed. Franz Böckle (Dusseldorf: Patmos, 1966); William A. Luijpen, *Phenomenology of Natural Law* (Pittsburgh: Duquesne University Press, 1966).

82. Perhaps the most synthetic explanation of Johann's thought on the particular question of natural law is found in an unpublished address given by him to the American Society of Christian Ethics, January, 1965. Also see, Robert O. Johann, S.J., "Responsible Parenthood: A Philosophical View," *Proceedings of the Catholic Theological Society of America,* 20 (1965), 115-128; Johann, "Love and Justice," in *Ethics and Society,* ed. R. T. DeGeorge (New York: Doubleday, 1966), p. 33 ff.

83. W. van der Marck, O.P., pp. 35-63.

84. Francis Simons, "The Catholic Church and the New Morality," *Cross Currents,* 16 (1966), 429-445.

85. John G. Milhaven, S.J., "Towards an Epistemology of Ethics," *Theological Studies,* 27 (1966), 228-241.

JOHN G. MILHAVEN

1. Here and throughout the essay "physical" does not mean "material" or "perceptible to the senses." By this term I mean the objective effect not yet considered in any relationship to a norm of morality. At the price of oversimplification and repetition, I am using consistently the phrase "as a means," in order to avoid the necessity of a detour into the complexities of another natural law principle, the principle of double effect, which is not pertinent to the purpose of this chapter.

2. See the *Dictionary of Moral Theology,* ed. P. Palazzini (Westminster, Md.: Newman, 1962), *sub voce;* Henry Davis, S.J., *Moral and Pastoral Theology* (New York: Sheed and Ward, 1943), I, pp. 62-63, and II, pp. 168-169; Marcellino Zalba, S.J., "The Catholic Church's Viewpoint on Abortion," *World Medical Journal,* Vol. 13, No. 3 (May-June, 1966), 88-89, 92-93.

3. For example, Joseph Sittler, *The Structure of Christian Ethics* (Louisiana State University Press, 1958), pp. 79-86; Dietrich Bonhoeffer, *Letters and Papers from Prison* (New York: Macmillan, 1962), pp. 17-19; Helmut Thielicke, *Theological Ethics. Volume I: Foundations* (Philadelphia: Fortress Press, 1966), pp. 578-647.

4. See Bonhoeffer's apparently absolute condemnation of abortion as murder in *Ethics* (New York: Macmillan Paperback,

1965), pp. 175-176. It shocked a more thoroughgoing situationist, Joseph Fletcher, as he states in his *Situation Ethics* (Philadelphia: Westminster, 1966), pp. 38, 74-75. Helmut Thielicke rejects the pragmatic slogan "to prevent something worse" as ethically destructive (*op. cit.,* pp. 624-625). Moreover, "although from the standpoint of justification 'all things are possible,' in human affairs there are from the human standpoint certain limits which cannot be transgressed" (p. 643). For example, there is no situation possible in which I would be justified in denying Christ or torturing a man to obtain some truth (pp. 643-667).

5. *Op. cit.,* p. 140.

6. Paul Lehmann, *Ethics in a Christian Context* (New York: Harper and Row, 1963); Joseph Fletcher, *op. cit.,* and *Moral Responsibility. Situation Ethics at Work* (Philadelphia: Westminster, 1967).

7. See John G. Milhaven, S.J., and David J. Casey, S.J., "Introduction to the Theological Background of the New Morality," *Theological Studies,* Vol. 28, No. 2 (June, 1967), pp. 224-244; also James M. Gustafson, "Christian Ethics," in *Religion,* ed. Paul Ramsey (Englewood Cliffs, N.J.: Prentice-Hall, 1965), pp. 287-354, especially, pp. 325-336, and "Context versus Principles: A Misplaced Debate in Christian Ethics," *Harvard Theological Review,* 58 (1965), pp. 171-202.

8. The genuine idea of natural law, Jacques Maritain recalls, is a heritage of Greek and Christian thought. In listing those who have contributed to its historical transmission and development, Maritain notes that St. Thomas Aquinas "alone grasped the matter in a wholly consistent doctrine . . ." *Man and the State* (University of Chicago Press, 1951), p. 85. Cf. Germain Grisez, *Contraception and the Natural Law* (Milwaukee: Bruce, 1964), pp. 60, 71 (with note 29).

9. E.g. *S. Th.,* II-II, q.64, a.6 and 7; q.154, a.2; q.66, a.5. The Marietti edition indicates parallel passages. To the point: "The end of the act itself [fornication] by its nature is disordered, even if the person acting could be intending a good end. The end intended does not suffice to excuse the act, just as is clearly the case with one who steals with the intention of giving alms." *De Malo,* q.xv, a.1, ad 3. (Unless otherwise indicated, all translations are my own.)

10. *Genesis,* XXII, 1-14. The pertinent texts of Thomas will be discussed below.

11. *Hosea,* I, 1-3.

12. *Exodus* III, 21-22; XI, 1-2; XII, 35-36.

13. *S. Th.,* II–II, q.64, a.5, and a.3. Cf. a.7.

14. *S. Th.,* Suppl., q.65, a.1, and q.67, a.2. In the course of

the present study, it will rather be the original form of the articles in the *Commentary on the Sentences* that will be considered: IV, d.33, q.1, a.1, and q.2, a.1.

15. E.g. Helmut Thielicke, *op. cit.,* pp. 664-667; Karl Barth, *Church Dogmatics,* II, ii, *The Doctrine of God* (Edinburgh: Clark, 1957), pp. 672 ff.; John Macquarrie, *Twentieth-Century Religious Thought* (New York: Harper and Row, 1963), pp. 222-223. Thielicke recalls the significance the Bible story had for Luther and Kierkegaard.

16. Cf. André Thiry, S.J., "Saint Thomas et la morale d'Aristote," in *Aristote et saint Thomas d'Aquin* (Louvain, 1957), pp. 229-258. Thiry could have indicated more clearly that it was ultimately from the Stoics that the medieval theologians inherited the notion of a science of ethics based on natural first principles and oriented towards purposes imposed on man by his nature and by God. Cf. Max Pohlenz, *Die Stoa* (Göttingen: Vandenhoeck and Ruprecht, 1959), pp. 243-245; also Heinrich Rommen, *The Natural Law* (St. Louis: Herder, 1947), pp. 16-40. Along lines similar to Thiry's: Etienne Gilson, *The Christian Philosophy of St. Thomas Aquinas* (New York: Random House, 1956), pp. 291, 302-305.

17. Although his theological problematic never exactly coincides with the one we are considering, the research of Dom Lottin provides valuable material on the development of our question in the medieval period before Thomas. Especially useful are "La loi naturelle depuis le début du XIIe siècle jusqu'à saint Thomas d'Aquin" and "Le problème de la moralité intrinsèque d'Abélard à saint Thomas d'Aquin," in *Psychologie et Morale aux XIIe et XIIIe siècles* (Louvain: Abbaye du Mont César, 1948), II, i, pp. 71-100 and 421-465. Both studies incorporate previously published work of Lottin. Much remains to be done. For example, there is still lacking, to my knowledge, a comprehensive, scholarly study that would analyze how Thomas' integration of the newly translated Aristotelianism differed from that of his mentor, Albert the Great.

18. Cf. O. Lottin, "La valeur des formules de saint Thomas d'Aquin concernant la loi naturelle," in *Mélanges Joseph Maréchal,* II (Paris: Desclée de Brouwer, 1950), p. 345.

19. Harry V. Jaffa's thesis is that, although Thomas generally interprets or explains statements of Aristotle in terms of other statements of the Greek philosopher, nonetheless, in so doing, he imputes non-Aristotelian principles to Aristotle. Cf. *Thomism and Aristotelianism* (University of Chicago, 1952), pp. 167-188. Jaffa (pp. 189-193) invokes for his support Frederick Copleston, S.J., *A History of Philosophy, Volume II, Mediaeval Philosophy: Augustine to Scotus* (Westminster, Md.: Newman Press, 1950),

Chapter XXXIX. Maritain admits that Thomas's doctrine on natural law "unfortunately was expressed in an insufficiently clarified vocabulary" and his respect for the stock phrases of the jurists causes some trouble, particularly when it comes to Ulpian (*loc. cit.*). Cf. M.-D. Chenu, O.P., *Towards Understanding St. Thomas* (Chicago: Regnery, 1964), pp. 126-149.

20. Some brief studies of Thomas's thought patterns in dealing with the cases: R. P. Sertillanges, *La philosophie morale de saint Thomas d'Aquin* (Paris: Aubier, 1946), pp. 110-113; Josef Fuchs, *Die Sexualethik des heiligen Thomas von Aquin* (Cologne: Bachem, 1949), pp. 170-178; Hans Meyer, *The Philosophy of St. Thomas Aquinas* (St. Louis: Herder, 1946), pp. 493-499. A longer, unfortunately unpublished study has been of assistance to me: John W. Healey, S.J., *The Mutability of the Natural Law in Selected Texts of Saint Thomas.* For a present-day Thomistic discussion of the question, see M. Zalba, S.J., *Theologiae Moralis Summa,* I, 2nd ed. (Madrid: Biblioteca de Autores Cristianos, 1957), pp. 232-236.

21. ". . . seipsum occidere est omnino illicitum triplici ratione" (*S. Th.,* II-II q.64, a.5, c.).

22. "As Augustine says, in the First Book of *The City of God,* when Samson crushed himself along with the enemy in the ruin of the building, he is excused only by the fact that the Spirit, who was working miracles through him, secretly commanded this. And he assigns the same reason for certain holy women who killed themselves in time of persecution and whose memory is celebrated in the Church" (*S. Th.,* II–II, q.64, a.5, ad 4).

"Augustine, in the First Book of *The City of God,* says that Samson is excused because it is believed that he did it on God's command. A sign of this is that he would not have been able to bring down so great a building by his own strength, but by the strength of God, who does not give assistance to the evil" (*Ad Hebr.,* c. XI, 1.7, 629 [Marietti]).

23. In "De Quinto Praecepto," *Duo Praecepta Caritatis et Decem Legis Praecepta,* 1261 (Marietti), Samson and the holy women are recalled by way of objection to argue that the prohibition to kill forbids the killing of another, but not the killing of oneself. Thomas quotes Augustine's reply, "Who kills himself certainly kills a man," and concludes, "If, therefore, it is not permitted to kill a man except by the authority of God, it is, consequently, not permitted to kill oneself except by God's command or the instinct [*instinctu*] of the holy Spirit, as is said of Samson."

"In reply to the sixth objection, it should be said that according to Augustine in the First Book of *The City of God,* no one is permitted to lay hands on himself for any reason unless perhaps it is done by divine instinct to give an example of courage in condemning death. Those concerning whom the objection has been made are believed to have brought death on themselves by a divine instinct. Wherefore their martyrdom is celebrated by the Church" (*In IV Sent.*, d.49, q.5, a.3, sol.2, ad 6).

By "instinct" Thomas means that motion of the holy Spirit in which, unlike prophecy, the human agent does not know what he is seeing or saying or doing; see *Ad Hebr.*, c. XI, 1.7, 631 (Marietti).

"Fornicatio dicitur esse peccatum, inquantum est contra rationem rectam. Ratio autem hominis recta est secundum quod regulatur voluntate divina, quae est prima et summa regula. Et ideo quod homo facit ex voluntate Dei, eius praeceptis obediens, non est contra rationem rectam, quamvis videatur esse contra communem ordinem rationis: sicut etiam non est contra naturam quod miraculose fit virtute divina, quamvis sit contra communem cursum naturae. Et ideo, sicut Abraham non peccavit filium innocentem volendo occidere, propter hoc quod obedivit Deo, quamvis hoc, secundum se consideratum, sit communiter contra rectitudinem rationis humanae; ita etiam Osee non peccavit fornicando ex praecepto divino. Nec talis concubitus proprie fornicatio debet dici: quamvis fornicatio nominetur referendo ad cursum communem" (*S. Th.*, II–II, q.154, a.2, ad 2).

24. Cf. his *Situation Ethics*, pp. 57-58.

25. "Quod vero dicitur ad Oseam: *Accipe tibi mulierem fornicariam*, etc., intelligitur secundum modum praecepti; sed praeceptum divinum facit ut non sit peccatum quod aliter esset peccatum. Potest enim Deus, ut Bernardus dicit (*de praec. et dispens.*, aliquant. a princ. lib.) dispensare in praeceptis secundae tabulae, per quae homo immediate ordinatur ad proximum; bonum enim proximi est quoddam bonum particulare. Non autem potest dispensare in praeceptis primae tabulae, per quae homo ordinatur in Deum, qui a se ipso alios non potest avertere: non enim potest negare se ipsum, ut dicitur II ad Tim. ii, quamvis quidam dicant, quod ea quae dicuntur de Osea, sunt intelligenda contigisse in visione prophetiae" (*De Malo*, q.3, a.1, ad 17).

"Respondeo dicendum, quod praeceptum est signum voluntatis divinae, respondens voluntati antecedenti, et non consequenti. Unde quod est praeter voluntatem consequentem cadit sub praecepto, non autem quod est praeter voluntatem antecedentem. Sed in hoc tamen considerandum est, quod aliquid secundum se acceptum est praeter voluntatem antecedentem, quod, aliqua conditione adveniente vel subtracta, est de voluntate antecedente, sicut illa quae secundum se considerata mala sunt; sed inquantum stant sub praecepto divino recipiunt quamdam rationem bonitatis, ut sic in ipsa voluntas tendere debeat: quod quidem in quibusdam per se malis contingit, et in quibusdam non. Bonum enim in rebus surgit ex duplici ordine: quorum primus et principalis ordo est rerum omnium ad finem ultimum, qui Deus est; secundus ordo est unius rei ad aliam rem: et primus ordo est causa secundi, quia secundus ordo est propter primum. Ex hoc enim quod res sunt ordinatae ad invicem, iuvant se mutuo, ut ad finem ultimum debite ordinentur. Unde oportet quod subtracta bonitate quae est ex ordine unius rei ad finem ultimum nihil bonitatis remanere possit. Sed subtracta bonitate quae est ex ordine unius rei ad rem aliam, nihilominus potest remanere illa bonitas quae est ex ordine rei ad finem ultimum: quia primum non dependet ex secundo, sicut secundum ex primo.

"Dico ergo, quod quaedam peccata nominant deordinationem unius rei ad rem aliam, sicut homicidium, odium fraternum, inobedientiam ad praelatum, et huiusmodi. Unde si talia bonitatem illam retinere possent quae est ex ordine ad finem ultimum, proculdubio bona essent et in ea voluntas ferri posset. Sed hoc non posset esse nisi virtute divina, per quam ordo in rebus institutus est. Sicut enim non potest fieri, nisi per miraculosam operationem virtutis divinae, ut quod recipit esse a primo agente, mediante aliqua causa secunda, habeat esse destructa vel subtracta causa secunda, ut hoc quod accidens sit sine subjecto, sicut in sacramento altaris: ita etiam non potest fieri, nisi per miraculum virtutis divinae, ut id quod natum est recipere bonitatem ex ordine ad finem ultimum mediante ordine ad rem illam, habeat bonitatem subtracto ordine qui erat ad rem illam; unde ille actus qui est occidere innocentem, vel resistere praelato, non potest esse bonus nec bene fieri, nisi auctoritate vel praecepto divino. Unde in talibus nullus dispensare potest, nisi Deus quasi miraculose. Quaedam vero peccata sunt quae dicunt deordinationem a fine ultimo immediate, ut desperare de Deo et odire eum, et huiusmodi; et illa nullo modo bonitatem habere possunt, nec etiam per virtutem divinam, sicut etiam virtute divina fieri non potest ut res esse habeat, cessante influentia primi agentis. Et ideo nulla dispensatione praecepto divino subjacent, quia nunquam bene fieri possunt. Et propter hoc dicitur quod contra praecepta primae tabulae, quae ordinant immediate in Deum, Deus dispensare non potest; sed contra praecepta secundae tabulae, quae ordinant immediate ad proximum, Deus potest dispensare; non autem homines in his dispensare potest" (*In I Sent.*, d.47, q.1, a.4, c).

"Ad secundum dicendum quod ipsa occisio innocentis prout substat deordinationi a fine, quae advenit sibi post speciem completam ab objecto proximo, est contra legem naturae, et non potest bene fieri; sed, remota tali deordinatione, est conveniens legi naturae, quae dictat omne illud esse faciendum quod est ordinatum et praeceptum a Deo" (*loc. cit.*, ad 2).

I am translating "dispensare contra" and "dispensare in," wherever they appear, as "dispense from"; but an analysis of the context is needed in each case to determine whether or not Thomas means dispensation in a strict legal sense. For our purpose, it suffices that he means, as he himself says, that what otherwise a man may not do because of natural law or the decalogue, he may now licitly do in virtue of the divine command or permission.

26. In translating or paraphrasing, I am rendering all Latin words of the stem "ord-" (e.g. ordo, deordinationem, ordinatae) by English words of the stem "ord-" (e.g. order, ordering). It makes for clumsy English, but seems the best way to convey the unity, various nuances, and occasional ambiguity of Thomas's expression.

27. "Ad quartum dicendum, quod nihil prohibet aliquem actum qui in se esset peccatum mortale, aliqua circumstantia addita fieri virtuosum; occidere enim hominem absolute peccatum mortale est; sed ministro judicis occidere hominem propter justitiam ex praecepto judicis, non est peccatum, sed actus justitiae. Sicut autem princeps civitatis habet disponere de hominibus quantum ad vitam et mortem et alia quaecumque pertinent ad finem sui regiminis, qui est justitia, ita Deus habet omnia in sua dispositione dirigere ad finem sui regiminis quod est ejus bonitas. Et ideo licet occidere filium innocentem de se possit esse peccatum mortale, tamen si hoc fiat ex praecepto Dei propter finem quem Deus praevidit et ordinavit, licet etiam sit homini ignotus, non est peccatum, sed meritum. Et similiter etiam dicendum est de fornicatione Oseae, cum constet Deum esse ordinatorem totius humanae generationis, quamvis quidam dicant, quod hoc non acciderit secundum veritatem rei, sed secundum visionem prophetiae" (*De Potentia Dei*, q.1, a.6, ad 4).

28. *In III Sent.*, d.37, a.4; *S. Th.*, I-II, q.100, a.8. The phrase in the question is "sint dispensabilia."

29. The cases of Hosea and the Israelite in Egypt ground the third objection raised in the *III Sent.* article and discussed in the corresponding reply. The same cases plus that of Abraham are discussed in the reply to the third objection in the *Summa* article.

30. "Ad tertium dicendum quod contra praecepta decalogi secundum quod ad decalogum pertinent, nunquam Deus fieri praecepit" (*loc. cit.*, ad 3).

31. The full reply to the second objection: "Ad secundum dicendum quod, sicut Apostolus dicit, *II ad Tim.* 2, 'Deus fidelis permanet, negare seipsum non potest.' Negaret autem seipsum, si

ipsum ordinem suae iustitiae auferret: cum ipse sit ipsa iustitia. Et ideo in hoc Deus dispensare non potest, ut homini liceat non ordinate se habere ad Deum, vel non subdi ordini iustitiae eius, etiam in his secundum quae homines ad invicem ordinantur."

32. Here, as in some other passages, Thomas takes "justice" in a wide sense, as prescribing whatever is due to another. He repeats the point at the beginning of the reply to the third objection and treats adultery there as a violation of justice.

"Nam praecepta primae tabulae, quae ordinant ad Deum, continent ipsum ordinem ad bonum commune et finale, quod Deus est; praecepta autem secundae tabulae continent ipsum ordinem iustitiae inter homines observandae, ut scilicet nulli fiat indebitum, et cuilibet reddatur debitum; secundum hanc enim rationem sunt intelligenda praecepta decalogi. Et ideo praecepta decalogi sunt omnino indispensabilia" (*loc. cit., corp.*).

"Ad tertium dicendum quod occisio hominis prohibetur in decalogo secundum quod habet rationem indebiti: sic enim praeceptum continet ipsam rationem iustitiae" (*loc. cit.,* ad 3).

In *Summa Contra Gentiles,* III, 128, Thomas takes "justice" in the same wide sense and applies it concretely to each of the precepts of the second table of the decalogue. In other places, Thomas understands justice in a narrower sense, distinct from virtue in general and chastity in particular, for example, in the passages quoted below in notes 36b and 51.

33. *Loc. cit.,* ad 2, cited in note 31.

34. "Sic igitur praecepta ipsa decalogi, quantum ad rationem iustitiae quam continent, immutabilia sunt" (*Loc. cit.,* ad 3). This sentence and its fuller context will come in for discussion subsequently.

35. The text of Aristotle that Thomas had before him, at least in later writings such as the *Summa,* is the version of Grosseteste as revised by William of Moerbeka. It can be found, for example, in the Marietti edition of Thomas's commentary on the Nicomachean Ethics, *ad locum.*

36. "Praecepta enim decalogi sunt de iure naturali. Sed iustum naturale in aliquibus deficit, et mutabile est, sicut et natura humana, ut Philosophus dicit, in *V Ethic.* Defectus autem legis in aliquibus particularibus casibus est ratio dispensandi, ut supra dictum est. Ergo in praeceptis decalogi potest fieri dispensatio" (*S. Th.,* I-II, q.100, a.8, 1; similarly *In III Sent.,* d.37, a.4, 2).

36a. The full reply to the objection in the *Summa* article: "Ad primum ergo dicendum quod Philosophus non loquitur de iusto naturali quod continet ipsum ordinem iustitiae: hoc enim nunquam deficit, iustitiam esse servandam. Sed loquitur quantum ad determinatos modos observationis iustitiae, qui in aliquibus fallunt."

36b. "Ad secundum dicendum quod iustum naturale est duplex, ut supra dictum est: quoddam quod semper et ubique est iustum, sicut hoc in quo consistit forma iustitiae et virtutis in generali, sicut medium tenere, rectitudinem servare et alia huiusmodi; quoddam vero est ex hoc profectum, secundum Tullium (in *II Rhet. de invent.*), et hoc in pluribus ita contingit sed potest in paucioribus deficere, ut dictum est. Quod contingit ex hoc quod huiusmodi iustum est applicatio quaedam universalis et primae mensurae ad materiam difformem et mutabilem et de huiusmodi iusto loquitur Philosophus" (ad 2).

37. The objection: "Praeterea, ea quae sunt secundum legem, iusta esse dicuntur, ut dicitur in *V Ethic.* Sed in eodem libro dicitur quod nihil est ita iustum apud omnes, quin apud aliquos diversificetur. Ergo lex etiam naturalis non est apud omnes eadem." The reply: "Ad secundum dicendum quod verbum Philosophi est intelligendum de his quae sunt naturaliter iusta non sicut principia communia, sed sicut quaedam conclusiones ex his derivatae, quae ut in pluribus rectitudinem habent et ut in paucioribus deficiunt" (*S. Th.*, I-II, q.94, a.4, 2 and ad 2).

38. "Et primo [Aristoteles] manifestat iustum naturale dupliciter. Uno modo secundum effectum vel virtutem, dicens: iustum naturale est quod habet ubique eandem potentiam et virtutem ad inducendum ad bonum et ad ‾arcendum a malo. Quod quidem contingit eo quod natura, quae est huius iusti causa, eadem est ubique apud omnes. Iustum vero ex positione alicuius civitatis vel principis apud illos tantum est virtuosum qui subduntur iurisdictioni illius civitatis vel principis. Alio modo manifestat hoc iustum secundum causam, cum dicit quod iustum naturale non consistit in videri vel non videri, id est non oritur ex aliqua opinione humana, sed natura. Sicut etiam in speculativis sunt quaedam naturaliter cognita, ut principia indemonstrabilia et quae sunt propinqua his; quaedam vero studio hominum adinventa, et quae sunt propinqua; ita etiam in operativis sunt quaedam principia naturaliter cognita quasi indemonstrabilia principia et propinqua his, ut malum esse vitandum, nulli esse iniuste nocendum, non furandum, et similia. Alia vero sunt per industriam hominum excogitata, quae dicuntur hic iusta legalia" (*In Decem Libros Ethicorum Aristotelis Ad Nicomachum Expositio*, lib. V, lectio xii, 1018; cf. 1023).

39. "Sed apud nos homines, qui sumus inter res corruptibiles, est aliquid quidem secundum naturam, et tamen quicquid est in nobis est mutabile vel per se vel per accidens" (*loc. cit.*, 1026; cf. 1027).

40. "Est tamen attendendum quod quia rationes rerum mutabilium sunt immutabiles, sic quicquid est nobis naturale quasi pertinens ad ipsam hominis rationem, nullo modo mutatur, puta hominem esse animal. Quae autem consequuntur naturam, puta dispositiones, actiones et motus, mutantur ut in paucioribus. Et similiter etiam illa quae pertinent ad ipsam iustitiae rationem nullo modo possunt mutari, puta non esse furandum, quod est iniustum facere. Illa vero quae consequuntur, mutantur ut in minori parte" (1029).

41. *Loc. cit.*, 1018.

42. *S. Th.*, I-II, q.100, a.8, *corp.*

43. Implied in *In V Eth.*, 1028.

44. *Loc. cit.*, 1018.

45. *S. Th., loc. cit.*, ad 3.

46. *Loc. cit.*, ad 1.

47. *In III Sent., loc. cit.*, ad 2.

48. *Ibid.*

49. An example of a "common principle of practical reason": "Apud omnes enim hoc rectum est et verum, ut secundum rationem agatur" (*S. Th.*, I-II, q.94, a.4, c).

50. *In V. Eth.*, 1018, 1023 and 1029.

50a. "Et ideo necesse est quod quicquid ex iusto naturali sequitur, quasi conclusio, sit iustum naturale; sicut ex hoc quod est, nulli est iniuste nocendum, sequitur non esse furandum; quod quidem ad naturale pertinet" (1023; cf. 1029, quoted above).

51. Here, as frequently elsewhere, I present the full Latin text in one place in order to bring out the context and unity of the whole. Sections of the text will be discussed in various places in the exposition.

"Ad secundum dicendum quod sicut Deus nihil operatur contra naturam, quia 'haec est natura uniuscuiusque rei quod in ea Deus operatur,' ut habetur in *Glossa Rom. XI*, operatur tamen aliquid contra solitum cursum naturae; ita etiam Deus nihil potest praecipere contra virtutem, quia in hoc principaliter consistit virtus et rectitudo voluntatis humanae quod Dei voluntati conformetur et eius sequatur imperium, quamvis sit contra consuetum virtutis modum. Secundum hoc ergo praeceptum Abrahae factum quod filium innocentem occideret, non fuit contra iustitiam, quia Deus est auctor mortis et vitae. Similiter nec fuit contra iustitiam quod mandavit Iudaeis ut res Aegyptiorum acciperent, quia eius sunt omnia et cui voluerit dat illa. Similiter etiam non fuit contra castitatem praeceptum ad Osee factum ut mulierem adulteram acciperet quia ipse Deus est humanae generationis ordinator, et ille est debitus modus mulieribus utendi quem Deus instituit. Unde patet quod praedicti nec obediendo Deo nec obedire volendo peccaverunt" (*S. Th.*, II–II, q.104, a.4, ad 2).

One sees here how two approaches of Thomas that seemed to conflict are united by him: the apparent nominalism according to which God's will is the sole determinant of what is moral (cf. *S. Th.*, II-II, q.154, a.2, ad 2, cited in note 23) and the insistence that God can will only what is just and virtuous (cf. *S. Th.*, I-II, q.100, a.8, and parallel passages quoted above).

52. "Hic est duplex quaestio. Una quia innocentem occidere est contra legem naturae et ita peccatum; ergo volendo offerre peccavit.

"Respondeo. Dicendum est, quod ille qui ex mandato superioris interficit, si ille licite praecipit, alius licite obedit, et potest licite exequi ministerium suum. Deus autem habet mortis et vitae auctoritatem. I Reg. II, 6: 'Dominus mortificat et vivificat.' Deus autem subtrahendo vitam alicui etiam innocenti, nulli facit iniuriam. Unde et quotidie, dispositione divina, multi nocentes et innocentes moriuntur. Et ideo Dei mandatum licite poterat exequi" (*Ad Heb.*, c. XI, 1. iv, 604).

Thomas uses an almost identical formulation in *S. Th.*, II-II, q.64, a.6, ad 1; here he terms it "God's dominion over life and death": "Ad primum ergo dicendum quod Deus habet dominium mortis et vitae: eius enim ordinatione moriuntur et peccatores et iusti. Et ideo ille qui mandato Dei occidit innocentem, talis non peccat, sicut nec Deus, cuius est executor. Et ostenditur Deum timere, eius mandatis obediens."

53. "Ad tertium dicendum quod occisio hominis prohibetur in decalogo secundum quod habet rationem indebiti: sic enim praeceptum continet ipsam rationem iustitiae. Lex autem humana hoc concedere non potest, quod licite homo indebite occidatur. Sed malefactores occidi vel hostes reipublicae, hoc non est indebitum. Unde hoc non contrariatur praecepto decalogi; nec talis occisio est homicidium, quod praecepto decalogi prohibetur, ut Augustinus dicit in *I de Lib. Arb.* Et similiter si alicui auferatur quod suum erat, si debitum est quod ipsum amittat, hoc non est furtum vel rapina, quae praecepto decalogi prohibentur.

"Et ideo quando filii Israel praecepto Dei tulerunt Aegyptiorum spolia, non fuit furtum, quia hoc eis debebatur ex sententia Dei. Similiter etiam Abraham, cum consensit occidere filium, non consensit in homicidium, quia debitum erat eum occidi per mandatum Dei, qui est Dominus vitae et mortis. Ipse enim est qui poenam mortis infligit omnibus hominibus, iustis et iniustis, pro peccato primi parentis; cuius sententiae si homo sit executor auctoritate divina, non erit homicida, sicut nec Deus. Et similiter etiam Osee, accedens ad uxorem fornicariam vel ad mulierem adulteram, non est moechatus nec fornicatus, quia accessit ad eam quae sua erat secundum mandatum divinum, qui est auctor institutionis matrimonii.

"Sic igitur praecepta ipsa decalogi, quantum ad rationem iustitiae quam continent, immutabilia sunt. Sed quantum ad aliquam determinationem per applicationem ad singulares casus, ut scilicet hoc vel illud sit homicidium, furtum vel adulterium, aut non, hoc quidem est mutabile: quandoque sola auctoritate divina, in his scilicet quae a solo Deo sunt instituta, sicut in matrimonio et aliis huiusmodi; quandoque etiam auctoritate humana, sicut in his quae sunt commissa hominum iurisdictioni. Quantum enim ad hoc, homines gerunt vicem Dei, non autem quantum ad omnia" (*S. Th.,* I-II, q.100, a.8, ad 3).

"Ad secundum dicendum quod naturali morte moriuntur omnes communiter, tam nocentes quam innocentes. Quae quidem naturalis mors divina potestate inducitur propter peccatum originale; secundum illud I *Reg.* 2, 'Dominus mortificat et vivificat.' Et ideo absque aliqua iniustitia, secundum mandatum Dei, potest infligi mors cuicumque homini vel nocenti vel innocenti. Similiter etiam adulterium est concubitus cum uxore aliena; quae quidem est ei deputata secundum legem divinitus traditam. Unde ad quamcumque mulierem aliquis accedat ex mandato divino, non est adulterium nec fornicatio. Et eadem ratio est de furto, quod est acceptio rei alienae. Quidquid enim accipit aliquis ex mandato Dei, qui est Dominus universorum, non accipit absque voluntate domini, quod est furari. Nec solum in rebus humanis quidquid a Deo mandatur, hoc ipso est debitum: sed etiam in rebus naturalibus quidquid a Deo fit, est quodammodo naturale, ut in Primo dictum est." (*S. Th.,* I-II, q.94, a.5, ad 2; the objection was that the incidents concerning Abraham, Hosea and the Jews in Egypt prove that the natural law can change.)

54. *De Pot.,* q.1, a.6, ad 4, quoted in note 27.

55. In three other passages Thomas describes God's command to Abraham as an unusual precept of God (*S. Th.,* II-II, q.154, a.2, ad 2, quoted in note 23), as a direct and miraculous ordering of the killing to God as man's final end (*In I Sent.,* d.47, q.1, a.4, c. and ad 2), and as a dispensation from a primary precept of the natural law (*In IV Sent.,* d.33, q.2, a.2, sol. 1, which will be discussed shortly). But in none of the three passages does he make an attempt to show how this fits in with inviolable principles of morality and justice.

56. *S. Th.,* II-II, q.104, a.4, ad 2, quoted in note 51. Similarly: "Ad octavum dicendum quod sicut propter praeceptum Dei, in cuius potestate sunt omnia, id quod alias fuisset furtum fuit non

furtum filiis Israel Aegyptios spoliantibus, ut dicitur *Exod.* XII, ita et propter auctoritatem ipsius Dei, qui est supra legem matrimonii, concubitus ille non fuit fornicarius, qui alias fornicarius fuisset. Unde dicitur uxor fornicationum et fornicationum filii non quia tunc esset fornicatio, sed quia alias fornicatio fuisset" (*De Malo*, q.XV, a.1, ad 8).

57. *S. Th.*, I-II, q.94, a.5, ad 2, quoted in note 53. Similarly: "Ad tertium dicendum quod contra praecepta decalogi, secundum quod ad decalogum pertinent, nunquam Deus fieri praecepit. Prohibitio enim furti ad decalogum pertinet inquantum res furata aliena est ab accipiente. Retenta ergo hac conditione, si res illa fiat ipsius accipientis, iam non erit contra decalogum. Hoc autem non solum Deus, qui est omnium Dominus, facere poterat, sed etiam quandoque homines auctoritatem habentes rem quae unius fuerat alteri conferunt aliqua ex causa. Potest tamen Deus in aliquibus factis conditiones contrarias decalogo auferre qui et naturam mutare potest, quod homo facere non potest; sicut ab ea quae non est matrimonio iuncta potest auferre hanc conditionem 'non suam,' sine hoc quod uxor plenarie fiat, ut sic accedere ad eam non sit contra decalogum" (*In III Sent.*, d.37, a.4, ad 3).

In two other passages, it is not clear whether Thomas is appealing to God's universal dominion in order to justify his command: "it was not stealing because it was due the Egyptians by God's sentence" (*S. Th.*, q.100, a.8, ad 3, quoted in note 53): "that something, belonging to another, be taken, secretly or openly, in virtue of the authority of a judge who decrees it is not stealing; for it becomes due to one by the very fact that it has been granted to him by judicial sentence. Wherefore much less was it stealing when the children of Israel took spoils of the Egyptians on the command of the Lord who was decreeing it for the afflictions which the Egyptians had brought on them without cause" ("Ad primum ergo dicendum quod accipere rem alienam vel occulte vel manifeste auctoritate iudicis hoc decernentis non est furtum, quia iam fit sibi debitum per hoc quod sententialiter sibi est adiudicatum. Unde multo minus furtum fuit quod filii Israel tulerunt spolia Aegyptiorum de praecepto Domini hoc decernentis pro afflictionibus quibus Aegyptii eos sine causa afflixerant. Et ideo signanter dicitur *Sap.* 10: 'Iusti tulerunt spolia impiorum' " [*S. Th.*, II-II, q.66, a.5, ad 1]).

58. *S. Th.*, II-II, q.104, a.4, ad 2, quoted in note 51. Similarly, in the *De Potentia* passage, Thomas justifies the action of God by his being "ordinatorem totius humanae generationis" (*De Pot.*, q.1, a.6, ad 4, quoted in note 27).

59. *S. Th.*, I-II, q.100, a.8, ad 3, quoted in note 53.

60. *De Malo*, q.15, a.1, ad 8, quoted in note 56.

61. *S. Th.*, I-II, q.94, a.5, ad 2, quoted in note 53.

62. *In III Sent.*, d.37, a.4, ad 3, quoted in note 57.

63. *In IV Sent.*, d.33, q.2, a.2, sol.1 and ad 2.

64. The entire second article is devoted to the question.

65. There are three other passages in which God's command to Hosea is discussed, but is not justified in terms of moral principles: *S. Th.*, II-II, q.154, a.2, ad 2; *De Malo*, q.3, a.1, ad 17; *In Matth.*, c. XIX (p. 255, Marietti, 1925). In the light of the analysis made earlier in our inquiry, it is not surprising that in the first passage (quoted in note 23) Thomas offers no specific moral justification of God's command, and that in the second passage (quoted in note 25) he merely applies the principle that "the good of the neighbor is a particular given good" and therefore God can bypass it, still ordering the man to his final good, God himself. In the third pasage, it is not clear to me in exactly what sense Thomas is comparing God's command to Hosea to the Mosaic dispensation for divorce, but in any case there is no reference to specific moral principles: "Ideo dicit Chrysostomus, quod a peccato abstulit peccati culpam. Et licet inordinatum quid esset, noluit tamen quod eis imputaretur ad culpam, ut Dominus Oseae praecepit, ut faceret filios fornicationis: unde permissio non fuit ex praecepto, sed ad vitandum majus malum."

66. The textual evidence concerns only the disposing of human generation. It says nothing of the possibility of God's authorizing non-generative sexual (for example, contraceptive or homosexual) activity.

67. "Respondeo dicendum quod res exterior potest dupliciter considerari. Uno modo, quantum ad eius naturam: quae non subiacet humanae potestati, sed solum divinae, cui omnia ad nutum obediunt. Alio modo, quantum ad usum ipsius rei. Et sic habet homo naturale dominium exteriorum rerum, quia per rationem et voluntatem potest uti rebus exterioribus ad suam utilitatem, quasi propter se factis; semper enim imperfectiora sunt propter perfectiora, ut supra habitum est. Et ex hac ratione Philosophus probat, in I *Polit.*, quod possessio rerum exteriorum est homini naturalis. Hoc autem naturale dominium super ceteras creaturas, quod competit homini secundum rationem, in qua imago Dei consistit, manifestatur in ipsa hominis creatione, *Gen.* 1, ubi dicitur, 'Faciamus hominem ad similitudinem et imaginem nostram, et praesit piscibus maris, etc.'

"Ad primum ergo dicendum quod Deus habet principale dominium omnium rerum. Et ipse secundum suam providentiam ordinavit res quasdam ad corporalem hominis sustentationem. Et propter hoc homo habet naturale rerum dominium quantum ad potestatem utendi ipsis." (*S. Th.*, II-II, q.66, a.1, c. and ad 1; the replies to the second and third objection develop the theme further.)

68. *In III Sent.*, d.37, a.4, ad 3, quoted in note 57. Similarly, in *S. Th.*, II-II, q.66, a.5, ad 1 (also quoted in note 57), Thomas compares God's authority in changing the ownership of the Egyptians' property to that of a human judge.

69. "Quidam dixerunt hic [by the fifth precept of the decalogue] prohibitum esse homicidium hominis omnino. Unde homicidas dicunt esse iudices saeculares, qui condemnant secundum leges aliquos. Contra quos dicit Augustinus quod Deus per hoc praeceptum non abstulit sibi potestatem occidendi. Unde *Deut.* XXXII, 39: 'Ego occidam et vivere faciam.' Est ergo licitum illis qui mandato Dei occidunt, quia tunc Deus facit. Omnis enim lex mandatum Dei est. *Prov.* VIII, 15: 'Per me reges regnant et legum conditores iusta decernunt.' Et Apostolus, *Rom.* XIII, 4: 'Si malum feceris, time: non enim sine causa gladium portat; Dei enim minister est.' Moysi quoque dicitur, *Exod.* XXII, 18, 'Maleficos non patieris vivere.' Id enim quod licitum est Deo, licitum est et ministris eius per mandatum ipsius. Constat autem quod Deus non peccat, cum sit auctor legum, infligendo mortem propter peccatum. *Rom.* VI, 23: 'Stipendia peccati mors.' Ergo nec minister eius. Est ergo sensus: 'Non occides' propria auctoritate" (*Duo Praecepta Caritatis Et Decem Legis Praecepta*, "De quinto praecepto," 1260 (Marietti); cf. *S. Th.*, II-II, q.64, a.2, c. and ad 2). Thomas uses the identical argument here that he did for God's command to Abraham; cf. the passages quoted in note 52.

70. Pertinent parts of the paragraph are quoted in note 22.

71. "Respondeo dicendum quod, sicut dictum est, occidere malefactorem licitum est inquantum ordinatur ad salutem totius communitatis. Et ideo ad illum solum pertinet cui committitur cura communitatis conservandae, sicut ad medicum pertinet praecidere membrum putridum quando ei commissa fuerit cura salutis totius corporis. Cura autem communis boni commissa est principibus habentibus publicam auctoritatem. Et ideo eis solum licet malefactores occidere, non autem privatis personis.

"Ad primum ergo dicendum quod ille aliquid facit cuius auctoritate fit, ut patet per Dionysium, 13 cap., *Cael. Hier.* Et ideo Augustinus dicit, in I *de Civ. Dei*, 'non ipse occidit qui ministerium debet iubenti sicut adminiculum gladius utenti.' Unde illi qui occiderunt proximos et amicos ex mandato Domini, non hoc fecisse ipsi videntur, sed potius ille cuius auctoritate fecerunt; sicut et miles interficit hostem auctoritate principis et minister latronem auctoritate iudicis" (*S. Th.*, II-II, q.64, a.3, c. and ad 1; cf. a.4, ad 1).

72. *S. Th.,* I-II, q.100, a.8, ad 3, quoted in note 53. A similar comparison of divine and human authority is made in *De Pot.,* q.1, a.6, ad 4, quoted in note 27.

73. "Respondeo dicendum quod aliquis homo dupliciter considerari potest: uno modo, secundum se; alio modo, per comparationem ad aliud. Secundum se quidem considerando hominem, nullum occidere licit, quia in quolibet, etiam peccatore, debemus amare naturam, quam Deus fecit, quae per occisionem corrumpitur. Sed sicut supra dictum est, occisio peccatoris fit licita per comparationem ad bonum commune, quod per peccatum corrumpitur. Vita autem iustorum est conservativa et promotiva boni communis, quia ipsi sunt principalior pars multitudinis. Et ideo nullo modo licet occidere innocentem" (*S. Th.,* II-II, q.64, a.6, c).

74. *S. Th.,* I-II, q.100, a.8, ad 3, quoted in note 53. In *S. Th.,* II-II, q.154, a.2, ad 2, quoted in note 23, Thomas quotes Augustine and places Hosea's act in the hierarchical network of authorities: "For as in the powers of human society the greater stands above the lesser to be obeyed, so God above all."

75. *Summa Contra Gentiles,* IV, 78, second paragraph in the Leonine edition.

76. *S. Th.,* I-II, q.100, a.8, ad 3, quoted in note 53. Similarly *In III Sent.,* d.37, a.4, ad 3, quoted in note 57, and *Summa Contra Gentiles,* III, 125.

77. Josef Fuchs, *Die Sexualethik des heiligen Thomas von Aquin* (Köln: Bachem, 1949), p. 175. Fuchs believes that in certain passages Thomas is appealing to divine positive law as complementing and determining natural law, but that often the distinction between the two seems to be denied.

78. "Ad duodecimum dicendum, quod actus generationis ordinatur ad bonum speciei, quod est bonum commune. Bonum autem commune est ordinabile lege; sed bonum privatum subjacet ordinationi uniuscuiusque. Et ideo quamvis in actu nutritivae virtutis, quae ordinatur ad conservationem individui, unusquisque possit sibi determinare cibum convenientem sibi, tamen determinare qualis debeat esse generationis actus non pertinet ad unumquemque, sed ad legislatorem, cuius est ordinare de propagatione filiorum, ut etiam Philosophus dicit in II *Polit.* Lex autem non considerat quid in aliquo casu accidere possit, sed quid convenienter esse consuevit. Et ideo licet in aliquo casu possit salvari intentio naturae in actu fornicario quantum ad generationem prolis et educationis, nihilominus actus est secundum se inordinatus et peccatum mortale" (*De Malo,* q.XV, a.2, ad 12; cf. ad 14 and *Summa Contra Gentiles,* III, 125, *fine*).

79. M.-D. Chenu, O.P., *Towards Understanding Saint Thomas* (Chicago: Regnery, 1964), p. 271.

80. "Respondeo dicendum quod, sicut ex praedictis patet, pluralitas uxorum dicitur esse contra legum naturae, non quantum ad prima praecepta eius, sed quantum ad secunda, quae quasi conclusiones a primis praeceptis derivantur. Sed quia actus humanos variari oportet secundum diversas conditiones personarum et temporum et aliarum circumstantiarum, ideo conclusiones praedictae a primis legis naturae praeceptis non procedunt ut semper efficaciam habentes, sed in maiori parte. Talis enim est tota materia moralis, ut patet per Philosophum in libris *Ethicorum*. Et ideo ubi eorum efficacia deficit, licite ea praetermitti possunt. Sed quia non est facile determinare huiusmodi varietates, ideo illi ex cuius auctoritate lex efficaciam habet, reservatur ut licentiam praebeat legem praetermittendi in illis casibus ad quos legis efficacia se non extendere debet. Et talis licentia dispensatio dicitur. Lex autem de unitate uxoris non est humanitus, sed divinitus instituta, nec unquam verbis aut litteris tradita, sed cordi impressa, sicut et alia quae ad legem naturae qualitercumque pertinent. Et ideo in hoc a solo Deo dispensatio fieri potuit per inspirationem internam, quae quidem principaliter sanctis patribus facta est et per eorum exemplum ad alios derivata est eo tempore quo oportebat praedictum naturae praeceptum praetermitti, ut maior esset multiplicatio prolis ad cultum Dei educandae. Semper enim principalior finis magis conservandus est quam secundarius. Unde cum bonum prolis sit principalis matrimonii finis, ubi prolis multiplicatio necessaria erat, debuit neglegi ad tempus impedimentum, quod posset in secundariis finibus evenire, ad quod removendum praeceptum prohibens pluralitatem uxorum ordinatur, ut ex dictis patet" (*In IV Sent.*, d.33, q.1, art.2, sol.). What Thomas means by "primary" and "secondary" precepts is brought out in the solution of article 1.

81. Q.1, a.3, sol.3 and replies; q.2, a.2, sol.2 and replies. Cf. above, the summary of Thomas' position on the Mosaic permission for divorce.

82. Cf. J.-M. Aubert, *Le droit romain dans l'oeuvre de saint Thomas* (Paris: Vrin, 1955), p. 111; J. Fuchs, *Die Sexualethik des heiligen Thomas von Aquin*, p. 177; J. Maritain, *Man and the State*, p. 85; O. Lottin, "La valeur des formules de saint Thomas d'Aquin concernant la loi naturelle," *Mélanges Joseph Maréchal*, II, pp. 351 ff.; O. Lottin, *Psychologie et Morale aux XIIe et XIIIe siècles*, II, i. p. 96.

83. "Sciendum est autem quod, sicut naturalis inclinatio est ad ea quae sunt ut in pluribus, ita et lex posita est secundum id quod in pluribus accidit. Non est praedictis rationibus contrarium si in aliquo aliter possit accidere; non enim propter bonum unius debet praetermitti bonum multorum, cum 'bonum multitudinis semper sit divinius quam bonum unius.' Ne tamen defectus qui in

aliquo uno posset accidere, omnino absque medela remaneat, residet apud legislatores et eis similes auctoritas dispensandi in eo quod communiter est statutum, secundum quod est necessarium in aliquo casu particulari. Et si quidem lex sit humana, per homines similem potestatem habentes dispensari potest. Si autem lex sit divinitus posita, auctoritate divina dispensatio fieri potest, sicut in veteri lege ex dispensatione indultum videtur uxores plures habere et concubinas et uxoris repudium" (*Summa Contra Gentiles,* III, 125; cf. *De Malo,* q.15, a.2, ad 12).

84. "Respondeo dicendum ad primam quaestionem quod dispensatio in praeceptis, praecipue quae sunt aliquomodo legis naturae, est sicut mutatio cursus rei naturalis, qui quidem mutari dupliciter potest. Uno modo ex aliqua causa naturali, per quam alia causa naturalis impeditur a cursu suo, sicut est in omnibus quae in minori parte casualiter accidunt in natura. Sed per hunc modum non variatur cursus rerum quae sunt semper, sed quae sunt frequenter. Alio modo per causam penitus supernaturalem, sicut in miraculis accidit; et hoc modo potest mutari cursus naturalis non solum qui est ordinatus ut sit frequenter, sed qui est ordinatus etiam ut sit semper, ut patet in statione solis tempore Josue et reditu eiusdem tempore Ezechiae et de eclypsi miraculosa tempore passionis Christi. Haec autem ratio dispensationis in praeceptis legis naturae quandoque est in causis inferioribus, et sic dispensatio cadere potest super secunda praecepta legis naturae, non autem super prima, quia illa sunt quasi semper existentia, ut dictum est de pluralitate uxorum et de huiusmodi. Aliquando autem est tantum in causis superioribus, et tunc potest dispensatio esse divinitus etiam contra prima praecepta legis naturae, ratione alicuius mysterii divini significandi vel ostendendi, sicut patet de dispensatione in praecepto Abrahae facto de occisione filii innocentis" (*In IV Sent.,* d.33, q.2, a.2, sol.1). Cf. q.1, a.2, sol. and ad 1, 2 and 3, where Thomas develops further, à propos of polygamy, how dispensations of the sort are possible where natural sequences hold only for the most part. On the other hand, the prohibitions of polyandry and of concubinage in the strict sense, that is, of fornication, are primary precepts of the natural law and not subject to dispensation of this sort: q.1, a.1, ad 8; q.1, a.3, sol.3 and ad 1.

85. Joannis de Lugo, *Tractatus de iustitia et iure,* disp. X, sect. I, 2.

86. *Loc. cit.,* 9.

87. Cf. R. P. Sertillanges, *La philosophie morale de saint Thomas d'Aquin* (Paris: Aubier, 1946), p. 95; Dietrich Bonhoeffer, *Letters and Papers from Prison* (New York: Macmillan Paperback, 1962), for example, pp. 190-191, 194-197; H. Richard Niebuhr,

The Responsible Self (New York: Harper and Row, 1963), e.g., pp. 66, 131.

88. *Loc. cit.*, 2.

89. Classic expressions of the contemporary vision are H. R. Niebuhr, *The Responsible Self*, for example, pp. 47-68, and Dietrich Bonhoeffer, *Letters and Papers from Prison*, especially the pages cited in note 87. In a sense, all of Niebuhr's book is an attempt to clarify the twentieth-century vision of man before God by putting the image of man-the-responder in a place of prominence over that of man-the-maker and that of man-the-citizen. Niebuhr observes that even the word "responsible" seems to have acquired its current moral sense only in the nineteenth and twentieth centuries (p. 47). It is interesting that there is no exact verbal equivalent in classical Greek and Latin for "responsibility" just as there is none for "loneliness."

90. Max Müller, *Existenzphilosophie im geistigen Leben der Gegenwart* (Heidelberg: Kerle, 1958), p. 140. In translating, I have availed myself of the context in order to make clear Professor Müller's meaning in the brief quotation.

CORNELIUS J. VAN DER POEL

1. Germain Grisez, "A New Formulation of a Natural-Law Argument against Contraception," in *The Thomist*, Vol. 30, No. 4, 1966, 356. Italics added.

2. Cf. J. P. Kenny, *Principles of Medical Ethics* (Newman, 1962), pp. 208 ff.

3. It is not necessary to give here an elaborate analysis of the human act and of the principle of the double effect. For this I may refer to L. Janssens, "Daden met meerdere Gevolgen," in *Coll. Mechliniensia* 17 (1947), 621-633 or J. Ghoos: "L'act à double effet," in *Ephemerides Theologicae Lovanienses*, 28 (1951), 30-52. Here I am mainly concerned with the application of the principle of the double effect as it occurs in so many of our manuals of moral theology.

4. H. Noldin, *Summa Theologiae Moralis*, 1962, Vol. I, No. 82: "Effectus malus, qui *ex natura actionis* sequitur ita ut actio alium effectum habere non possit, item effectus malus *intentus*, sive in se, sive ut medium ad alium, semper imputatur."

5. *Theologia Moralis*, I (Marietti, 1939), No. 58, 13th ed.

6. Van Zunderen, quoted in W. van der Marck, *Love and Fertility* (Sheed & Ward, 1965).

7. E. Regatillo and M. Zalba, *Theologiae Moralis Summa,* Vol. I (Madrid, 1952), No. 1876: "Sic imputatur medico mors fetus, quando peragit craniotomiam ad salvandam matrem; et revera cum vult craniotomiam, quae non habet alium effectum immediatum nisi mortem infantis, vult hanc mortem in se, etsi non propter se."

8. For a concise philosophical description of man, cf. Engelbert J. van Croonenburg, C.S.Sp.: *Gateway to Reality* (Pittsburgh: Duquesne University Press, 1963), especially pp. 39-118.

9. Edward Schillebeeckx, "Wereld an Kerk," *Theologische Peilingen,* III (Nelissen, Bilthoven, 1966), p. 253.

10. Cf. W. van der Marck, *op. cit.,* pp. 46-48.

11. Jan H. Walgrave, "Is Morality Static or Dynamic?" in *Moral Problems and Christian Personalism, Concilium,* Vol. 5, p. 29; cf. J. Ghoos, "Fundamentele opdrachten en geboden," in *Dynamische perspectieven der christelijke moraal,* pp. 121-125.

12. Edward Schillebeeckx, "God an Mens," *Theologische Peilingen,* II (Nelissen, Bilthoven, 1965), p. 184.

13. P. Anciaux, F. D'Hoogh, J. Ghoos, *Dynamische perspectieven der christelijke moraal,* ed. Lannoo, pp. 114 ff.

14. Hubert Bonner, *Group Dynamics* (New York: Ronald Press, 1959), p. 46.

15. Jan H. Walgrave, "Standpunten en stromingen in de hedendaagse Moraal Theologie," in *Tijdschrift voor Theologie,* 1 (1961), 66.

16. Walgrave, *op. cit., p.* 67.

17. W. van der Marck, "De autonome menselijke samenleving als sacrament van de Godsgemeenschap," in *Tijdschrift voor Theologie,* 4 (1964), 165; also *Love and Fertility,* p. 53; and cf. Bruno Schuller, "Wie weit kann die Moral Theologie das Naturrecht entbehren," in *Lebendiges Zeugnis,* 1965, No. 1/2, pp. 58-62; Georg Teichtweiler, "Eine neue Moraltheologie," in *Lebendiges Zeugnis,* 1965, No. 1/2, pp. 84-89.

18. B. Häring, *The Law of Christ,* III (Newman, 1964), p. 208.

19. John McCarthy, *Problems in Theology* II (Westminster, Md.: Newman Press, 1960), pp. 119-124. All the definitions and examples in the next paragraph are taken from McCarthy, who also includes other bibliographical material on the notion of direct and indirect killing. For a critique of the principle of double effect by a theologian who also disagrees with the present emphasis on the physical structure of the act, cf. P. Knauer, S.J., "La Determination du bien et du mal par le principe de double effet," *Nouvelle Revue Théologique* 87 (1965), 360.

20. McCarthy, *loc. cit.*

21. E. Schillebeeckx, "De Natuurwet in verband met de katholieke Huwelijksopvatting," in *Jaarboek 1961 van het werkgenootschap van der katholieke theologen in Nederland.*

22. Ad. Peperzak, "Wijsgerige notities ten behoeve van een theologische etiek," in *Tijdschrift voor Theologie*, 4 (1964), 276.

23. Cf. E. Schillebeeckx, "Wijsgerig-theologische beschouwingen over man en vrouw," in *Katholiek Artsenblad*, 1961, pp. 85-94.

24. W. van der Marck, *Love and Fertility*, p. 57.

25. *Op. cit.*, p. 56.

26. *Loc. cit.*

27. P. Knauer, *op. cit.*, p. 369.

28. I am aware of the fact that I use the term "indirect voluntary" in a wider sense than is usually done in the manuals of moral theology. But even in the manuals there is no strict uniformity in the use of this term. I include in the term "indirect voluntary" all those aspects of human action which in themselves are not the purpose of the action but which are either the means to or the concomitant effects of the human action. They are the regretted but unavoidable aspects of the total act. They themselves are willed, but only because and insofar as the totality of the act demands them.

29. Erich Fromm, *Man for Himself, An Inquiry into the Psychology of Ethics* (New York: Holt, Rinehart and Winston, 1964), p. 29.

30. *S. Th.*, II-II, q.8, a.2.

31. W. van der Marck, "De autonome menselijke samenleving als sacrament van de Godsgemeenschap," in *Tijdschrift voor Theologie*, 4 (1964), 162.

32. I do not will them for their *own* value, but I *do* will them as inseparable parts of my effort to see the panorama.

33. The human will intends the excision, but in such cases the will is not directed to it as to an independent value. The excision is only willed insofar as it makes the future implantation possible. The implantation gives the *human* meaning to the excision.

34. W. van der Marck, *op. cit.*, p. 165.

35. Jan H. Walgrave, "Standpunten en stromingen in de hedendaagse Moraal Theologie," in *Tijdschrift voor Theologie*, 1 (1961), 56.

36. F. D'Hoogh, "Algemene morele waarden en concrete normen," in *Dynamische perspectieven der christelijke moraal*, p. 90.

37. W. van der Marck, "Het Christusgeheim in de menselijke samenleving," *Romen en Zenen* (Roermond, 1966), pp. 52-53.

38. E. Shillebeeckx, "God en Mens," *Theologische Peilingen* II, p. 24. For the specific aspect of the "purpose" of human action

it is of major importance to study Thomas Aquinas, *S. Th.,* I-II, q.1-5. God is the transcendent goal of human existence (as he is of all existence), but he is also the "immanent" goal of human existence and action. This means that man by developing himself in his specific and proper *human* way contributes to the manifestation of the glory of God. Thomas stresses that God's self-manifestation in and through man is different from his self-manisfestation in any other creature: *"sic in hoc fine hominis non communicant creaturae irrationales . . ."* (q.1, a.8). This has its impact upon the activity of man: *"ut tendat in finem quasi se agens vel ducens ad finem . . ."* (q.1, a.2). Man will reach God to the degree of his "being human," that is, "by knowing and loving," but this "knowing and loving" means to know God and to love him.

39. E. Shillebeeckx, *ibid.,* p. 25.

40. Father Schillebeeckx describes this: "we are involved in a dialogue-in-acts between God and man. In this dialogue it is as if the world and history are placed by God between him and us as a translation of his speaking to us internally. Moreover, they are also the means in which and through which man is explicitly made aware of this internal communication, and finally they are the space within which man can give his response to this invitation" ("God en Mens," p. 187).

41. Al. van Rijen, "De christen in de wereld," in *Tijdschrift voor Theologie,* 6 (1966), 329.

42. *S. Th.,* I-II, q.1, art.3, a.3.

43. For a more detailed study of the proportion which must exist between the means and the end in the individual act, we may refer to P. Knauer, "La determination du bien et du mal par le principe de double effet," in *Nouvelle Revue Théologique,* 87 (1965), especially pp. 367-371.

44. Even the so-called "solitary sin" is still an isolation of "self" which by its nature is either a result of or a prelude to the frustration of communication with others.

45. W. van der Marck, *Het Christusgeheim in de menselijke samenleving,* p. 97.

46. Gabriel Mardinier, "De mens en zijn geweten," *Spectrum* (Utrecht, 1964), p. 77.

47. *Loc. cit.*

48. P. Anciaux, "Dynamische perspectieven in de Moraal," in *Dynamische perspectieven der christelijke Moraal,* p. 49; cf. also E. Schillebeeckx, *Marriage: Human Reality and Saving Mystery* (Sheed & Ward, 1965), especially pp. 89-91.

49. E. Shillebeeckx, "God en Mens," *Theologische Peilingen* II, p. 211; for a more detailed study, see John T. Noonan, "Au-

thority, Usury and Contraception," in *Cross Currents,* Vol. XVI (1966), No. 1, pp. 55-81.

50. *A New Catechism. Catholic Faith for Adults* (authorized edition of *The Dutch Catechism*) (New York: Herder and Herder, 1967), p. 397.

51. "The Changing Vision of Christian People concerning Marriage," in *Katholiek Archief,* 1965, kol. 1089, and in *ido-c, Doss.* 66-4/5.

52. In no way do we exclude the manifestation of God through special revelation. But in such special intervention God either creates means or uses created means in order to convey to man such particular knowledge about himself.

53. Genesis 1:28.

DENNIS DOHERTY

1. V. J. Pospishil explores the question in his *Divorce and Remarriage: Towards a New Catholic Teaching* (New York: Herder and Herder, 1967); the appendices and bibliography are especially helpful. The subtitle (not the author's own), however, is not especially accurate since the teaching is not really new; see p. 134: "One should be grateful to O'Connor for having quite cogently shown that at least the Church does possess such divine authority" (to dissolve a sacramental consummated marriage). The reference is to W. R. O'Connor, "The Indissolubility of a Ratified, Consummated Marriage," *Ephemerides Theologicae Lovanienses,* 13 (1936), 692-722.

2. Cf. I. Lepp and D. Doherty, "The Problem of Divorce and Remarriage," *Marriage* 48 (July, 1966), 7-18.

3. See, for example, L. Fanfani, *Manuale Theorico-Practicum Theologiae Moralis* IV (Romae: Libraria "Ferrari," 1950), pp. 676-682. Cf. Pius XI, *Casti Connubii, AAS,* 22 (1930), 539-592, at pp. 553f.

4. *The Documents of Vatican II,* ed. W. Abbott (New York: Guild Press, 1966), "Pastoral Constitution on the Church in the Modern World," n. 47, p. 249.

5. *Ibid.,* n. 48, p. 250.

6. *Ibid.,* n. 50, p. 255.

7. Abbott, *op. cit.,* n. 11, p. 502.

8. A. Abate, *The Dissolution of the Matrimonial Bond in Ecclesiastical Jurisprudence* (Romae: Desclée & Co., 1962), p. 7.

9. F. Kearney, *The Principles of Canon 1127* (Wash., D.C.: Catholic University Press, 1942), p. 59.

10. *Codex Juris Canonici* (Westminster, Md.: Newman, 1944), Docum. VIII, p. 824: "Populis ac nationibus nuper ex gentilitatis errore ad fidem catholicam conversis expedit indulgere circa libertatem contrahendi matrimonia, ne homines, continentiae servandae minime assueti, propterea minus libenter in fide persistant, et alios illorum exemplo ab eius perceptione deterreant." Cf. Pius XII's "Allocution to the Rota," Oct. 3, 1941, *AAS*, 33 (1941), 421-426, at p. 426; and J. J. O'Rourke, "Marginal Notes Concerning the Privilege of the Faith," *Jurist,* 20 (1960), 437-440, especially p. 439.

11. Kearney, *loc. cit.;* cf. Fanfani, *op. cit.,* p. 686: "a facto ad posse valet illatio." The fact that the Church does something would indeed seem to indicate that it has the power to do it. But the fact that it does not do or has not done something means only *that* it has not done something, not that it does not have such a power; to the contrary, see Abate, *op. cit.,* p. 23 (italics added): "By its practice rather than by its doctrine . . . the Church has marked out the *limits* within which it *must* remain in applying its jurisdiction." The dissolution of the bond by Pius XII in the first "Fresno" case (July 18, 1947) ended the long dispute over papal power to grant such a dissolution. The dispute concerning the pope's power to dissolve a sacramental consummated marriage may eventually be similarly terminated so that, in retrospect, "a facto ad posse . . ." will solve all difficulties. See F. J. Connell, "Basic Courses in the Institute on Christian Marriage," *Christian Marriage: Some Contemporary Problems,* ed. V. Nugent (New York: St. John's University Press, 1961), pp. 1-16, at p. 7: "This power (to dissolve) was given to the Church by Christ and preserved in tradition. It seems to have been left to the Church's authority to determine in what type of cases it can be used, and the Church decided never to use it in the case of a marriage between two baptized persons that has been consummated, for this represents perfectly the union between Christ and the Church, but to use it (for the benefit of the faith) in other types of marriage."

12. E. Schillebeeckx, *Marriage: Secular Reality and Saving Mystery,* II (London: Sheed and Ward, 1965), p. 74. Or see the American edition, *Marriage: Human Reality . . .* (New York: Sheed and Ward, 1965), p. 287.

13. Abbott, *op. cit.,* n. 46, p. 248 (Preface to Part II of *Gaudium et Spes*).

14. Can. 1013, § 2.

15. Can. 1118.

16. Cf. my doctoral study, *The Sexual Doctrine of Cardinal Cajetan* (Regensburg: Pustet, 1966), pp. 242f.

17. For a summary consideration of this see A. McNevin,

"The Indissolubility of Marriage as Effected by Consummation," *Resonance* (Spring, 1967), 16-34.

18. A. Vermeersch, *What Is Marriage?*, cited by T. L. Bouscaren and A. C. Ellis, *Canon Law: A Text and Commentary* (Milwaukee: The Bruce Publishing Co., 1957), pp. 591f. Cf. Suppl. 66, 1 ad 3; and Abate, *op. cit.*, p. 29: "It is certain that consummation, like sacramentality, does not add any fuller perfection to the indissolubility of the validly contracted bond. What it does is to actuate, in a more adequate manner, the symbolism existing in a marriage between the baptized. The marriage that is solely sacramental represents the union of Christ with the soul through grace, a union which can be destroyed by mortal sin. The marriage crowned by consummation, however, represents the unbreakable union of Christ with human nature. It is only on account of this element that the ratified and consummated marriage is asserted to be absolutely indissoluble, both extrinsically and intrinsically."

19. In his *Concordantia, PL* 187, 1407: "Cuncta ergo, quae de non separando conjugio inducta sunt, de perfecto intelliguntur, quod sponsali conventione est initiatum, et officio corporalis commixtionis est consummatum. Illa vero, quibus separabile conjugium ostenditur, de initiato intelliguntur, quod nondum officio sui perfectum est." Cf. also McNevin, *op. cit.*, pp. 28f.

20. Bouscaren-Ellis, *loc. cit.*

21. *Ibid.*

22. Cf. Fanfani, *op. cit.*, p. 685: "Igitur statim ac matrimonium fuerit consummatum, etiamsi id factum sit per vim aut fraudem, nullus est amplius locus matrimonii dissolubilitati q ʾʾad vinculum."

23. Cf. T. Bouscaren and J. O'Connor, *The Canon Law Digest* (Milwaukee: The Bruce Publishing Co., 1934-   ), 1959 Supplement, cans. 1068 and 1119.

24. *CIC,* can. 1013, § 1.

25. Can. 1067, § 1.

26. *Ibid.*, § 2.

27. *CIC,* can. 1082.

28. Pospishil, *op. cit.*, p. 117.

29. *Ibid.* For the sake of background we may note here that Pospishil's discussion of "spiritual union" is clearly a reference to *Time* (July 22, 1966, p. 65). The editors chose that expression in reporting an idea suggested by the present writer in *Marriage* (*op. cit.*, p. 14). Their choice of expression was approved in a phone interview. We may note too that while Msgr. Pospishil rejects spiritual union as impossible of definition and classifies it under the heading "inadequate solutions," two pages later (p. 119) he

finds it more reasonable to suggest (italics added) that legally invalid second marriages be presumed valid "because of some general, canonical, *undefinable* ground of invalidity in respect to first marriages."

30. Cf. L. Gerke, *Christian Marriage, A Permanent Sacrament* (Wash., D.C.: Catholic University Press, 1965, Second Series, No. 161), pp. 19-27, at p. 26: "Hence it is clear that actual love, any form of real love, is not the essence of marriage. However, conjugal love is not wholly outside the essence of marriage; it must be said to be essential in the sense that it is the essential *object* of the juridical bond, of the rights and obligations which constitute the essential core of matrimony: . . . The obligation to a shared common life of mutual help will be truly human in the degree as it is animated and permeated by love." This is said by way of comment on F. Diekamp's statement, p. 25: "For the *juridical* permanence of a validly contracted marriage, the *actual* existence of any kind of love is not essential. However, the spouses have the serious *obligation* to show one another the respect and love such as the full union of life (which marriage is) demands." (See also *infra*, n. 31, *in fine*.) Gerke's assertion (p. 25) that "the freely given and duly expressed marital consent is essentially an act of love, if it is at all sincere (which it must be in order to be valid)" is somewhat ambiguous. That consent, to be valid, must be sincere is true. That it is essentially an act of love is not necessarily true; nor need it be such in order to be valid.

31. M. J. Faraon, *The Metaphysical and Psychological Principles of Love* (Dubuque: Wm. C. Brown Co., 1952), p. 54. With regard to the direction which love takes, see pp. 58f.: "the subject is inclined out of itself toward the object for the sake of real union with it in its concrete existence. Thus there must be a definite proportion between the object as capable of perfecting and the subject as perfectible. . . . It is because the object is what it is that it happens to be good for the subject. For it is precisely the object as it is in its concrete existence toward which the loving subject is inclined. . . . In other words, the beloved would not be good for the lover, and hence attract the lover, if it were not in the first place proportioned to the lover in its being; not in its being which is knowable, its '*ratio speciei*,' but in its being which is lovable, its '*esse quod habet in rerum natura*' (*De Ver.*, q.21, a.1). Therefore, it is that suitability, fitness (*convenientia*), or similarity possessed by the object in its *esse naturae* for the perfecting of the subject, which is the root cause of love." On p. 71 of this splendid work the author says, "love is not essential to marriage." Cf. B. Lavaud, "The Interpretation of the Conjugal Act and the Theology of Marriage," *Thomist*, 1 (1939), 360-380, especially p. 379. ·

32. L. Gerke, *op. cit.*, p. 124.

33. See, for example, the fine articles by V. Coburn, "Homosexuality and the Invalidation of Marriage," *Jurist*, 20 (1960), 441-459; and C. Ritty, "Possible Invalidity of Marriage by Reason of Sexual Anomalies," *Jurist*, 23 (1963), 394-422.

34. Cf. *CIC*, can. 1083, § 2; Coburn, *op. cit.*, pp. 454-457; and *infra*, n. 41.

35. J. Keating, "The *Caput Nullitatis* in Insanity Cases," *Jurist*, 22 (1962), 394-411, at p. 399; cf. by the same author, "Marriage of the Psychopathic Personality," *Chicago Studies*, 3 (1964), 19-38, at p. 30: "It is inaccurate to define the impediment of impotence as the physical inability to place *actus per se aptos ad prolis generationem;* it is rather the *moral* inability to assume the right and obligation" (to place such acts).

36. Cf. Bouscaren-O'Connor, *op. cit.*, IV (1958), pp. 348f.; V (1963), pp. 540f.

37. For a discussion of three diagnostic categories of incompatibility resulting from psychopathology, see R. McAllister, "Psychological Incompatibility," *Marriage: A Psychological and Moral Approach*, ed. W. Bier (New York: Fordham University Press, 1965), pp. 185-193.

38. Cf. M. Jugie, "Mariage dan l'Eglise Gréco-Russe," *Dict. de théol. chrét.* IX, 2323-2328.

39. Cf. Ritty, *op. cit.*, pp. 395f.; and Keating, "Marriage of the Psychopathic Personality," pp. 27f.

40. Pospishil, *op. cit.*, p. 112.

41. See, for example, the explanation of simple error as syllogized by Bouscaren-Ellis, *op. cit.*, p. 549: "Distinguish the major premise: the will embraces its object as represented by the mind; that is, the will cannot embrace an object which is in no way represented, I grant; the will embraces the object under every aspect in which the mind represents it, I subdistinguish: it does so *explicitly*, I deny; *implicitly*, I subdistinguish again: it does so implicitly *if there is no actual prevailing intention to the contrary*, I grant: it does so implicitly *even in the face of an actual prevailing intention to the contrary*, I deny."

42. Pospishil, *loc. cit.;* cf, *supra*, n. 29.

43. Cf. Aertnys-Damen, *Theologia Moralis* II (Romae: Marietti, 1950, ed. 16), n. 439, 1º: "Omittenda est monitio . . . v.g. si uxor quidem posset de nullitate matrimonii sui admoneri sine ullo periculo, sed pericula formidanda essent, prout ordinarie continget, a parte mariti," and Bouscaren-Ellis, *op. cit.*, pp. 463f.

44. A. Bride, "Le pouvoir du souverain pontife sur le mariage des infidèles," *Revue de Droit Canonique*, 10-11 (1960-1961), 52-101, at p. 99.

45. Cf. *supra*, n. 6; and D. von Hildebrand, *Marriage* (London: Longmans, Green and Co., 1942), pp. 23-27.

46. In *S. Th.*, III, q.29, a.2, asking about the marriage between Mary and Joseph, St. Thomas distinguishes a twofold perfection of a thing, the first of which is its form: "Forma autem matrimonii consistit in quadam indivisibili coniunctione animorum, per quam unus coniugum indivisibiliter alteri fidem servare tenetur." Just as the union of souls is possible without physical consummation, as in a virginal marriage, physical consummation is equally possible without a union of souls. It is this latter union, therefore, which should be the criterion of a consummated marriage since it looks to persons as persons, not to persons as biologically pro-creative agents.

47. Cf. Bouscaren-O'Connor, *op. cit.*, IV, pp. 350-352.

48. Aertnys-Damen, *op. cit.*, I, n. 489: "Ratio cur votum semper valide irritetur est, quia votum iam non esset honestum, si limitaret ius alterius. . . . votum non est honestum, si non attendat ad ius tertii."

49. *Ibid.*, n. 487.

50. In the words of Cardinal Suenens at Vatican II: "Many repeat that the bishop is 'wed to his diocese'; yet if this is taken literally the Council hall is full of bishops divorced two or three times over." Cf. M. Novak, *The Open Church* (New York: The Macmillan Co., 1964), p. 245.

51. Cf. Pospishil, *op. cit.*, pp. 83-91.

52. J. Mahoney, "Do They Intend Marriage?" *Homiletic and Pastoral Review,* 67 (October, 1966), 41-45.

53. J. T. Catoir, "The Church and Second Marriage," *Commonweal* (April 14, 1967), 113-117; cf. P. Shannon, "Changing Law in a Changing Church," *America* (February 18, 1967), 248-250.

MARTIN NOLAN

1. *AAS*, 44 (1952), p. 787.

2. *Aristotle, Politics,* Book 1, c.2.

3. See Mt 5:2.

4. St. Thomas Aquinas, *Summa contra Gentiles,* III, cc. 112-113, *Summa theologica,* I, q.60, a.5 in corp.; James of Viterbo, *Quodlibetalia,* II, a.20; John Duns Scotus, *Summa theologica,* I, q.60, a.5, etc. Cf. M. Nolan, *The Principle of Totality in the Writings of Pope Pius XII* (Rome: Pontifical Gregorian University, 1960), "An Historical Introduction to the Principle of Totality," pp. 14 ff.

5. *AAS*, 44 (1952), pp. 787-788.

6. *AAS*, 44 (1952), p. 784.

7. *AAS*, 35 (1944), pp. 221-222; *Discorsi e Radiomessaggi*, 6 (1944-45), pp. 186-187; *AAS*, 43 (1951), pp. 838-839; *AAS*, 43 (1951), p. 857; *AAS*, 44 (1952), pp. 781-782, 784-788; *AAS*, 45 (1953), pp. 747-748; *AAS*, 46 (1954), pp. 590-595; *AAS*, 48 (1956), pp. 461-462; *AAS*, 48 (1956), pp. 678-680; *AAS*, 50 (1958), p. 279.

8. Cf. A. Hitler, *Mein Kampf* (München, 1933), pp. 433, 446.

9. (Author's name withheld), "Sterilization Law in Germany," *The Ecclesiastical Review*, 95 (1936), p. 50. The source is *Deutsche Justiz, Rechtspflege* 57, n. 21, Edition A, May 24, 1935, pp. 780-782; *ibid.*, Appendix 1, p. 12, 1. of the law.

10. A reaction to these unjustified incursions is seen in the Holy Office decrees of February 24, 1940 (*AAS*, 32 (1940), p. 73) and December 20, 1940 (*AAS*, 32 (1940), pp. 553-554).

11. II-II, q.64, a.2 in corp.

12. Cf., n. 4.

13. Cf. Gillon, L.-B., O.P., "L'argument du tout et de la parité après Saint Thomas d'Aquin," *Angelicum*, 28 (1951), pp. 214-218. James of Viterbo, 1.c.

14. Scotus, 1.c.

15. Nicholas of Occam, *Quodlibeta*, ms. Assisi., 158, ff. 239-243.

16. P. Laymann, S.J., *Theologia Moralis* (Monachii, 1626), L.III, Tr. III, Pars III, c.1, p. 200.

17. Discourse to the 13th Congress of the International Society of Applied Psychology, April 10, 1958, *AAS*, 50 (1958), p. 278.

18. *AAS*, 44 (1952), p. 787.

19. *Ibid.*, pp. 784 ff.

20. Cf. *AAS*, 48 (1956), pp. 461-462.

21. *AAS*, 44 (1952), p. 786; *AAS*, 48 (1956), p. 461.

22. *AAS*, 44 (1952), p. 788.

23. Cf. J. J. Shinners, *The Morality of Medical Experimentation on Living Human Subjects in the Light of Recent Papal Teaching* (Dissertation, Catholic University of America, Washington, D.C., 1958), pp. 88-103.

24. E. Tesson, S.J., "Reflexions Morales," *Cahiers Laënnec*, 12 (1952), p. 167.

25. G. Kelly, S.J., "Pope Pius XII and the Principle of Totality," *Theological Studies*, 16 (1955), p. 383.

26. J. Ford, S.J., "Notes on Moral Theology," *Theological Studies*, 6 (1945), p. 563.

27. *AAS*, 48 (1956), pp. 459-467.

28. L. Bender, O.P., "Ancora sul trapianto di organi," *Perfice Munus*, 31 (1956), p. 484; C. Borg, "Del trapianot di un membro," *ibid.*, 30 (1955), pp. 165-166; A. Tabone, "De transplantatione organorum humanorum," *Melita theologica*, 9 (1956), p. 87; M. Zalba, "La mutilació y el trasplante de organos a la luz del magistero eclesiastico." *Razón y Fe*, 153 (1956), p. 541; C. J. McFadden, *Medical Ethics*, 4th Edition (Philadelphia: F. A. Davis Co., 1956), pp. 314-315; J. Madden, "Mutilation of the Human Body: Transplantation of Members," *The Australasian Catholic Record*, 33 (1956), pp. 138-147; G. Sölch, O.P., "Uerpflanzung menschlicher Organe," *Die Neue Ordnung*, 8 (1954), pp. 378-380; G. Perico, "Il problema dei trapianti umani," *Aggiornamenti sociali*, 6 (1955), pp. 337-352; T. A. Iorio, *Theologia moralis*, editio, 4a (Naples: D'Autia, 1954), p. 112; F. X. Hürth, S.J., *De re matrimoniali*, editio 2a (Rome: Gregorian University, 1955), p. 104.

29. *AAS*, 46 (1954), p. 594.

30. G. Kelly, S.J., l.c., p. 394; L. Scremin, *Appunti di morale professionale per i medici*, 3a edizione (Rome: 1947), pp. 194-195; D. P. Bongiovanni, S.D.B., "Del trapianto di un membro," *Perfice munus*, 29 (1954), p. 701; L. Babbini, "Moralità del trapianto di un organo pari," *Palestra del Clero*, 34 (1955), p. 361; L. M. Simeone, O.F.M., Min. Conv., "De mutilatione quaedam," *Miscellanea Franciscana*, 35 (1955), p. 81; J. F. Groner, O.P., "Die Organverpflanzung beim Menschen in moralischer Sicht," in *Der Mensch unter Gottes Anruf und Ordnung: Festgabe für Theodor Müncker*, ed. R. Jauser and F. Stolz (Düsseldorf, 1958), p. 199; G. B. Guzzetti, "Il trapianto degli organi," *La scuola cattolica*, 84 (1956), p. 259; P. Palazzini, "I trapianti," *Studi cattolici*, 2 (1958, n. 7), p. 66; B. J. Cunningham, C.M., *The Morality of Organic Transplantation* (Dissertation: Catholic University of America, Washington, D.C., 1944).

31. *AAS*, 50 (1958), pp. 593-694.

32. *Ibid.*

33. *Confessions*, Bk 1, c.1.

34. *Summa theologica* I-II, q.1, a.2, 3.

35. Mt 22:40.

36. Rom 13:8-10.

37. Cf. Augustine's statement about his quest for God: "Et ecce intus eras et ego foris" (*Confessions* X, 27). A failure to realize one's own relationship to God is a failure to realize one's own true identity.

38. Pius XII to the Eighth Assembly of the World Medical Association, 30th September, 1954, *AAS*, 46 (1954), pp. 594-595.

39. *Ibid.*

40. Cf. R. J. Nogar, O.P., *The Wisdom of Evolution* (Garden City, New York: Doubleday and Co., 1963), *passim*.
41. Gen. 1:28.
42. Nogar, 1.c., pp. 196 ff.
43. Cf. Vatican II: *Gaudium et spes*, n. 5.
44. Gen. 1.c.
45. Cf. Pius XII, Christmas Message, 24th December, 1942, *AAS*, 35 (1943), p. 13.
46. On this problem cf. van Melzen, A.G.M., "Natur und Moral," in *Das Naturrecht im Disput* (ed. Fr. Böckle, Düsseldorf: Patmos-Verlag 1966), pp. 61 ff.
47. Cf. *AAS*, 44 (1952), p. 787.
48. III., 64, 97.
49. Lk 21:1-4.
50. Mt 7:1 ff.
51. 1 Cor 13.
52. *AAS*, 50 (1950), pp. 693-694.
53. Hb 10:5-7.
54. Mk 10:41 ff.
55. Jn 12:32.
56. Jn 16:22.
57. Jn 17:21 ff.
58. Jn 14:15 ff., 26 ff.; Acts 1:8.
59. Acts 2:1 ff.
60. Romans 5:5.
61. Cf. Romans 8:11; 1 Cor 13:8 ff.
62. Romans 12:1.

KIERAN NOLAN

1. Werner Schöllgen, "Die Norm arztlichen Handelns im Lichte einer Wesenlehre vom Menschen," *Konkrete Ethik* (Düsseldorf, 1961), p. 424f.
2. Karl Rahner, *Theology of Death* (New York: Herder and Herder, 1965), 32-35.
3. Cf. F. X. Durrwell, *The Resurrection* (Sheed and Ward, 1960); David M. Stanley, S.J., *Christ's Resurrection in Pauline Soteriology*, Analecta Biblica, 13 (Rome: Pontifical Institute, 1961); K. Rahner, S.J., "The Resurrection of the Body," in *Theological Investigations*, 2 (Helicon Press, 1963), pp. 203-216.
4. The situation of modern mechanized medicine in relation to the dying was somewhat dramatically presented, anonymously, in

the *Atlantic Monthly*, "A Way of Dying," Vol. 199, No. 1 (January, 1957), 53 ff.

5. John J. Farrell, M.D., "The Right of a Patient to Die," *The Journal of the South Carolina Medical Association*, Vol. LIV, No. 7 (July, 1957), 231 ff.

6. Edward Rynearson, M.D., "The Patient Who Is Dying of Cancer," *The Manitoba Medical Review*, Vol. 42, No. 2 (February, 1962), 77 ff.

7. John Cavanaugh, M.D., "Bene Mori: The Right of the Patient to Die with Dignity," *The Linacre Quarterly*, Vol. 30, No. 2 (May, 1963), 60 ff.

8. The main papers delivered in Rochester, Minnesota, in April, 1967, at the Consultation on Medicine and Theology, were not available at the time of this writing. The chief speakers included Dr. Edward M. Litin, head of the Psychiatry Section at the Mayo Clinic, Dr. Joseph Fletcher, Professor at Episcopal Theological Seminary, Cambridge, Mass., and Dr. Edward Rynearson.

9. George Hanzel, M.D., "Modern Medico-Moral Problems," *Homiletic and Pastoral Review* 67 (April, 1967), 591.

10. Article 22 of *Ethical and Religious Directives for Catholic Hospitals* (St. Louis: The Catholic Hospital Association of the United States and Canada, 1955) states: "The failure to supply the ordinary means of preserving life is equivalent to euthanasia."

11. Gerald Kelly, S.J., "The Duty of Using Artificial Means of Preserving Life," *Theological Studies*, 11 (1950), 203-220. Father Kelly's work is of great value in that it provides a review of the thinking of the past with the varied opinions which were current at a time when so many of our present problems first arose.

12. *Loc. cit.*

13. C. Capellmann, *Pastoral Medicine* (New York, 1882), 20-28.

14. Thomas J. O'Donnell, S.J., *Morals in Medicine* (Newman Press, 1959), p. 67.

15. G. Kelly, S.J., *op. cit.*, p. 218.

16. Joseph P. Donovan, C.M., "Intravenous Feeding," *Homiletic and Pastoral Review*, 49 (August, 1949), 904.

17. G. Kelly, S.J., *op. cit.*, p. 218.

18. Joseph V. Sullivan, *Catholic Teaching on the Morality of Euthanasia* (Washington, D.C., 1949), pp. 65 and 72.

19. Thomas J. O'Donnell, S.J., *op. cit.*, p. 71.

20. John R. Cavanaugh, *op. cit.*, 63.

21. *Ibid.* Of interest in this connection is the concern of Robert Ettinger in freezing bodies of those dying and thereby freezing life. He expounds his theory in his book *The Prospect of Immortality* (Doubleday, 1964). Reactions to Ettinger's theory

vary considerably. Leon Putnam commented, "In spite of my reservation we need to take seriously what Ettinger and others are saying, for questions regarding death are likely to increase as the boundary lines between religion and science grow less distinct in a technological age . . ." (*Christian Century*, 82 [1965], 1550-1552). Holding the opposite view was E. Jackson, who wrote: "In view of the status of scientific research in this matter (cryogenic preservations) it would seem unwise to encourage the assumption that we are on the verge of a great breakthrough in cryogenic internment. The scientific study of the matter does not appear to warrant such an assumption. An exploration of the personal, legal, social and religious implications of cryogenic internment seems to be not only premature but unfortunately misleading" (*Christian Century*, 83 [1966], 183).

22. K. Rahner, S.J., *The Christian of the Future*, (Herder and Herder, 1967), pp. 42 ff.

23. Joseph V. Sullivan, *op. cit.*, p. 65; Thomas J. O'Donnell, S.J., *op. cit.*, p. 58.

24. Eugene G. Laforet, M.D., "The Hopeless Case," *Linacre Quarterly*, Vol. 29 (August, 1962), 131. In an address on anesthesia, February 24, 1957, Pope Pius XII spoke of relieving pain in the dying, even though the anesthetic induces unconsciousness and indirectly hastens death. For the complete text in English, cf. *Catholic Medical Quarterly*, April, 1957, 51-66.

25. J. McCarthy, "Taking of Insulin to Preserve Life," *The Irish Ecclesiastical Record*, Vol. 58 (1964), 552-554.

26. George Hanzel, M.D., *op. cit.*, 593; Hanibal Hamlin, M.D., "Life or Death by EEG," *Journal of the American Medical Association*, Vol. 190 (1964), 112-114.

27. Addressing the First International Congress on the Histopathology of the Nervous System on September 13, 1952, Pope Pius XII spoke of methods which degrade man "to the level of a purely sensory being—a being of acquired reflexes or a living automaton." Cf. Gerald Kelly, S.J., *Medico-Moral Problems* (St. Louis: The Catholic Hospital Association of the United States and Canada, 1958), pp. 280-281.

28. Edward Rynearson, M.D., *op. cit.*, 78f.

29. Cf. Message of Pope Paul VI, at the close of the Ecumenical Council, to the Poor, the Sick, and All Who Suffer. *The Documents of Vatican II*, edited by Walter Abbott, S.J. (New York: America Press, 1966), pp. 734f.

30. Dwight J. Ingle, "The Biological Future of Man," *Chicago Today*, Vol. 3, No. 2 (Spring, 1966).

31. Eugene Laforet, M.D., *op. cit.*, 128.

32. Cf. P. H. Long, "On the Quantity and Quality of Life,"

Resident Physician, Vol. 6, April, 1960, 69-70; May, 1960, 53-61; June, 1960, 51-53.

33. Euthanasia is defined as a "theory that in certain circumstances, when owing to disease, senility or the like, a person's life has permanently ceased to be either agreeable or useful, the sufferer should be painlessly killed either by himself or by another." H. J. Rose, "Euthanasia," *Encyclopedia of Religion and Ethics* V, 598-601.

34. In his recent book treating various aspects of dying, Professor John Hinton commented, "It seems a terrible indictment that the main argument for euthanasia is that many suffer unduly because there is lack of preparation and provision for the total care of the dying." Cf. *Dying* (Penguin, 1967), p. 146. Professor Hinton has done a service to a better understanding of dying both through his own thoughtful chapters as well as through the numerous helpful references.

INDEX

313